THE 28TH INFANTRY DIVISION IN THE HÜRTGEN FOREST

THE 28TH INFANTRY DIVISION IN THE HÜRTGEN FOREST

FORGOTTEN SACRIFICE

Walter S. Zapotoczny Jr.

First published in Great Britain in 2026 by
Fonthill
An imprint of
Pen & Sword Books Ltd
Yorkshire—Philadelphia
www.fonthill.media

ISBN 978-1-03615-665-7

A CIP catalogue record for this book is available from the British Library.

Typeset by Simon and Sons ITES Services Pvt. Ltd., Chennai, India.
Printed and bound in the UK by CPI Group (UK) Ltd, Croydon, CR0 4YY

The Publisher's authorised representative in the EU for product safety is Authorised Rep Compliance Ltd., Ground Floor, 71 Lower Baggot Street, Dublin D02 P593, Ireland.
www.arccompliance.com

For a complete list of Pen & Sword titles please contact

PEN & SWORD BOOKS LIMITED
47 Church Street, Barnsley, South Yorkshire, S70 2AS, England
E-mail: enquiries@pen-and-sword.co.uk
Website: www.pen-and-sword.co.uk
or
PEN AND SWORD BOOKS
1950 Lawrence Rd, Havertown, PA 19083, USA
E-mail: Uspen-and-sword@casematepublishers.com

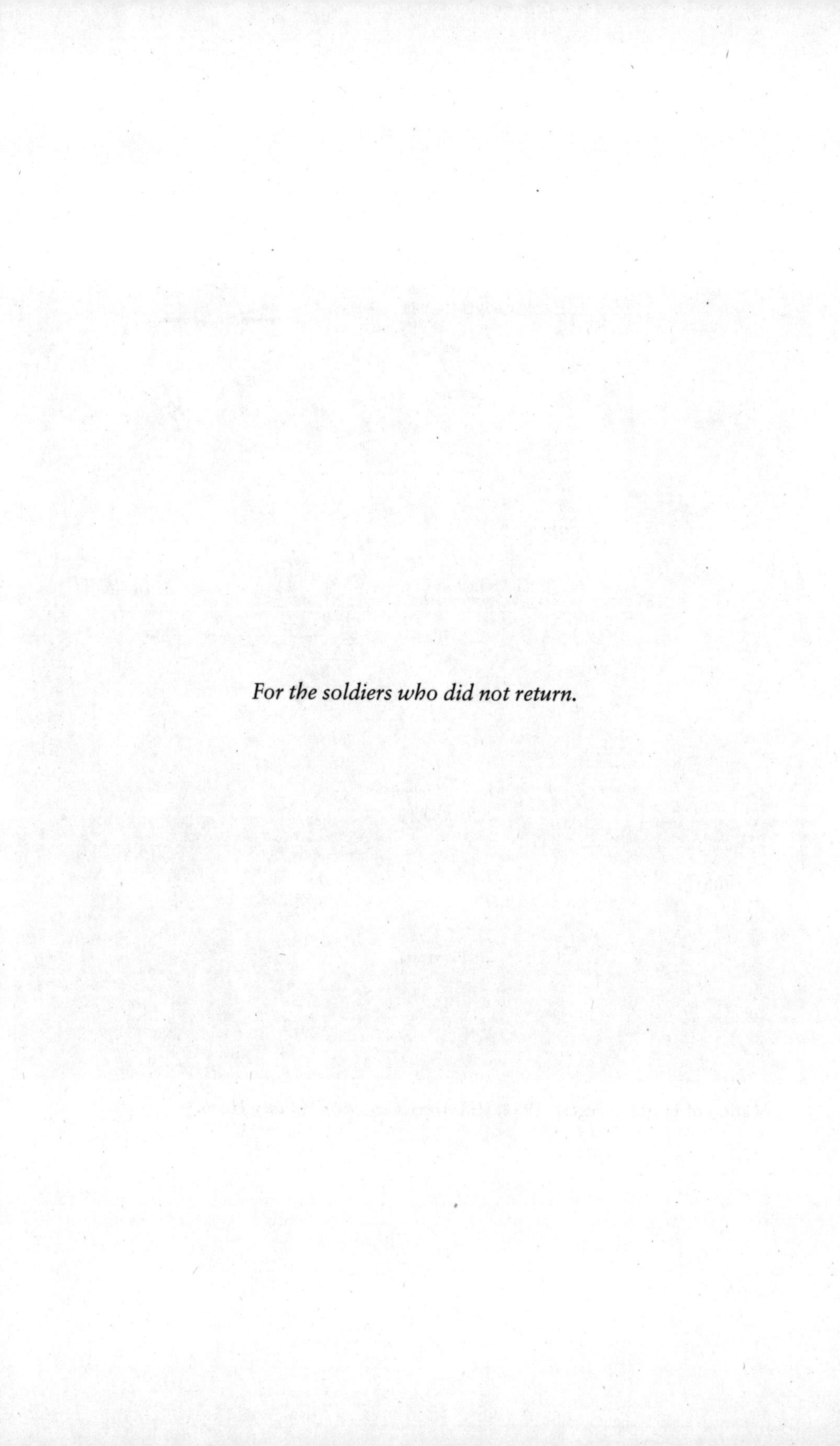

For the soldiers who did not return.

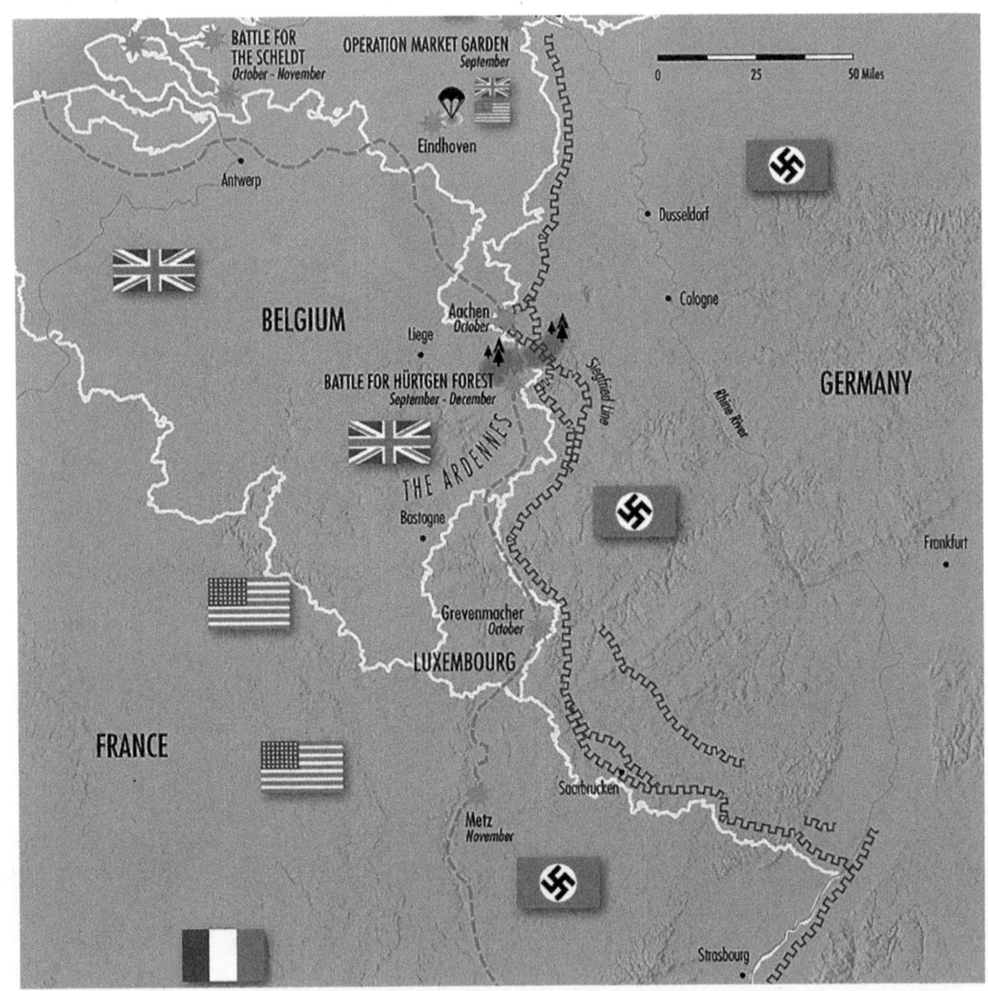

Location of Hürtgen Forest, 1944. (*US Army Center of Military History*)

Preface

The Battle of Hürtgen Forest has remained largely overlooked since World War II, lacking the in-depth examination given to more prominent European battles such as the D-Day invasion or the Ardennes Offensive (Battle of the Bulge). Although the battles in the Hürtgen Forest did not significantly alter the overall outcome of the war, they had considerable operational consequences by securing for the Germans their northern flank, facilitating their offensive through the Ardennes in December 1944.

By November 1944, Allied Command believed conditions were ripe for a significant breakthrough towards Cologne in the German lowlands. However, they encountered unexpectedly fierce German resistance, which thwarted this plan. The Allies aimed to seize the Ruhr and Saar industrial regions and had just achieved a hard-fought victory in capturing Aachen. The US First Army, poised to advance across the Rhine River plain into Germany, faced the Hürtgen Forest on its southern flank. Clearing the forest of German troops was deemed necessary to secure their right flank for the advance beyond Aachen.

Moreover, the strategic significance of the Hürtgen Forest was heightened by the presence of the Roer River and its critical dams. The Americans needed to capture these dams to prevent the Germans from potentially destroying them, which would flood the area and sever any troop crossings. Control of the dams was essential for ensuring the Allies could safely advance over the Roer River.

The Allies attacked with the First and Ninth US Armies and parts of the British Second Army—seventeen divisions in all. At the peak of the battle, ten US divisions were massed in the 40-kilometer-wide Gelsenkirchen-Monschau sector. The main effort of the Allied attack was concentrated in the Hürtgen Forest. In his book, *The Battle of the Rhineland*, Reginald W. Thompson writes:

> No other Army ever encountered a more determined enemy. No section along the entire Allied front, from Switzerland down to Arnhem, held so many horrors

> and difficulties of terrain as did the Hürtgen area, and I daresay that no other section was of greater tactical importance than this area which was the key to the plain of Cologne and the northern Rhineland.[1]

A colossal American artillery preparation on November 2 at 8:00 AM marked the beginning of one of World War II's fiercest battles, which can only be compared with the battles of Verdun in World War I and of Sevastopol in World War II. The 28th Infantry Division started offensive operations with its 109th, 110th, and 112th Infantry Regiments along with attached units.

This is the story of tremendous bravery and the forgotten sacrifice of those who fought in the Hürtgen Forest, illuminated for the first time through a compilation of studies, after-action reports, interviews, German publications, and the memories of both 28th Division and German soldiers. After examining these accounts, it becomes clear why so many veterans referred to the Hürtgen Forest as "the green hell," while others labeled it a "death factory." These descriptions capture the harrowing conditions and relentless challenges faced by troops, emphasizing the brutal reality of warfare in this unforgiving terrain. Their stories are a testament to the resilience and courage that defined this conflict, and it is essential to remember their sacrifices as we seek to understand the true cost of war.

Acknowledgments

Thank you Tom Scholtes from the Circle of Studies on the Battle of the Bulge (CEBA) for the tour of the Kall Trail and the inspiration for this book. Thank you Albert Trostorf from the Hürtgen Forest Museum for the reports and materials for the book.

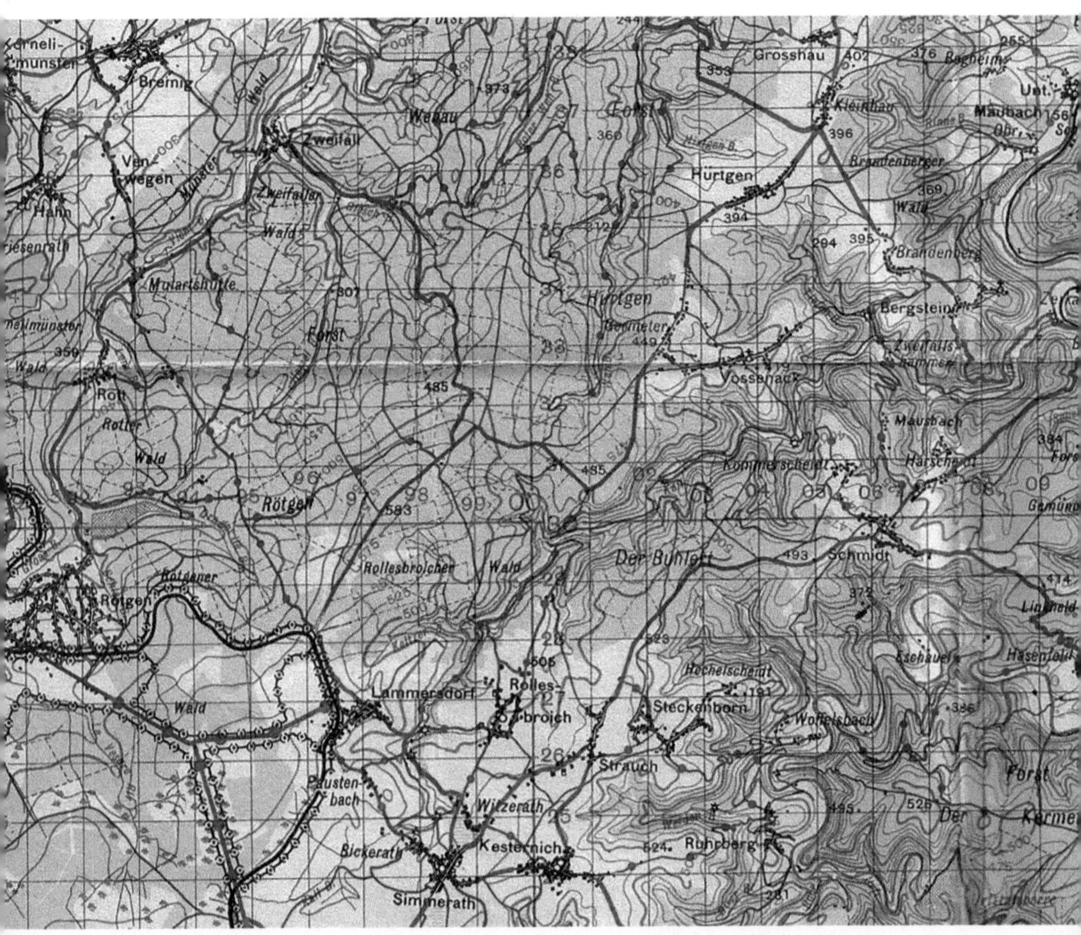

Topographic Map of the Hürtgen Area, 1944. (*Hürtgen Forest Museum*)

Contents

Maps

Abbreviations and Definitions

(-)	following a unit's name indicates that the unit is "understrength" or missing some of its organic elements
APC	armor-piercing composite. An armor-piercing composite round combines different materials in one projectile to improve performance. Instead of being made from a single piece of steel, it typically has a very hard, dense core (often tungsten or similar material) and a lighter outer casing or body (usually steel or alloy)
BAR	Browning automatic rifle. A portable automatic rifle that can fire continuously (fully automatic) or in controlled bursts. It was intended to give individual soldiers the ability to provide mobile suppressive fire—something between a standard rifle and a machine gun
blaze bomb	a type of incendiary bomb designed to cause fires
Blutig Eimer	"Bloody Bucket"—a grim German nickname for the 28th Infantry Division, reflecting how costly and punishing its operations appeared to the opposing side during the Hürtgen Forest battles
Bn	battalion
breech raceway	the slot or mechanism where the shell is loaded into the gun
DIN A4	standardized paper size (approximately 8.27 in. × 11.69 in.)
Dragon's teeth	pyramidal concrete fortifications used to slow down or stop the advance of tanks and other armored vehicles
FA	field artillery
Fala	President Franklin D. Roosevelt's dog

FLAK (*Flugabwehrkanone*)	acronym derived from German term for "anti-aircraft cannon"
Füsilier battalion	unit in the German army consisting of light infantry troops
GI (Government Issue)	refers to an American soldier
G-2	US intelligence officer, division level and higher
G-3	US operations officer, division level and higher
G-4	US logistics officer, division level and higher
H-hour	time of day an attack is planned to begin
Hauptmann	German term for "captain"
HE	high explosive
Heerestruppen Kampfgruppe	German term for "combat group"
hedgehog defense	military tactic in which defending force creates multiple mutually supportive strongpoints in a defense in depth, designed to sap enemy strength and break momentum of attack
HERA	high explosive rocket-assisted. After being fired, a small rocket motor ignites in flight, giving the projectile an extra push and allowing it to travel further than a standard shell
ladder fire	method of adjusting artillery or mortar fire by firing three rounds in rapid succession with the same deflection but at different ranges
Kampfgruppe	a flexible, ad hoc military formation, literally meaning "combat group," used by the German Army (Wehrmacht) in World War II. It was not a permanent unit like a division or regiment, but a temporary grouping assembled for a specific mission or operational need
LD	line of departure. The point on the battlefield from which troops begin an attack or advance. It is usually a clearly marked starting line on maps or in the field, aligned with the mission plan
MAC	mission assurance coordinator. Oversees activities to make sure that a mission meets its objectives even under challenging or unexpected conditions
MO	medical officer
MSR	main supply route
Muckefuck	coffee substitute made from roasted grains, like barley or chicory

Oberstleutnant	German term for "lieutenant colonel"
PAK (*Panzerabwehrkanone*)	acronym derived from German term for "anti-tank guns"
Panzerschreck	German term for "shoulder-type rocket launcher," which was used as an anti-tank weapon
Panzenjägerabteilung	German term for tank-destroyer battalion
Passchendaele	the Battle of Passchendaele was a campaign in World War I
phase line	terrain feature extending across zone of action used to control and coordinate a military advance or withdrawal
POW	prisoner of war
RAD camp	German term for "barracks," an abbreviation of *Reichsarbeitsdienst*
RCT	regimental combat team. A regiment-sized unit reinforced with additional support units to operate independently in combat. It is designed to have all the necessary combat, fire support, and logistics elements to complete a mission without relying on higher headquarters for immediate support
S-2	US intelligence officer, brigade/battalion level
S-3	US operations officer, brigade/battalion level
S-4	US logistics officer, brigade/battalion level
SHAEF	Supreme Headquarters Allied Expeditionary Force
SS (*Schutzstaffel*)	German term for protection squads. Created in 1925 as a small personal bodyguard unit for Adolf Hitler, it was initially tasked with protecting Nazi Party leaders at rallies and events
Stalag	German prisoner-of-war camp
Sturmgeschütz	refers to a series of German assault guns
TC	tank commander
Uferstraße	German term for riverside/lakeside/coastal road
Unteroffizier	German term for "sergeant"
VB	stands for *Vorgeschobener Beobachter*, which translates to "forward observer"
Weiße Wehe	9-mile-loop trail near Hürtgenwald, Germany
Wilde Sau	literally "wild boar," a specific German Luftwaffe tactical concept in World War II

NOTE: See Map 2 (Topographic Map of the Hürtgen Forest Area) for the locations of all map coordinates referenced throughout the book

Brief Chronology, November 2–14, 1944

November 2
The 1st Battalion of the 109th Infantry Regiment pushes into the woods, while the 3rd Battalion is halted by the Wilde Sau minefield. German engineers launch a counterattack. The 110th Infantry faces resistance from the Westwall bunkers along the Schill Line near Raffelsbrand. The 2nd Battalion of the 112th Infantry moves forward with tank support through Vossenack, positioning two of its three companies in trenches in the fields to the east of the town and one company within the town.

November 3
The 3rd Battalion of the 112th Infantry navigates the Kall ravine toward Schmidt, while the 1st Battalion sets up in Kommerscheidt. The narrow pathway in the Kall ravine limits tank movement, hampering support for the 112th Infantry in Schmidt.

November 4
Three M4 Sherman tanks from A Company of the 707th Tank Battalion reach Schmidt, with the remainder of the company stuck on the trail. In the morning, German Panzergrenadier-Regiment 156 launches attacks on Vossenack but fails to penetrate the town. American companies positioned outside suffer heavy artillery fire from the Germans. Schmidt comes under attack from three directions by units of the German 89th Infantry Division, backed by Sturmgeschütz Brigade 341. The remaining defenders of the 3rd Battalion, 112th Infantry hold out in the southern part of town until they are finally overwhelmed in the early afternoon, when nine German Panzer IV tanks from the 2nd Panzer Regiment 16 arrive to support the assault. Later in the afternoon, forces from the 2nd Panzer Regiment 16 and Sturmgeschütz Brigade 241 charge out of Schmidt to attack Kommerscheidt but incur significant losses and retreat back to Schmidt.

November 6
Task Force Ripple, including the 3rd Battalion of the 110th Infantry, tries to bolster defenses in Kommerscheidt and is the last unit to arrive before the Germans cut off the Kall ravine. As the US 20th Engineer Battalion works to improve the Kall ravine trail, Panzer Aufklärungs-Abteilung 16 and Panzergrenadier Regiment 1056 strive to seal off the ravine by capturing Mestrenger Mill, which controls the only bridge in the area. Eventually, the 3rd Battalion of Panzergrenadier-Regiment 1056 secures the mill. A pre-dawn assault on Vossenack by two Panzergrenadier regiments from the 116th Panzer Division is delayed, but the bombardment of two outlying companies of the 2nd Battalion, 112th Infantry causes a disorganized retreat back into town. By noon, panzergrenadiers enter the eastern sections of the town, with intense house-to-house fighting continuing into the night. The American 146th Engineer Battalion is dispatched to Vossenack to support the faltering 2nd Battalion, 112th Infantry; most of the panzergrenadiers are pushed out, and the 2nd Battalion, 109th Infantry takes over the town's defenses.

November 7
Kommerscheidt is attacked by Kampfgruppe Bayer and Panzergrenadier Regiment 1056, while the 16th Panzer Reconnaissance Battalion advances from the rear through Kall ravine. US defenses in Kommerscheidt collapse after four hours of fighting. The battle results in a stalemate, with both sides exhausting themselves in combat.

November 8
The 2nd Battalion of the 112th Infantry, authorized for about 850 personnel, receives 515 replacements. The battalion is assigned the mission to launch an attack the following morning.

November 9
General Cota convenes a briefing for all regimental and battalion commanders at the division command post. Effectively, the 28th Infantry Division's engagement in the Hürtgen Forest concludes on this day. Offensive operations cease, but for the next week, the division focuses on consolidating positions west of the Kall Trail and accounting for the many missing soldiers throughout its sector.

November 14
The Hürtgen ordeal finally ends for the 28th Infantry Division. The 8th Infantry Division moves in, relieving the Keystone Division and preparing for its own challenges. The 28th Infantry Division relocates to a quieter area 40 miles to the southwest in Luxembourg, tasked with defending a 25-mile-wide sector.

Introduction

Never think that war, no matter how necessary, nor how justified, is not a crime. Ask the infantry, ask the dead.

—Ernest Hemingway

The Battle of Hürtgen Forest is a lesser-known chapter of American history, with some preferring to overlook it entirely. The events there went largely unreported in the media back home, and many high-ranking commanders left this episode out of their memoirs. American soldiers referred to the whole forested region south of Aachen as Hürtgen Forest, comprising not only Hürtgen Forest itself, but also Wenau Forest and Rötgen Woods. This area spans an 80-square-kilometer triangle defined by the towns of Aachen, Düren, and Monschau.

The commitment of the 28th Infantry Division men was about to be tested as never before as they entered the dark, damp Hürtgen Forest in Germany. War correspondent Ernest Hemingway called it, "Passchendaele with tree-bursts."[1] But not even Hemingway could quite capture the true description of this awful place. In these harsh conditions, morale plummeted, and many soldiers found the psychological pressure overwhelming. Some retreated to the rear, while certain commanders were removed from their positions for refusing to lead an attack or failing to rally their troops. The men faced the ultimate test. Still, most soldiers continued fighting, driven by a sense of duty not only to themselves but also to those waiting for them back home.

The 28th Infantry Division's grueling experience in Hürtgen Forest endures as a powerful reminder of the unwavering determination displayed by both the German defenders and the American soldiers locked in this intense conflict. The campaign took place under conditions where the relentless resolve of German forces intersected with challenging terrain and harsh weather, highlighting the unforgiving nature of warfare on enemy soil.

Fighting within German territory, American troops faced an adversary equally committed to defense. This fierce clash of wills transformed the forest into a crucible of combat, where both sides were resolute in holding their ground regardless of the cost. The Hürtgen Forest thus became a scene of relentless close combat, where soldiers faced environmental adversity, relying on their ingenuity and camaraderie to overcome the obstacles before them.

The terrain added yet another level of difficulty. Dense undergrowth and forested areas created hidden dangers and opportunities, turning each step into a potential trap—demanding constant vigilance against ambushes. The forest masked enemy movements, requiring soldiers to be ready for sudden encounters at any moment. In this challenging landscape, they had only their skills, weaponry, and unity to rely upon. Close-range combat pushed soldiers to the edge of physical and mental endurance, heightening the intensity of the struggle and the sacrifices required, surpassing even the seasoned expectations of 28th Division veterans.

The fierce battles of the Normandy breakout paled in comparison to those of Hürtgen Forest. The 109th and 110th Infantry Regiments faced the unique challenges of forest combat, including dispersed formations, limited command and control, and constant confusion. Small German units were determined to inflict maximum casualties and disrupt American advances. Across the Kall River, the 112th Infantry Regiment was positioned in Schmidt on an exposed plain, caught between German fire and isolation from their fellow regiments.

By late September 1944, the 60th Infantry Regiment of the 9th Division had already tested the forest and withdrawn bloodied by small, resolute German units. Attempting to move directly through the woods to capture the Hürtgen-Kleinhau road network along the forest's eastern ridges, a single regiment was overpowered by an enemy expertly exploiting the forest's defensive advantages. As October began, the First Army aimed to tie up loose ends before launching a broader offensive. The Hürtgen Forest remained a fortified and unconquered obstacle on the route to the Roer River, challenging the right flank of VII Corps.

As the 9th Infantry Division prepared to attack in early October, few in American command appeared to recognize the critical significance of a related objective that the capture of Schmidt might uncover. This was a multiple objective, a series of seven dams near the headwaters of the Roer River. Though three of the seven are on tributaries of the Roer, all came to be known collectively as the Roer River Dams (see Map 3).

The importance of the Roer River dams to Germany's defense strategy was highlighted a few days before the 9th Division's October offensive by Major Jack A. Houston, the division's G-2 officer. Major Houston explained that by controlling water discharge from the various dams, Germany could create "bank overflows and destructive flood waves" along the Roer River.[2] Destroying some of the dams, he noted, would unleash powerful flood waves that could devastate the populated industrial areas along the Roer, extending to the Meuse and into Holland. The implication was clear—if the Allies crossed the Roer downstream of the dams, the Germans could release the stored waters to flood the area, wiping out tactical bridges and isolating any Allied forces east of the river, leaving them vulnerable to concentrated attacks from German reserves.

The 9th Infantry Division, operating under VII Corps, launched its attack on October 6 at 11:30 AM, and it quickly became clear that the effort would be met with significant resistance. The offensive began along the Siegfried Line near Roetgen, Germany, with towns like Rott and Zweifall among those captured. As the division advanced toward Germeter, located west of Vossenack and north of Simonskall in North Rhine-Westphalia, it was abruptly confronted by a powerful German counterattack from the north and northeast originating from Hürtgen (Map 4 shows the first attack on Schmidt).[3]

At least one battalion was cut off from the main body of the division, which had suffered heavy casualties throughout the action. The line was stabilized toward the end of the third week in October just west of the main road running north and south through Germeter to Hürtgen. As a result of the heavy casualties it had sustained, plans were made to replace the 9th Division with the 28th Division, who had been resting and re-fitting at Elsenborn, Belgium after their encounter with the German Siegfried Line.[4] On October 10, Private Kensler wrote in his diary to his wife Cindy. He said he had just received a lecture on how to handle prisoners of war. He told her how he missed the things they had back home. "That is the honor and misery of war, I guess. We are here to make sure we keep those things," he wrote.[5]

In *Siegfried: The Nazis' Last Stand*, Charles Whiting reflected on the aftermath of the 9th Infantry Division's fighting in the Hürtgen Forest in early October 1944, during the opening phase of the larger Hürtgen campaign.

> Unrelenting German artillery and mortar fire had twisted the trees in the 9th Infantry Division sector into weird shapes. Graves registration personnel were completely overwhelmed due to the number of deaths and the terrain. The bodies of 9th Infantry Division soldiers lay throughout the sector. Trash and equipment that had been discarded was everywhere.[6,7]

The ragged appearance of 9th Division soldiers and the experiences they related were sufficient to unnerve many of the 28th Division men, especially those without combat experience.[8]

As part of the broader strategy from which the V Corps and 28th Division attack emerged, the US First Army was tasked with an offensive aimed at crossing the Roer River, capturing Düren, and then advancing toward Cologne and deeper into Germany. About a week prior, V Corps was to initiate a well-supported attack with the 28th Infantry Division to secure the key crossroad town of Schmidt. After taking Schmidt, the division would push south and southwest to clear the towns of Straunch and Steckenborn.[9]

In the attack's second phase, units of the 5th Armored Division were to launch a coordinated offensive from around Lammersdorf, advancing northeast to link up with the 28th Division as it drove south.[10] The V Corps plan called for the attack to begin on October 31. Bad weather prevented its launch until November 2, when, under orders from the First Army, the attack was launched despite bad weather. The bad weather almost completely prevented artillery observation and grounded air support until well after the attack had begun.[11]

In the V Corps sector, with a part of the lower portion of the VII Corps sector assigned to V Corps for this attack, the 28th Division entered the deadly forest. The entire western front was quiet when the 28th Division attacked. As a result, the Germans were unhampered in bringing in reserves, additional infantry, artillery and armor to confront the 28th Division's advance. Opposing the 28th Division was the German 275th Infantry Division, 275th Fusilier Battalion, 1412th Infantry Battalion, 89th Fusilier Battalion, and the Kampfgruppe Trier.[12]

Starting about 5 miles southeast of Aachen, the Hürtgen Forest spanned roughly 200 square miles, extending southward to the village of Steckenborn. The forest lay across high plateaus intersected by the gorges of the Kall and Roer Rivers and open farmland. Three prominent ridges rose across this sector of Germany, directly confronting the US First Army. Along the forest's eastern edge, a line of German fortifications stretched through the trees in a double layer. These defenses included concrete pillboxes with interlocking fields of fire, camouflaged log-and-earth bunkers, reinforced command posts, concealed machine gun nests, and tall concrete pylons to block armored vehicles. The area was also strewn with minefields and booby traps.

On November 1, the 28th Division was in a relatively inactive sector and was almost at full strength, but still attempting to integrate new replacements. The division had been in combat three-plus months and had seen heavy fighting in France in August and at the Westwall in September. The cumulative casualties as of November 1 were 8,775, including 6,130 battle losses.[13]

For the attack on Schmidt, the division had been reinforced by the 630th and 893rd Tank Destroyer battalions, equipped with the M10 Tank Destroyer, and the 707th Tank Battalion, equipped with the M4 Sherman Tank. The division also received forty-seven M29 Weasels (See Appendix B) in recognition of the rugged terrain in which resupply would have to be conducted. Eight battalions and a separate battery of V and VII Corps artillery were available for fire support (Map 5 shows the 28th Division attack plan).

When the 28th Division arrived in the Hürtgen Forest, an assessment of supply and evacuation capabilities revealed that the division's mission could not be completed with their existing transportation resources. This presented two options: using horses with pack saddles, M29 Weasel cargo carriers, or a combination of both. Since appropriate pack saddles were unavailable from the Army Quartermaster Class II supply, the horse option was abandoned, and forty-seven M29 Weasels were requested instead.[14]

For direct and general support, the corps placed eight battalions and a separate battery of artillery to support the 28th Division attack. Using five fighter-bomber groups and a night fighter group, IX Tactical Command was to direct its main effort toward air support of the division.[15] After a heavy artillery bombardment from six battalions of VII Corps artillery on the morning of November 2 from 8:00 AM to 9:00 AM, with more than 12,000 rounds fired under misty, overcast skies, the attack commenced (Map 6 shows the second attack on Schmidt).

The 2nd Battalion, 112th Infantry, supported by D Company of the 707th Tank Battalion, advanced through Germeter toward Vossenack. Meanwhile, the US 1st Division, positioned in the northern half of VII Corps' sector, fired mortars and artillery to mislead the Germans into thinking the attack spanned the entire front. The 2nd Battalion encountered minimal resistance in its eastward push, reaching Vossenack's northeast section by early afternoon. Two of the battalion's attacking companies established defensive positions on the forward slope of the ridge, while the reserve company cleared out bypassed stragglers and snipers.

The German's well-observed artillery fire took a heavy toll on the division companies, reducing them considerably. It was already evident that American artillery was unable to effectively neutralize the German observation posts and positions on the commanding ridges because the shells were coming into the town from three major points of the compass. Companies reported German armor in the town of Schmidt.[16]

After several days of intense fighting, moving in and out of basements in Vossenack and Germeter, the 109th Regiment received orders to launch an assault northeast of Hürtgen. The route passed entirely through dense forest, so the regiment concentrated all available .30- and .50-caliber machine guns to lay interdictory fire on the roads surrounding the town. They even removed .50-caliber guns from kitchen trucks, manned by headquarters and kitchen personnel, to boost firepower. As they advanced through the forest, they established a ladder-type barrage to support the movement.

The attack started off successfully, with the 109th Regiment making significant progress in coordination with the 112th Infantry, managing to neutralize fifteen pillboxes and capture over two hundred prisoners. The 1st Battalion advanced 2,700 yards northeast toward Hürtgen, while the other assault battalion heading in the same direction could only cover 500 yards due to dense minefields and wire obstacles, which were protected by sweeping fire from German automatic weapons.[17]

The 109th Infantry achieved partial success. One battalion managed to secure most of its objectives by the end of the day, while the other battalion was unable to reach its goal due to unexpected minefields and fierce resistance from previously undiscovered German strongpoints. The 2nd Battalion, 112th Infantry Regiment took its objective by 10:30 AM and proceeded to dig in. Opposition had been light. The rest of the 112th Infantry Regiment ran into unexpected opposition south of Vossenack and was unable to advance further that day.

The 110th Infantry Regiment launched an assault against formidable German positions but did not achieve significant success. The attacking battalions were met with intense mortar and artillery fire from the Germans, which hampered their progress, due to heavily booby-trapped defensive setups, pillboxes, dug-in wooden bunkers, and other fortified positions. They managed to advance only about 200 yards. On the morning of November 3, the 2nd Battalion and the 3rd Battalion launched another attack. While American mortar and artillery units heavily bombarded the front, the assault battalions still could not penetrate the fortified positions.[18]

On November 3, the 112th Regiment continued its attack, with the 1st and 3rd battalions successfully reaching Kommerscheidt and Schmidt. The two battalions established defensive positions in both towns. Meanwhile, the 109th Infantry Regiment renewed its assault, deploying a previously uncommitted reserve battalion, but was unable to achieve success throughout the day. In the morning, a strong counterattack from the direction of Hürtgen against the regiment's left flank forced a slight withdrawal. According to the November summary of activities from the 28th Infantry Division's regiments, the G-2 Section reported that while the 2nd Battalion of the 109th Regiment did not make significant progress, their preliminary attack in the 109th area had effectively drawn in the Germans.[19]

Such daily summaries from the 28th Division headquarters might have confused riflemen in the battalions of the 109th Infantry Regiment. They did not feel they had sucked in the German counterattack or foiled their enemies. As they stumbled blindly through the battle area following inadequate maps, they might have marveled to know the divisional headquarters prided itself on letting every man know what he was supposed to do. Yet, without good maps or clear guidance, the men did the best they could. The 110th Infantry Regiment again attacked but suffered heavy casualties and gained no ground.[20]

On November 4, German artillery fire intensified across the entire division area. A counterattack on the positions in Schmidt forced the 3rd Battalion of the 112th Infantry Regiment to retreat. Initially, the counterattack split the battalion in two, with one company vanishing into the woods south of the town. The sound of exploding artillery shells striking Kommerscheidt and Schmidt drove the men of L Company into their foxholes, where they hurriedly dug to make them larger while there was still time, fully intending to hold their position.

Artillery fire was particularly heavy to their south. Due to a hill and the sloping terrain between them, they were unable to fully understand the difficulties K Company was encountering. Along with the artillery fire, they were also facing German tank fire. L Company's 2nd Platoon was positioned on a forward slope facing east, with the town of Schmidt directly behind them. Through the morning fog, the men spotted about fifty Germans approaching over a rise approximately 600 yards ahead.[21]

During this operation, Captain Linguiti, a medical officer of the 112th Infantry Regiment, relocated his aid station to a small, abandoned house overlooking Kommerscheidt to ensure prompt medical attention for the wounded. As the fighting intensified, division infantry and tanks positioned themselves near the house where Captain Linguiti's aid station was located.

On November 5 at 5:00 AM, a resupply convoy for the 1st Battalion arrived in Kommerscheidt and unloaded its supplies in front of the medical personnel's battalion aid station. For the next two hours, Captain Linguiti, the unit surgeon, became increasingly frustrated as he observed company supply parties arriving to collect their ammunition and rations. He was deeply worried that these activities would jeopardize his efforts, fearing that German artillery would target the area without realizing that an aid station was situated amid the commotion.[22]

The Germans, positioned on the far slopes of the surrounding hills and noticing the increased activity around the house, launched an artillery and mortar barrage on the aid station and its vicinity. Recognizing the need to move the aid station to ensure the safety of his staff and the casualties crowding their facilities, Captain Linguiti decided to evacuate after dark. He led his staff and patients along the road out of Kommerscheidt toward the river.

The Germans managed to score direct hits on the house three times, resulting in the deaths of medical officers and two aidmen, as well as the destruction of all food supplies and most medical equipment. Despite the ongoing artillery fire, Captain Linguiti continued to receive, treat, and evacuate the wounded. When German artillery struck the already damaged house again, rendering it nearly unusable, he relocated to join the 3rd Battalion aid station, located in a log-and-dugout bunker. Linguiti left eight litter bearers in Kommerscheidt to gather casualties and transport them to the dugout.[23]

As the dugout became increasingly unlivable and troops began to withdraw, the chaplains of both battalions chose to remain in the dugout, where many wounded soldiers were calling out for spiritual support. These men wanted to practice their faith even while lying on stretchers. Chaplain Alan P. Madden from the 1st Battalion and Chaplain Ralph E. Maness from the 3rd Battalion stayed in the dugout until November 9, doing their best to minister to those brought to the bunker. They represented the two major Christian denominations, with Father Madden attending to Roman Catholics and Reverend Maness serving Protestants.[24] Father Madden was eventually captured by the Germans.

Captain Linguiti's decision to advance his aid station into the village enabled seventy-seven casualties to be given immediate medical treatment, a factor which saved many lives. Captain Linguiti was listed as missing in subsequent action against the Germans and was posthumously awarded the Silver Star for his actions that day.[25]

The remainder of the battalion withdrew to the northern edge of Schmidt, where they faced renewed German attacks. Unable to hold their position, they retreated to Kommerscheidt. There are indications that some soldiers were unwilling to maintain their positions. The defensive line at Kommerscheidt was bolstered by personnel from the 3rd Battalion of the 112th Infantry Regiment and held until the morning of November 7.[26]

The 110th Infantry Regiment launched another attack but did not achieve significant success. As the daily German artillery barrages began, the men of the 110th hurried to their foxholes. In the distance, they could hear mortars firing. Typically, the Germans would fire about eighteen rounds, with the shells landing moments later. After the debris from the explosions settled, someone would peek out of their hole to check if anyone was injured. Eventually, the Germans realized that the Americans were counting the shell rounds, so while the expected eighteen rounds were landing, they added three additional rounds into their mortar tubes.[27]

On November 4, the 1st Battalion of the 110th Infantry, which had remained unengaged until that morning, successfully conducted a flanking attack and captured its first two objectives. However, they soon found themselves confronted by German forces in fortified positions, which cut them off from the rest of their regiment. Efforts to clear the area over the next nine days were only partially successful, and the regiment was finally relieved from the front lines on November 13.[28] The division's men were thankful to be out of combat, even if only for a few hours or days. On November 6, the Germans launched a counterattack in Vossenack. The 2nd Battalion of the 112th Infantry abandoned its positions without clear evidence of strong infantry assaults, succumbing to extremely heavy artillery fire—some of which was direct. Simultaneously, the Germans captured the main supply route to Kommerscheidt, effectively isolating the 112th Infantry and the newly formed Task Force Ripple, which included the 3rd Battalion of the 110th Infantry, a company of tank destroyers, and two tank companies.[29]

American soldiers faced a nightmarish situation as shells exploded in the tops of 100-foot fir trees and mines detonated from the forest floor. The impact of a tree-burst sent shrapnel and debris raining down, while foxholes offered little protection. Many GIs became casualties of their own artillery fire. Navigating the minefields was particularly hazardous, as engineers would mark cleared paths with white tape—which the wind could easily displace or snow and mud could obscure. When US armor finally arrived to support the infantry, the dense trees and minefields restricted the tanks to a few narrow, muddy forest roads and logging trails. However, those roads were also mined, and a single disabled tank or truck could block an entire convoy. In addition to facing enemy forces and severe weather, the Americans contended with exhaustion, hunger, pneumonia, and trench foot. They lacked sufficient boots and winter clothing, with many struggling to find a dry place to sleep. Soldiers in forward positions endured long, freezing nights in open foxholes. To the surprise of the British troops nearby, the GIs relied on cold C-rations for sustenance.[30]

Overcoats drenched with water and caked in frozen mud became excessively heavy, while moisture infiltrated radio sets, rendering them inoperative. The forest floor was so entangled with brush and debris that soldiers struggled under the physical burden of carrying weapons, transporting supplies, and evacuating the wounded. Combat often occurred at such close range that hand grenades were the only effective weapons. Booby traps hidden in abandoned foxholes and ditches turned potential safe havens into deadly traps for the unsuspecting. The Germans even set explosives beneath fallen American soldiers.

One seriously injured GI lay motionless on a booby trap for seventy-two hours, fighting to stay conscious in order to warn anyone who might come to help him. Eventually, someone did arrive, and he survived. While the living fought for survival, the bloated, frozen bodies of the dead lay scattered in grotesque positions, beyond any care.[31]

Even amidst what appeared to be a hopeless situation, the courage of some individuals remained unwavering. During a bombardment in which six hundred German artillery shells struck within a 30-minute span, Staff Sergeant Paul Kerekes, from M Company, 110th Infantry, rushed out from his cover to fix damaged communication lines. Meanwhile, as army air force planes approached to bomb and strafe German positions, Staff Sergeant Arthur Johnson, from K Company, pulled panels indicating American positions into sight, helping pilots distinguish between German and American forces.[32] Both men were awarded the Distinguished Service Cross for their efforts.

As German tanks advanced toward the Americans, they forced the soldiers from their foxholes, prompting a chaotic retreat. Sergeant Tony Kudiak from Headquarters Company was determined not to surrender easily. Recognizing the urgency of stopping the Germans, he grabbed a bazooka and fired at an approaching tank. When the Germans emerged from the wreckage, Kudiak and his men shot them with rifles and drove off other German tanks that had pinned down the soldiers. As the German forces pressed on, Sergeant Kudiak held his ground, climbed into a tank destroyer, and repelled the German grenadiers. When the weapon jammed, he abandoned that tank destroyer and got into another. When that gun also malfunctioned, he resorted to his M-1 rifle, targeting as many German infantry soldiers as he could.[33] Sergeant Kudiak was awarded the Silver Star for his actions that day.

The 109th Infantry Regiment was replaced in its area by the 12th Infantry Regiment from the 4th Infantry Division, allowing the 110th Regiment to take over positions in the Vossenack region. A task force composed of the 3rd Battalion, 109th Infantry Regiment was dispatched to rescue the encircled 112th Infantry and Task Force Ripple in Kommerscheidt, but the mission was unsuccessful. Some units became lost in the thick forest, while others faced unexpected resistance, causing the hastily formed task force to become scattered. Ultimately, they established a defensive position on the southern slope of a hill south of Vossenack and helped cover the withdrawal of the 112th Infantry during the night of November 8.[34]

On November 10, the Germans sent a captured American into the lines of the 3rd Battalion, 109th Regiment with a demand from the German commander that the unit should surrender. The 3rd Battalion commander, Major Howard Topping, answered with American artillery batteries, in which the artillery battalions of the corps pounded German positions.[35] The commander of 1340th Combat Engineer Battalion, Lieutenant Colonel Truman Setliffe, was at the site of the demolished Kall Bridge on November 10. When he told his engineers of the German ultimatum to surrender or be slaughtered, they said they would "stick it out and fight. That is what they came for."[36]

The evacuation process was challenging, with heavy casualties. Medical evacuations were especially complex and perilous. Vossenack served as a crucial junction for three major roads and was essential for accessing the Schwammenauel Dam across the Roer River, earning it the nickname "artillery alley." During a 24-hour period, German self-propelled, railroad, and field guns unleashed between 2,000 and 3,000 artillery rounds on the 1st Battalion, 112th Infantry Regiment, while the only road leading into Vossenack was subjected to shelling every hour.

Despite the intensity of the conflict, both sides paused, surprisingly, for humanitarian reasons. The fighting was so brutal and the casualties so high that there were three separate ceasefires over five days to facilitate the evacuation of the wounded. The first occurred on November 7 at Kall Bridge in Schmidt, while the second, organized by Major Albert Berndt, the regimental surgeon, took place on November 9, with the third coming two days later, allowing for the unimpeded transport of casualties to medical facilities in the rear.[37]

With the withdrawal of the 112th Infantry Regiment, the attack on Schmidt was temporarily abandoned. On November 10, the 28th Division was instructed by V Corps headquarters to secure a line along the north and west banks of the Kall River. It was in the fighting for this ground that the 1st Battalion, 110th Infantry Regiment suffered its heaviest casualties. On November 14, all attacks by the division had ceased. The men were exhausted. Many of the officers stated that they felt no further attacks could have been carried out even had they been ordered.[38]

The soldiers of the 28th Division encountered significant challenges during their time in the Hürtgen Forest. For much of the fighting, they were hampered by rain and fog, with snow adding to the difficulty in the later stages. On the few days it did not rain, low-hanging clouds and ground haze hindered the effective use of the substantial air support designated for the division. The rain rendered the narrow firebreak trails unsuitable for supply routes or for maneuvering armored vehicles, transforming them into rutted, slippery bogs. Even vehicles like jeeps and M29 Weasels, designed to operate in snowy conditions, became immobilized. The relentless wet conditions left the inadequately equipped troops vulnerable to trench foot.[39]

On average only 10–15 percent of the men per company were equipped with all-weather boots. The overwhelming majority endured the entire action without them. Foxholes turned into veritable artesian wells during the latter part of the action. The ground became so thoroughly soaked that it was impossible for the men to keep dry. The 28th Division Surgeon's Report of Casualties shows 750 cases of trench foot.[40]

The soldiers of the 28th Division encountered challenging terrain throughout their operations. Their assault took place within the dense pine of Hürtgen Forest, where visibility was generally limited to 150–200 yards, and in some areas less than 25 feet. As the attack continued, relentless artillery and mortar bombardments uprooted trees, brought down others, and created such a buildup of debris on the ground that visibility and movement were severely restricted.

Bringing warm food through the muddy terrain and thick woods was impossible until hours after it had been prepared, resulting in cold and spoiled meals upon arrival. Additionally, the attack occurred in an area dominated by German-held high ground to the north, east, and south. This placement enabled the Germans to observe the division's assault and, in some cases, deliver artillery fire from a full 180-degree arc. According to Lieutenant Colonel Thomas E. Briggs, the 28th Division's G-3, this was a significant factor contributing to the troops' inability to succeed.[41]

The road network in the area was limited and inadequate for employing armor. The route from Vossenack through the draw across the Kall River to Kommerscheidt and Schmidt was little more than a trail. As it turned out, this trail caused the breakdown of the supply movement and armored support to the Kommerscheidt area.[42]

Communications, always a problem in battle, was never adequate during the 28th Division operation. The heavy German artillery and mortar fire constantly knocked out wire communications from battalions to companies, and several times for prolonged periods from regiments to battalions. The most exhausting and tireless efforts of the communications personnel to keep communications open and lines repaired were unable to keep pace with the rate of communications being knocked out.

At night, messengers would, again and again, grope their way through the tangle of shot-down treetops along the frazzled telephone line in order to patch it up. The lack of communications effected the entire situation. Lack of situational awareness hampered quick, effective decisions on the part of commanders, increasing demoralization among the men. Orders from commanders were slowed or not received at all, delaying vital redeployments and other actions.[43]

Finally, the performance of the 28th Division's inexperienced personnel significantly hindered the division. Although the division had received replacements during the month of October, bringing it up to full strength, after its attempts to penetrate the Siegfried Defenses in September, many of the men were not trained infantry soldiers. Rifle company officers and noncommissioned officers, in many cases, had been drawn from anti-tank companies, anti-aircraft units, air force ground personnel, and other non-infantry organizations. Even during the period of comparative quiet that the division enjoyed for a brief period at Camp Elsenborn, Belgium in October, these deficiencies had not been sufficiently remedied according to Colonel Theodore A. Seely, 110th Infantry Regiment commander.[44]

As a result of the inexperienced personnel, when the attack began and casualties mounted, the loss of the few remaining trained men immediately became apparent. Some infantry soldiers broke and ran into Schmidt, Kommerscheidt, and Vossenack. Author Ernest Hemingway spent eighteen days on the front in the

Hürtgen Forest. He later wrote, "It was a place where it was extremely difficult for a man to stay alive even if all he did was be there."[45]

As the operation progressed, the rapid attrition of companies, the loss of experienced officers, commissioned and otherwise, and the complete absence of trained replacements all contributed to the mission's failure. On the German side, they were mounting a fervent defense in terrain they knew intimately. In turn, they fought fiercely, relinquished some ground, but frequently counter-attacked. And although they suffered significant losses, they managed to stop and devastate the advance of the 28th Infantry Division.

Many American soldiers arrived in Europe expecting that German forces were demoralized and would offer little resistance. They quickly learned, however, that German soldiers were determined and fearless fighters.[46] The 28th soldiers were fatigued from exposure to the cold and rain and the heavy artillery fire pounding for hours on end. Self-care had become all but impossible. Often the dead could not be buried because there were not enough men available and because the ground was either too sodden, solidly frozen, or rocky. Constantly suffering casualties, the strength of the teams manning the positions was increasingly sapped. And yet the men held their positions, went out on patrols, attacked, overcame their fears, and faithfully performed their duty. Some exhibited bravery that earned them battlefield promotions and awards for valor. Their shared experience created a spirit of fellowship among them such that each man was prepared to do his utmost to defeat the Nazis.

The soldiers of the 28th Division were worn out from the cold, rain, and continuous artillery fire that persisted for hours. Self-care was nearly impossible, and often there were not enough personnel to bury the dead due to the sodden, frozen, or rocky ground. As casualties mounted, the strength of the defending units decreased. Still, the soldiers held their ground, carried out patrols, launched attacks, faced their fears, and fulfilled their responsibilities. Many showed remarkable bravery, earning battlefield promotions and honors for their valor. Their shared experiences created a strong sense of camaraderie, driving each man to do everything he could to defeat the Nazis.

The Battle of Hürtgen Forest was defined by fierce resistance from both sides, compounded by rugged terrain and harsh weather conditions. Close combat was frequent, and soldiers had to rely solely on themselves in a forest filled with tangled branches and underbrush, always facing the risk of surprise. Most engagements occurred at close range, requiring them to be quick and decisive with their weapons to survive. Often, success hinged on the actions of a few brave individuals who inspired and guided younger, inexperienced soldiers, helping them navigate and stand firm in the eerie darkness of the forest.[47]

The second attack on Schmidt had developed into one of the costliest US divisional actions in the whole of World War II. After the action in the Hürtgen Forest, the 28th Infantry Division was destroyed as an effective fighting force.

Division combat casualties totaled 6,184. Losses included 614 killed, 2,605 wounded, 855 missing, 245 captured, and 1,865 non-battle casualties. More than 750 of the non-battle casualties were from trench-foot alone.[48]

Given the difficulties it faced, the 28th Infantry Division fought well against all odds. For fourteen days its men struggled over steep hills and fought off infantry and tanks while enduring endless artillery barrages. They crossed the ridges between Vossenack and Schmidt using no more than a narrow, twisting trail. They briefly captured the towns of Vossenack, Kommerscheidt, Schmidt, and Simonskall. The private soldiers, noncommissioned officers, and company-grade officers who fought on those ridges were brave, courageous, and resourceful.

On November 14, 1944, Ivan (Cy) Peterman of *The Philadelphia Inquirer*, who was embedded with the 28th Division, watched the survivors emerge from their struggle with German forces in the Hürtgen Forest and wrote:

> They crouched in their vehicles, staring straight ahead. If there were heroics to recount, someone else had to talk. The men of this unit (28th Infantry) would not. Too many of their companions remained behind, too many were dead or missing. Too many grievously wounded and shattered in nerves and spirit. If they never saw the Hürtgen Forest again it would suit them. . . . They had enough.[49]

The soldiers of the 28th Division carried a strong belief, shaped by wartime propaganda, that they were invincible and could overcome any challenge with ease. While this perception boosted their confidence, it faced a harsh reality in the Hürtgen Forest. Confronted by the tough terrain and determined German defenders, they encountered an enemy not easily subdued. The Hürtgen Forest became a harsh teacher, challenging their earlier beliefs with the brutal truths of combat on foreign soil. Their unwavering commitment reflected their resilience and core values.

Even as the forest's difficulties and the enemy's persistence shattered some of their illusions, the soldiers remained determined to uphold the principles and freedoms of their nation. The hardships they faced in the Hürtgen Forest ultimately strengthened their resolve rather than diminished it. This experience highlighted the complexities of warfare, where idealism often collides with harsh reality.

Emerging from the Hürtgen Forest, the soldiers gained a deeper understanding of the sacrifices involved in defending their homeland. Their steadfast dedication to the American way of life endured, serving as a powerful testament to the human spirit's ability to persevere and triumph in the face of adversity. In the wake of the intense battles in the Hürtgen Forest, strategic plans were devised to orchestrate the relief of the battle-weary 28th Division by the 8th Infantry Division. From November 16 to 21, this intricate transition took place.

The baton of responsibility was passed, signaling a respite for the 28th Division, which embarked on a journey southward to Luxembourg, where rest and refurbishment awaited. As the 28th Division prepared to face new trials, their resilience and determination would be tested once more. The echoes of previous battles resonated within them, a poignant reminder of the forgotten sacrifices made and the ideals for which they fought.

1

The Need to Secure the Roer River Dams

While German Field Marshal Walter Model was busy organizing the defense of the Hürtgen Forest, Allied commanders were deliberating their next move. They faced a crucial decision—should they continue attacking German forces to try to end the war quickly, or should they wait until after winter, when conditions would be more favorable for an assault?

If General Eisenhower chose to delay, he could take the opportunity to secure his supply lines and allow his troops much-needed rest, but this would also give the Germans time to strengthen their defenses and develop new weapons. Despite the fall of Aachen on October 21, the Siegfried Line remained largely intact elsewhere. Ultimately, Eisenhower made his decision based partly on optimism.

He aimed to strike the enemy with all available force in an effort to divide their armies west of the Rhine, hoping that, once they reached the river, the morale of the German Reich would falter and lead to the war's conclusion. His plan involved the Twelfth Army Group launching an attack north of the Ardennes with the First and Ninth Armies, while the Third Army would strike south of the wooded barrier. All three were to push to the Rhine and seize the crossings there if they could.

General Omar Bradley commented:

> For a plan like this to succeed, the Allies must control the Roer River dams. Patton's attack from Metz through the Saar would be fine, but the First and Ninth Armies would have to cross the Roer River in order to reach the Rhine. Montgomery's troops in the north would also have to cross the Roer. The first time that the dams are mentioned by an American in writing is late September. Bank overflows and destructive flood waves can be produced on the Roer River by regulating the discharge from various dams. By Demolition of some of them great destructive waves can be produced which would destroy everything in the populated industrial valley of the Roer known as the Meuse and into Holland.[1]

General Omar Bradley, based on his comments regarding the attack on Schmidt, seemed to be aware of the dams by early November. In the autumn of 1944, securing the Roer River dams became a key goal for the Allied forces. These dams were strategically important, as they could control water levels in the area, impacting both military operations and civilian infrastructure.

As the 9th Division prepared to launch its attack in early October, few in the American command seemed to recognize the critical significance of another objective that capturing Schmidt could reveal—a series of seven dams located near the headwaters of the Roer.[2] Though only three of the seven are on tributaries of the Roer, all came to be known collectively as the Roer River Dams (see Map 3).

The two principal dams are the Urft and the Schwammenauel. Constructed just after the turn of the century on the Urft River between Gemuend and Ruhrberg, the Urft Dam is capable of impounding approximately 42,000 acre-feet of water. Built in the mid-thirties near Hasenfeld, about 2 miles downhill from Schmidt, the Schwammenauel Dam creates a reservoir encompassing about 81,000 acre-feet. The Schwammenauel is constructed of earth with a concrete core. Both the principal dams were designed for controlling the Roer River and providing hydroelectric power for Düren and other cities downstream to the north.[3]

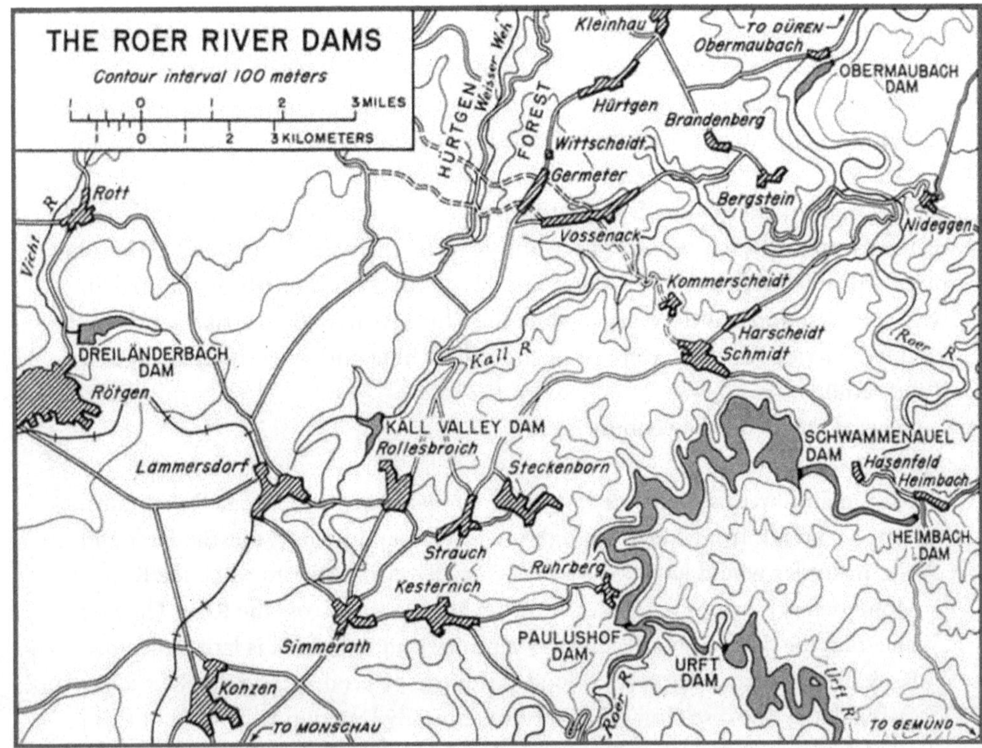

Roer River Dams, 1944. (*US Army Center of Military History*)

Downstream from the Schwammenauel, the lesser dams at Heimbach and Obermaubach were primarily constructed to serve as water management systems for industrial needs further downstream.[4] Among the other three dams, the Paulushof Dam, located near where the Roer River meets the Urft at Ruhrberg, was mainly built to manage water levels at the Schwammenauel reservoir's headwaters. The Kall Valley Dam, situated on the upper Kall River, near Lammersdorf, has a limited capacity, while the Dreilaenderbach Dam creates the Hauptbecken Reservoir near Roetgen at the headwaters of the Vicht River. The Dreilaenderbach Dam was already under American control prior to the 9th Division's attack in October.[5]

The value of the Roer River Dams to German defense was outlined several days before the 9th Division's October attack by the division G-2, Major Jack A. Houston.

> Bank overflows and destructive flood waves can be produced on the Roer River by regulating or demolishing its dams, creating waves capable of destroying everything in the populated industrial valley of the Roer, extending to the Meuse River and into Holland.[6]

The warning was fairly obvious—should the Allies cross the Roer downstream from the dams, the Germans could release the impounded waters to produce a flood that would demolish tactical bridges and isolate any force east of the Roer. Allied troops beyond the river would be exposed to destruction by German reserves.[7]

Despite this hazard, the Roer River Dams were not a formal objective of the 9th Division's October attack. As the division prepared to attack, advisers to the First Army commander minimized the defensive value of any floods which might be produced. On October 3, the day after the 9th Division's appraisal appeared, the First Army's intelligence section believed that if all of the dams in the entire First Army sector were blown, they would cause, at most, local flooding for about five days—counted from the moment the dam was blown until all the water had receded. Two days later a First Army engineer amended this view somewhat with the opinion that widespread flooding might result. But not for a long time were American commanders to appreciate the true value of the dams to the Germans.[8]

One explanation might rest in the fact that during October all reservoirs in the system were considerably drawn down, to an estimated 30–50 percent of total capacity. Yet as late as November 28, after water level in the reservoirs had risen as high as two thirds of capacity, the First Army G-2 still expressed the theory that the economic importance of the dams to life in Rhine River cities could prevent the enemy blowing them up as part of a "drowned earth" policy.[9]

Closer to reality was an early appraisal by a XIX Corps engineer. Aware that his corps eventually was to cross the Roer downstream from the dams near Jülich, where riverbanks are low, he warned his corps commander on October 8: "If one or all dams were blown, a flood would occur in the channel of the Roer River that would reach approximately 1,500 feet in width and 3 feet or more deep across the entire corps front—the flood would probably last from one to three weeks."[10] Unfortunately, the XIX Corps engineer went on to dismiss the subject because all the dams were in the VII Corps zone. The VII Corps, he noted, "could be requested to capture and prevent destruction although they can be presumed to do so as their area is affected also."[11]

On the contrary, General Collins and the VII Corps at this time were engrossed in plans to subdue Aachen and to send the 9th Division through the Hürtgen Forest. They paid scant attention to an objective like the dams, which did not lie along the planned route to the Roer and the Rhine.

SHAEF, General Eisenhower's headquarters, remained aloof on the subject of the dams until October 20, several days after the 9th Division's Hürtgen Forest attack had ended. On that date the SHAEF G-2 repeated and enlarged upon information originally obtained by the V Corps from a German prisoner. In Düren, the prisoner said, a persistent ringing of the city's church bells was to mean the dams had been blown. The people were to evacuate the city, because the flood there would reach a depth of almost 20 feet. Turning to photographic files, SHAEF noted that air cover of all dams except the Urft had existed since September 10. Allied air officials, SHAEF remarked, were prepared to study the question of [air] attack.[12]

Similar to the First Army, General Bradley's headquarters at the Twelfth Army Group downplayed the potential impact of a flood. In October, like SHAEF, the Twelfth Army Group viewed the dams primarily as an issue for the air force. A realistic perspective on the Roer River Dams took time to develop. Throughout October and November, the First Army, followed later by the Ninth Army, focused on strengthening their positions along the west bank of the Roer downstream from the dams, without making a concerted effort to seize them. However, neither army could cross the Roer until the dams were either captured or destroyed.[13]

The extent of time it took American command to adopt a realistic perspective on the dams becomes clear only after the First Army's operations concluded in October, November, and into December. As one examines the developments in the Hürtgen Forest and further north in the villages of the Roer River plain, it becomes increasingly obvious how significant these dams were in German strategy and how resolute the German defense of the dam region needed to be before American commanders recognized the threat they posed.[14]

The attack of the 28th Infantry Division to seize the Vossenack-Schmidt-Strauch area was the preliminary phase of a plan by V Corps to gain control of two large dams on the Roer River east of Monschau. If the Vossenack-Schmidt-Strauch triangle could be secured it would be possible to dominate the crossings of the Roer in this vicinity and a large portion of the major roads leading up from the east side of the river bottom. Further, the success of this operation, followed by exploitation across and east of the upper bends of the Roer River, would give the Allies control of the dams and prevent the enemy from blowing them up and flooding the middle reaches of the river. In its new sector, the 28th Division faced east in the Hürtgen Forest with its regiments disposed as follows: 109th Infantry to the north, 112th Infantry in the center and 110th Infantry to the south.[15]

2

The Battle for Aachen and the First Attempt in the Hürtgen Forest

The Siegfried Line (known as Westwall by the Germans) was a continuous series of pillboxes and emplacements stretching along Germany's western borders, from Kleve on the Dutch frontier to Lorrach near the Swiss border.

Built in 1939 and 1940, it predated the German military doctrine of strongpoints exemplified by the heavy defenses along the Atlantic and English Channel coasts. It was completed before the Russians taught the Germans the concept of an all-around hedgehog defense. As a result, the Siegfried Line primarily featured numerous reinforced concrete pillboxes designed for machine guns and 37mm antitank guns. There was minimal preparation for open earthworks for heavier artillery, and only limited field fortifications hastily constructed for infantry.[1]

The Siegfried Line was constructed along the first natural barrier east of the German frontier, with the densest concentration of pillboxes located where this barrier was weakest. The underlying strategy for the placement of pillboxes and anti-tank barriers was straightforward: to enhance the defensive capabilities of the terrain along the German border. Defenses were minimal in areas where attack would be challenging for tanks and infantry, such as across the Rhine River.

In contrast, regions with natural attack corridors—like the Belfort Gap, the Moselle River Valley, and the Aachen Plain—featured the most robust defenses.[2] The concrete structures generally measured 20–30 feet by 40–50 feet horizontally and stood 20–25 feet high, with at least half, and often more, situated underground. Their walls and roofs were 4–8 feet thick and sometimes reinforced with steel. Each pillbox included living quarters for its usual personnel. Fields of fire were limited; the path of fire generally did not exceed a 50-degree arc. Pillboxes were mutually supporting.

Four years of neglect during the high tide of German conquest had made the camouflage superb. Undergrowth and disuse made it extremely difficult to spot some of the boxes. Pillboxes occurred wherever the terrain indicated a profitable use of a machine gun or anti-tank gun. The real defense was to be an aggressive counterattacking force basing its offense from the Siegfried Line. The object of the defenses was not to stop the enemy but to slow him up and to tire him in the attack and then hit him with strong counterattacks.[3]

Although there were minor offensive operations on other portions of the army front during the first two weeks of October, the major effort of the army was confined to the Aachen area. The defensive line consisted of anti-tank dragon's teeth, barbed wire, mines, and pillboxes, a formidable, fixed defense. An equally arduous task facing the First Army was the taking of the city of Aachen. This was the first major German city American troops would attack. Aachen held an allure for American commanders. Regrettably, it also had great value for the Germans as well.

Aachen, also known as Aix-la-Chapelle in French, was previously the capital of the Carolingian Empire under Charlemagne, one that its defenders had to hold at all costs. Due to its significance, Hitler ordered that the German military defend the town of 160,000 to the last man.[4]

Capturing Aachen during World War II held significant strategic and symbolic importance for several reasons. First, Aachen was located near the borders of Belgium and Germany, making it a critical point for advancing into the heart of Germany. Its capture would allow Allied forces to secure a foothold for further operations. Second, Aachen was considered a gateway to the Ruhr industrial region, Germany's industrial heartland. Controlling Aachen meant the Allies could disrupt German supply lines and manufacturing capabilities.

The First Army's plan involved encircling the city using a double-wing envelopment strategy. This approach aimed to surround Aachen from two sides, effectively cutting off German forces and controlling access to the city. This maneuver would allow for a coordinated attack, maximizing pressure on the enemy and facilitating a more efficient capture of the city.

Although Aachen was not heavily fortified, its medieval layout made it conducive to defense, deterring commanders from launching a direct assault that would lead to intense house-to-house combat. Therefore, the strategy would involve Corlett's XIX Corps breaking through the Siegfried Line and, upon reaching the vicinity of the German town of Würselen, turning south to prepare for a meeting with the US VII Corps. The VII Corps was also tasked with breaching the Siegfried Line south of Aachen and, once east of the city, would pivot north to connect with the XIX Corps near Würselen.

On October 2, the Americans began their offensive, achieving significant progress in the first five days. However, during the following week, the Germans managed to thwart the Americans' plans to link up near Würselen. Nevertheless, by October 16, the encirclement was complete, and for the next five days, American forces relentlessly attacked the defenders from both ground and air. The city surrendered on October 21, marking the Allies' first major capture of a German city in the war. However, while Aachen lay in ruins, the leading US divisions, the 1st and the 30th, had suffered considerable losses in their rifle companies. Despite the Allies having breached the Siegfried Line, the rising casualties indicated a decline in their overall strength.[5]

As the battle for Aachen raged on, the First Army was also depleting its strength in another offensive. A series of attacks in the wooded region south of Aachen and north of the Ardennes, in the Hürtgen Forest, forced the US army into a style of warfare reminiscent of World War I. The operations in the Hürtgen Forest are considered one of the most perplexing episodes of the European Campaign. According to the official history of the First Army, "the original source of the idea to clear the forest remains unknown."[6] First Army Commander Lieutenant General Hodges, along with Major General William B. Kean (Hodges' chief of staff) and VII Corps Commander Major General Joseph Collins, were all apprehensive about the potential threat a German force could pose to the VII Corps' flank as it moved up the Stolberg corridor.

To safeguard this flank, Hodges and Collins suggested conducting an operation to clear the forested area of German units, an operation oddly reminiscent of the Argonne Forest campaign in 1918.[7] Despite the wealth of information available today, it remains challenging to comprehend why the Americans fought a battle in that area. One issue was that the objectives shifted throughout the course of the battle, and after the war, senior officers involved crafted a narrative about the campaign and its goals.

As the campaign progressed from September into October, it became increasingly apparent that the Roer Dams could be significant military targets. The Americans needed to capture the Hürtgen Forest, as it served as the gateway to the Roer Dam complex. It was not until the first week of November that the dams were clearly recognized as a threat, necessitating their capture.[8] Now in the second month of the campaign, the Roer Dams had become the primary objective, rather than that of preventing a German incursion into the VII Corps' flank.[9]

Conventional military wisdom would advise against launching an attack when the enemy has a clear advantage in a particular time or place. However, the American campaign in the Hürtgen Forest disregarded this, as the defenders in this damp forest held every advantage. A study from the US Army's Combat Studies Institute highlighted that the terrain's sharp, roller coaster-like ridges, valleys, and gorges exacerbated the disorienting effects of combat in the woods.[10] This naturally defensible area was filled with numerous well-fortified bunkers and pillboxes. The dense forests dominated the landscape, and the road network was often poor in some sections and nonexistent in others. The German defenders were entrenched in a formidable, dark, and dense manmade forest that had been planted before the war.[11]

Such terrain was, therefore, hardly an ideal setting for the most mobile and mechanized army in the European Theater to launch an attack, as it diminished the crucial advantages of mobility and tactical airpower that the US army possessed. The failure to grasp the challenges posed by the terrain may have been just one aspect of a broader oversight by First, Fifth, and Seventh Army headquarters.

The Allies believed that the German army was on the brink of collapse and that the war's conclusion was imminent. While it was true that the German army had suffered significant losses, its soldiers were no longer fighting in foreign lands; they were now defending their homeland. The experiences of Allied forces during Operation Market Garden and the tough defense of Aachen provided little insight into the true capabilities of the Germans. As American planners readied for an offensive into the Hürtgen, intelligence officers assumed the forest was held by weak units made up of exhausted soldiers and young recruits. In September, when the 9th Infantry Division launched its attack, the German 353rd Infantry Division consisted of a mix of second-tier troops stationed in the Hürtgen.

By October, when operations in the Hürtgen began in earnest, the 275th Infantry Division was responsible for its defense. Staff officers did not regard this division as a crack German unit. One author noted, "What the German division lacked in combat power, it recouped in the advantages the forest gave to the defender."[12] First Army planners failed to recognize that even second tier units can perform extremely well in terrain that is highly defendable. Regrettably, for far too many American soldiers, it would take two bitter lessons, the Hürtgen and the Ardennes, to reinforce the fact that the Germans were not yet defeated.

The first division to assault the Hürtgen was the 9th Infantry Division, led by Major General Louis A. Craig. Major General Collins aimed to breach the Siegfried Line before winter set in, so he instructed Craig to clear the northern part of the Hürtgen and capture the villages of Hürtgen and Kleinhau. This would help prevent a German attack on the flank of the 3rd Armored Division, which was advancing south of Aachen into the Stolberg area.

Craig's attack began in September.[13] Although the American division made progress by capturing the villages of Zweifall and Schevenhütte, the ninth was assigned competing priorities by higher headquarters. Two of Craig's regiments were reassigned to support the assault on the Aachen suburb of Stolberg, leaving only the 60th Infantry responsible for the attack in the Hürtgen. While the 9th Division was engaged in this offensive, two other operations were occurring on the Allied left flank: the assault on Aachen and Operation Market Garden, all targeting the area north of the Ruhr River. Fighting by elements of the 9th Division continued into the third week of September, with the original goals of the operation becoming increasingly obscured by a series of tactical challenges typical of the dense forest.

In early October, the 9th Infantry Division refocused on the Hürtgen as Collins ordered the attack to restart, this time with two regiments. The 47th Regiment was held in reserve to support the 3rd Armored Division. During this period, the G-2 of the 9th Infantry Division assessed the region and noted the importance of the Roer Dams, but First Army staff dismissed this report. Instead, the VII Corps instructed two regiments from the 9th Division to advance through the forest to capture Vossenack and Kommerscheidt, with the ultimate goal of reaching the town of Schmidt. The assault began shortly before noon on October 6, but progress was impeded by mud, dense forest, bunkers, and both mortar and artillery fire. Despite these challenges, American infantry units reached the outskirts of Germeter by October 9. However, the two regiments faced slim chances of reaching Vossenack or Schmidt. Intense fighting followed for the next four days, with both sides launching attacks and counterattacks, bolstered by reinforcements.

By October 13, a classic stalemate had developed on the battlefield. The division's objective remained the crucial road junction in Schmidt, but this goal was far from attainable. Overall, elements of the 9th Division spent nearly thirty days in the Hürtgen Forest, suffering about 4,500 casualties, both battle-related and otherwise. Despite the sacrifices made, they gained only slightly over 3,500 yards of territory and failed to clear the Hürtgen of German forces or capture the vital town of Schmidt. The setback in the American push into the Hürtgen Forest was just one of the many challenges facing the Twelfth Army Group, particularly the US First Army.[14]

In October, the First Army faced a critical shortage of supplies. Ammunition was particularly limited, raising significant concerns as the scarcity of artillery rounds restricted support for troops engaged with the enemy. Supply issues extended beyond ammunition, affecting rations, trucks, and tanks. A major part of the problem was the logistics of transporting supplies, especially since the deep-water port at Antwerp, Belgium was not yet operational, making the journey from Normandy beaches to the Hürtgen lengthy. Eisenhower's push to maintain pressure along the front, along with Bradley's orders for both the First and Third armies to remain in attack mode, contributed to these significant supply shortages.

By October 20, the 1st Division had nearly completely occupied Aachen. In the six days between encirclement and surrender, over 1,000 German prisoners were captured, and 5,000 civilians were evacuated from the combat zone.

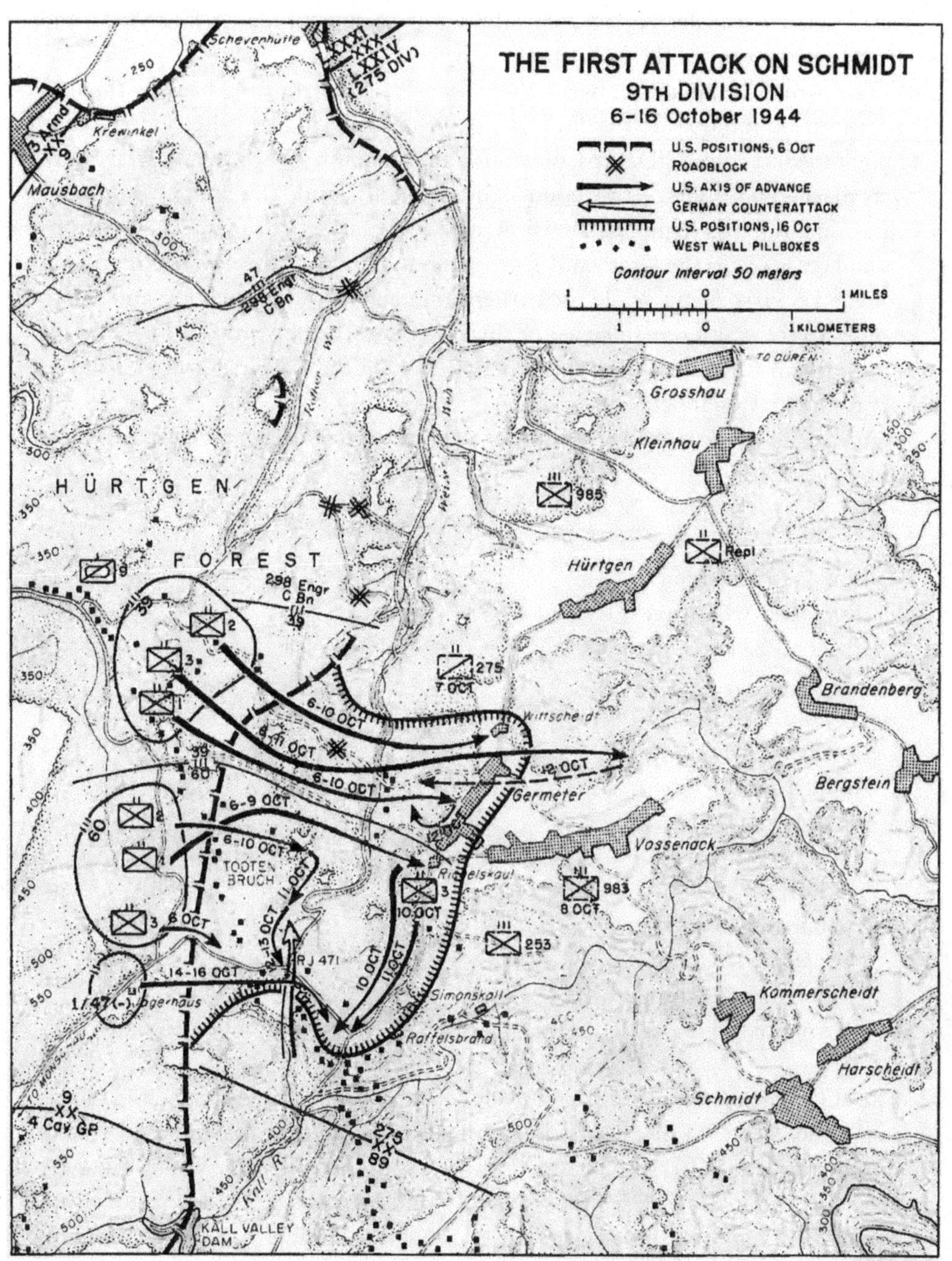

First Attack on Schmidt, 1944. (*US Army Center of Military History*)

On October 22, steps were initiated for regrouping and reorganizing ahead of future offensives into the lower Rhineland. On that day, Ninth Army Headquarters transferred control of the southern zone to the US First Army and took over the zone of the XIX Corps to the north.

The former boundary between the VII and XIX Corps now became the new northern boundary for the First Army, separating it from the Ninth Army. Simultaneously, the VIII Corps, previously on the south side of the US First Army, was placed under First Army control, including the 2nd, 8th, and 83rd infantry divisions, the 9th Armored Division, and other attached units. The previous boundary between the Ninth and Third armies established the new southern limit for the US First Army, while the earlier boundary between the First and Ninth armies to the south remained as the division between the V and VIII corps. This re-allotment of control over zones of action gave the US First Army a front of approximately 60 miles.

As a result of these changes the order of battle of the major combat units of the army was as follows:

V Corps
4th Infantry Division
28th Infantry Division
5th Armored Division

VII Corps
1st Infantry Division
9th Infantry Division
3rd Armored Division

VIII Corps
2nd Infantry Division
8th Infantry Division
83rd Infantry Division
9th Armored Division[15]

The V Corps' positions stretched from Monschau, including Hofen and Alzen, to the edge of the Monschau Forest, with patrols from the 5th Armored Division monitoring the front. The 102nd Cavalry Group patrolled the wooded border area for about 5 miles southeast, while units from the 28th Division were stationed along the frontier just west of Neuhof, covering roughly 5 miles. This front, aligned north to south and facing east, traversed heavily wooded terrain, closely following the frontier boundary south of Alzen. The primary strength of the corps was located in the 28th and 4th infantry divisions, which occupied the southern half of the zone.

Although Aachen had fallen, marking the end of the first phase of the operation outlined in the First Army's orders from September 29, the advance toward Düren and ultimately the Rhine River was still necessary. Before resuming the offensive, it was crucial to replace the fatigued 9th Division, which had suffered heavy losses during the month of combat in the Hürtgen and Rotgen Forests. Consequently, the 4th Infantry Division, which had been stationed in a quieter sector, was assigned to take over most of the front held by the 28th Infantry Division. The 28th Division would then relieve the 9th Division, excluding the 47th Regimental Combat Team, which was attached to the 3rd Armored Division.

On October 21, the Twelfth Army Group had ordered a general eastern attack, with the First Army tasked to reach the Rhine near Cologne and Bonn and secure a bridgehead if possible. Following this directive, the First Army issued instructions on October 26, confirming the changes within V and VII corps.

After an initial operation by V Corps to secure the Vossenack-Schmidt-Strauch area, a coordinated attack by VII Corps was planned towards Düren and Cologne to penetrate enemy positions and reach the Rhine. Once V Corps secured the Vossenack-Schmidt-Strauch area, they were to be ready to advance on Bonn, following orders from the army after VII Corps had successfully breached the enemy's main positions. VIII Corps was tasked with maintaining an aggressive defense and preparing to advance on Koblenz.

The target date for the preliminary operation was set for November 1, contingent on ammunition availability and favorable weather for air operations. The main operation was scheduled for November 5 or later, also dependent on supplies and troop readiness, aiming to leverage significant air support to clear a path through enemy defenses in front of Düren.

After the VII Corps failed to achieve its objectives in the Hürtgen, a second, perplexing phase of fighting began, as part of a plan from Twelfth Army Group headquarters. This plan aimed for an attack through the Stolberg corridor to position American forces on the west bank of the Rhine River and potentially secure a bridgehead.

Hodges' First Army was responsible for this operation, supported by V and VII Corps, with Collins' corps leading the main effort and VII Corps attacking the northern section of the Hürtgen via the Stolberg corridor. Following boundary adjustments in late October, Gerow took command of the upcoming attack, directing 28th Infantry Division to launch a supporting attack for VII Corps' primary effort.

The 28th began moving into an area east of Rott, Germany on October 25, replacing the exhausted 9th Infantry Division. The V Corps headquarters gave the 28th the following direction:

1. Relieve the 9th Infantry division on 26–27 October.
2. Prepare to attack the Germans, with the significant objectives being Kommerscheidt and Schmidt.[16]

Unlike the 9th Infantry Division, the 28th was able to employ all three of its regiments, actually regimental combat teams (RCTs), to achieve its objectives. Each RCT from the 28th would have specific objectives.[17]

The 109th RCT would attack toward and capture the town of Hürtgen. The division staff sent the 110th RCT to advance toward the town of Simonskall. The 112th RCT was to secure the ridge that led to Vossenack. The overall objective for the 28th, however, was to secure the town of Schmidt and draw German attention and reserves away from VII Corps' main effort. The 28th's action was supposed to be a supporting attack rather than the main effort.[18] The V Corps commander and his staff developed the overall plan for the 28th Division's attack.

All available evidence seems to indicate that the 28th Infantry Division commander, Major General Norman "Dutch" Cota and his staff, had little input on the plan, and Cota objected to the plan, primarily due to concerns about the terrain and the readiness of the troops. The corps staff ignored his objections.[19]

VII Corps was unable to get prepared to conduct the main effort on November 5, as initially planned. The corps staff rescheduled the attack for November 10 and then postponed it an additional six days. Despite these delays, the 28th Infantry Division's drive was not cancelled or rescheduled and began as ordered on November 2, even though it was supposed to support a main effort that, by that time, had become nonexistent.

This meant that on November 2 the 28th's attack was the only push along a 27-mile section of the front, such that for a few days, the division's attack was the only one on the 170-mile Western Front.[20] This allowed the Germans to focus their attention on a solitary division action, rather than on the collective elements of two corps.

As was typical of many major US offensives in the European Campaign, 28th Infantry Division staff believed that they would receive significant air and artillery support. However, such plans merely demonstrated the army and corps planners' ignorance of the Hürtgen's terrain. The heavy forest prohibited accurate close air support, while the forest and terrain complicated observed artillery fire. In addition, at the time of the planned attack, the weather was poor.

Planners did recognize the tough task assigned to the 28th, and V Corps did provide additional assets to the 28th. The 707th Tank Battalion, equipped with Sherman M4A1 tanks (See Appendix C), and the 893rd Tank Destroyer Battalion, equipped with M10 tank destroyers (See Appendix D), provided additional firepower on the ground. Given the strength of the German position and the terrain, the 117th Engineer Group, three artillery battalions, and a 4.2-inch mortar battalion were attached to the division as well.

3

The Terrain and Preparations

A significant portion of the Federal Republic of Germany is forested, and various factors such as topography, soil type, tree species (including underbrush), and the accessibility of roads and paths influence combat operations in these areas.

For military units operating in forests, it is crucial to understand both the benefits and challenges of fighting in wooded terrain. Many of Germany's forests are located in hilly regions of moderate elevation, which typically makes them well-suited for defensive positions.[1] The Hürtgen Forest marked the northern end of the 390-mile Westwall. This densely wooded mountainous region features steep elevations exceeding 500 meters. Beyond the enemy lines lay three small clearings: 1. the area with the villages of Grosshau and Hürtgen; 2. directly south, the village of Vossenack; and 3. to the southeast, an elongated clearing that includes the village of Kommerscheidt and the road hub of Schmidt.

A large, forested hill and ravine divide Schmidt from the expansive cleared area stretching from Lammersdorf and Monschau to the upper Roer River, which arcs northeast toward Schmidt. The village of Strauch, situated on elevated ground in the northern part of this open area, overlooks the wooded ravines along the Roer to the east.[2]

The timber in that area was considered the finest and most beautiful in Germany. Fast-flowing mountain streams and rivers traverse densely forested, steep ravines and folds. The presence of nearly impenetrable underbrush, rocky slopes, and treacherous swampy areas created a challenging and intricate landscape for military operations.

Ralph Johnson from the 28th Division Service Company, described it this way:

> The Hürtgen Forest was a dank dark and impossible place; a pine forest with trees so thick that the sun did not penetrate until about 10:00 AM and disappeared again at 3:00 PM The ground underfoot was 10 inches deep in wet pine needles and moss.[3]

Small arms were effective only at close range, prompting the Germans to create designated firing lanes. The defenders fortified the area with makeshift blockhouses, minefields, barbed wire, and booby traps, all concealed by mud and snow. Numerous concrete bunkers, primarily part of the Siegfried Line's deep defenses, also served as centers of resistance. The thick forest facilitated infiltration and flanking maneuvers, making it challenging to establish a clear front line or to ensure that an area was free of enemy forces. The limited routes and clearings in the forest allowed German machine gun, mortar, and artillery teams to accurately pre-range their weapons.[4]

The American superiority in numbers (up to 5:1), armor, mobility, and air support was significantly diminished by the weather and terrain. In the forest, a relatively small contingent of well-prepared and resolute defenders could be very effective. The thickly wooded landscape restricted tank operations and offered concealment for German anti-tank teams armed with Panzerfaust shaped-charge grenade launchers.[5]

The forested hilly terrain in this area offered excellent cover for concealing movements. German defenders had fortified the region with makeshift blockhouses, minefields, barbed wire, and booby traps, all obscured by mud and snow. Additionally, numerous concrete bunkers, primarily part of the deeper defenses of the Siegfried Line, served as strongholds. From the small German border villages southeast of Aachen, the Hürtgen Forest appears as an almost impenetrable expanse, a vast, undulating sea of dark green stretching endlessly.[6]

The 28th Infantry Division's mission extended beyond merely capturing the high ground around Schmidt. Along with securing this elevation, the plan aimed to breach the 2nd Westwall line in the Simonskall-Kallbrück-Ochsenkopf-Raffelsbrand area and advance into the Rollesbroich region. Utilizing forces that secured Schmidt, the objective was to infiltrate behind German positions at Simmerath and Monschau in the Monschau corridor, facilitating a broader offensive south of Aachen after neutralizing these enemy forces. To support this effort, a combat command from the 5th US Armor Division was later slated for deployment. Additionally, another advance by the 28th Division sought to capture the high ground southwest of Hürtgen, which would have simplified the logistics of troop deployment and supply delivery, as they would gain control over the main roads and paths.[7]

This led to an operational plan characterized by conflicting attack directions, determined by both the overall intent and specific tactical details for V Corps' forces. Drawing from prior experiences with the counterattack by the German 172nd Division's Wegelein Regiment at the Siegfried Line, the 109th Infantry Regiment was tasked with securing the left flank. Once it captured its objective southwest of Hürtgen, the regiment would address any potential threats to the division's flank. Additionally, the 2nd Battalion of the 112th Infantry Regiment

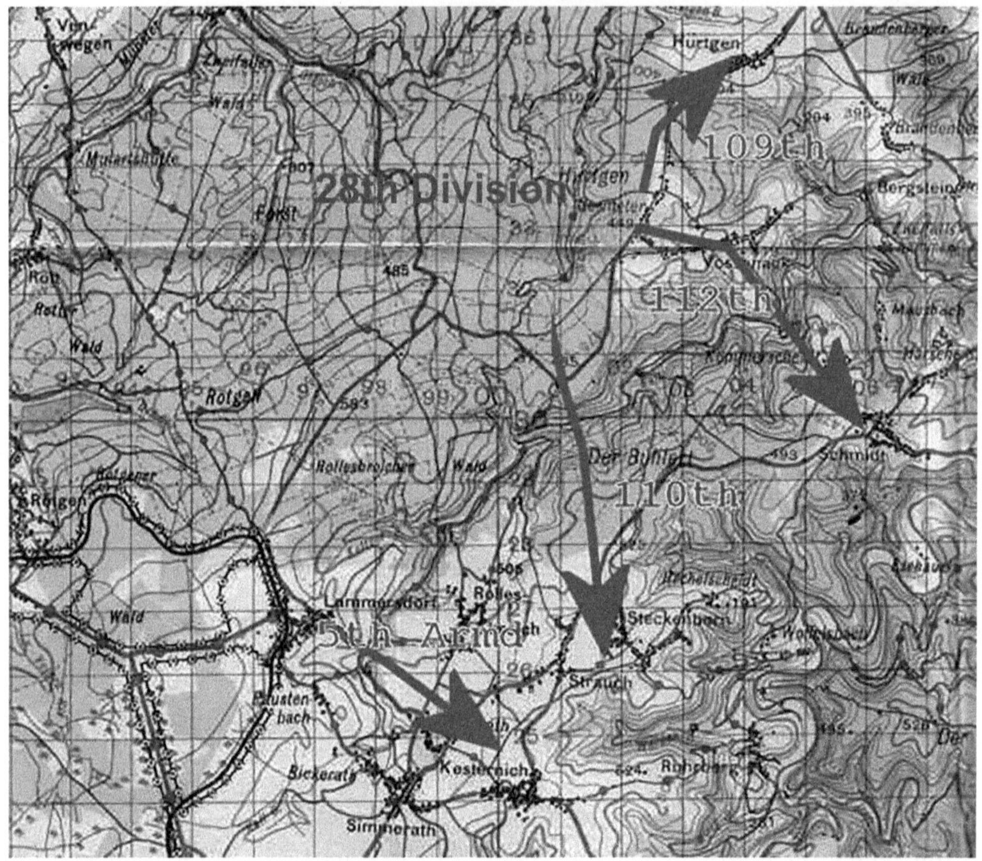

The 28th Division Attack Plan, 1944. (*US Army Center of Military History*)

was assigned to secure the extended northern flank toward the Tiefenbach Valley and Brandenberg following the capture of Vossenack.[8]

The primary emphasis was on the 112th Infantry Regiment, which was tasked with advancing toward Schmidt through Kall Gorge and the village of Kommerscheidt. Meanwhile, the 110th Infantry Regiment was to capture the bunkers around Raffelsbrand-Ochsenkopf before proceeding to assault the Monschau corridor. The only reserve available to the 28th Division was the 3rd Battalion of the 110th Infantry.[9]

Due to the challenging mission and the fact that the 28th Division was the only unit required to attack along a 260km front from Nijmegen to Metz, it received significant reinforcements from V Corps. In addition to extra artillery and tank units, the division had an entire engineer group comprising three battalions under its command. Artillery support came from two regiments of the V Corps and one from the VII Corps, totaling seven battalions equipped with 105mm, 110mm, 155mm, and 203mm artillery. Additional assistance was provided by five fighter-bomber squadrons and one night fighter squadron from IX Tactical Air Command. The division was fully supplied and equipped with bulk consumables, along with a large number of armored supply vehicles to navigate the challenging terrain.

The Order of Battle for 28th Infantry Division was as follows:

109th Infantry Regiment
110th Infantry Regiment
112th Infantry Regiment
28th Reconnaissance Troop (Mechanized)
103rd Engineer Combat Battalion
103rd Medical Battalion
28th Division Artillery
107th Field Artillery Battalion (105mm Howitzer)
109th Field Artillery Battalion (105mm Howitzer)
229th Field Artillery Battalion (105mm Howitzer)
108th Field Artillery Battalion (155mm Howitzer)
Special Troops
728th Ordnance Light Maintenance Company
28th Quartermaster Company
28th Signal Company
Military Police Platoon
Headquarters Company
Band
Attachments:
707th Tank Battalion
Co D 87th Chemical Battalion
86th Chemical Mortar Battalion
20th Engineer Combat Battalion, 1171st Combat Engineer Group
1340th Engineer Combat Battalion, 1171st Combat Engineer Group
146th Engineer Combat Battalion (- Company B)
Battery A 987th Field Artillery Battalion (155mm Gun)
76th Field Artillery Battalion (105mm Howitzer)
12th Combat Team (4th Division)
    42nd Field Artillery Battalion (4th Division) (105mm Howitzer)
    1st plat Co B 4th Engineer Combat Battalion (4th Division)
    Co A 801st Tank Destroyer Battalion (Self Propelled)
2nd Ranger Infantry Battalion
893rd Tank Destroyer Battalion (Self Propelled) (—Company A)[10]

The mission of the German LXXIV Corps remained the same, with expectations that the forthcoming Allied attack would target the Aachen area. The German

Corps continued to defend their positions using three infantry divisions, listed from north to south as the 275th Infantry Division, 89th Infantry Division, and 347th Infantry Division. After two months on the Westwall, the combat strength of the 89th Infantry Division had diminished to approximately 3,000 men, replenished only by replacement troops and air force personnel. To address this, the 272nd Volksgrenadier Division was assigned to take its place, with the transition set to begin on November 3. The 89th Division would then be rotated to a rear position for reconstitution.[11]

There were also no changes in their intentions or operational plans. Following the initial clashes in the Hürtgen Forest and around Aachen, the infantry divisions—particularly the 275th Infantry Division—focused on securing their positions, reorganizing their disheveled forces, building up reinforcements, and training personnel. To support this, they continued to deepen their positions. The 116th Panzer Division was redeployed to the Monchengladbach area as a reserve, where it would receive replacement units and supplies from disbanded Panzer Brigade 108. Additionally, the reinforced 156th Panzer Grenadier Regiment was kept on standby as an alarm and intervention reserve.[12]

All the remaining forces of the German 275th Infantry Division stationed in the Germeter-Vossenack-Raffelsbrand area were consolidated into the 983rd Infantry Regiment. The 984th Infantry Regiment still retained most of its personnel. The 942nd Infantry Regiment was renamed the 985th Infantry Regiment, which incorporated remnants of the Luftwaffe Fortress Battalion XX and parts of the 275th Fusilier Battalion, along with other sub-units from different units. The 275th Artillery Regiment was once again considered a fully operational unit.[13]

The two infantry units of the German 89th Infantry Division had not yet been reorganized into the structure of the Standard Infantry Division 44 (consisting of three units of two battalions each). They included personnel from replacement and training unit 416, as well as former Luftwaffe fortress battalions IX and XIV, along with Russian volunteer battalions. Artillery unit 189 was equipped with fifteen 105mm field howitzers and some captured 122mm Russian field howitzers.

Within the German 116th Panzer Division, the 156th Panzer Grenadier Regiment (motorized) was strengthened as an intervention force with a Panzer Pioneer Company from the 675th Panzer Pioneer Battalion, a Motorized Artillery Battalion from the 146th Motorized Artillery Regiment, and the 228th Tank Destroyer Battalion, which was not originally part of the division. The division, which had been withdrawn after Aachen's fall, was still in the process of being refreshed.

The companies had an average combat strength of eight to ninety men. In some cases, they relied on horse-drawn vehicles instead of motorized transport, and many units had only wheeled vehicles instead of armored personnel carriers.

Only the 60th Panzer Grenadier Battalion could truly be considered a panzer grenadier battalion due to its equipment of armored personnel carriers. The 116th reconnaissance detachment was a strong, mechanized unit but was depleted and only had a portion of its tracked and armored vehicles. The 24th Panzer Regiment, which was equipped with Panther V tanks, was under the division's command.[14]

The main attack by the US First Army was planned for November 5, which meant that October 31 was the latest date for the 28th Infantry Division to initiate its assault. However, like the 9th US Infantry Division in October, poor weather hindered these plans. The adverse conditions made it impossible for the US air force to provide air support. Nevertheless, it was deemed essential to prevent German armored reserves from being deployed along the Rur section to secure the battlefield.

Additionally, efforts were needed to eliminate German artillery observation on the heights of Brandenberg-Bergstein and Schmidt, particularly through Allied air strikes. As a result, the attack was delayed until November 2. However, on the morning of November 2, expectations for air support were still low due to overcast skies, light drizzle, and temperatures just above freezing. Further postponement was not feasible.[15]

4

109th Infantry Operations

As the month of November 1944 began, the 109th Regiment was still awaiting word from the division to attack. All preparations had been completed for several days, but the attack was delayed because of bad weather. It was estimated that the strength of the Germans to the regiment's immediate front was approximately seven hundred to nine hundred men. The German reconnaissance patrols sent into the 109th sector had not been very aggressive and were repelled with very little fire.

Analysis of the German capability concluded that they could delay any advance of the regiment by covering the river and all possible bridging and fording sites with fire from their fortifications. Although well-positioned, the concrete pillboxes had already been damaged in earlier action, but it was assumed that some of them had been repaired or replaced with dug-in positions. The Germans also controlled the high ground around the 109th Regiment positions and continually laid down observed mortar and artillery fire on the 109th forward positions with all types of mortar and artillery as well as sporadic harassing fire on the division's rear installations and supply and communication lines.[1]

The 109th Infantry Regiment, with attached units, was to attack with the 3rd Battalion on the right, 1st Battalion on the left, and the 2nd Battalion in reserve. The 2nd Battalion was to be prepared to protect the left rear flank of the regiment and to assist the assault battalions, if ordered. The general plan was for the battalions to follow an artillery barrage provided by the 107th Field Artillery Battalion from H-60 to H-hour and the 76th Field Artillery Battalion from H-10 to H-hour. Other mortar fires were to precede the troops and lift as they became masked by obstacles or terrain. A 4.2-inch chemical mortar company was in direct support with one platoon assigned to each battalion. In addition, the battalions were to use all organic weapons, including .50 caliber machine guns.[2]

On November 2, the division ordered the regiment to attack at 9:00 AM with the mission of advancing approximately 1,500 yards toward the town of Hürtgen. The 28th Division's artillery started firing preparatory fires over the division front and the direct support artillery and all organic support weapons of the regiment fired a preparation to the regiment's front. The attack started at 9:00 AM and progressed very well, with a small number of prisoners being taken. The 3rd Battalion was astride of the Hürtgen-Germeter road.[3]

The 1st Battalion under the command of Major Robert Ford jumped off at 9:00 AM. B Company was on the left, guiding on the fire break, A Company was on the right, and C Company followed B Company. The companies were in a formation of two platoons abreast with one platoon back. D Company was supported with the 81mm mortars. All the heavy machine guns were under regimental control and firing from the left flank in front of the troops, while 81mm mortars were under battalion control and were emplaced and firing on selected targets as called for. After the battalion jumped off and had progressed about 200 yards, they ran into German machine-gun and small arms fire coming from a draw. This slowed the attack down, but did not stop it.

A Company swung to the right and got on the enemy's flank, and B Company moved straight ahead and cleaned out the draw, capturing about 100 prisoners. The attack continued, with rather heavy resistance being met from small pockets of Germans. One small pocket was bypassed and had to be cleaned up by the reserve company. By moving forward as fast as possible, the attacking companies escaped a lot of German artillery fire, but the reserve company caught an excessive amount of fire, as it seemed as if the Germans were able to follow an advancing unit with artillery and mortar fire.[4]

A Company crossed the line of departure with their 1st Platoon on the right, their 2nd Platoon on the left, and the 3rd Platoon in support. The 2nd Platoon was in a T formation; the 1st Platoon used a wedge formation as they had more ground to cover. From the line of departure to the Germans was about 200 yards, and of that distance, 50 yards was open terrain. The plan was that each man would shoot a full clip from his M1 Rifle at 9:00 AM and to keep firing as they moved toward the enemy. They got to the bottom of the draw in the open space. First Lieutenant Samuel J. Leo, 1st Platoon leader, held the platoon up as he decided to cross the open area in one wave. One squad was slow, so Leo sent a guide back to move them up in line with the others.

After the platoon got across the open area, the squad on the right started getting some heavy machine gun fire from log bunkers full of Germans. The 3rd squad had moved forward without much opposition. Initially the squad on the left had moved forward and taken seven prisoners, but the Germans in the log bunkers would not come out, so they tossed some hand grenades in and the Germans came out. Until this point the platoon had no casualties.

The squad on the right was pinned down by heavy machine gun fire. The 2nd Platoon had reached the company phase line and had gotten into the open space and were pinned down and could not move. They were suffering casualties from the machine gun fire coming from the bunker.[5] Lieutenant Leo approached the ridge above the German bunkers, firing his carbine. When it jammed, he kept on going and tossed a grenade at the Germans. It landed in the bunker and wounded five Germans. Then he yelled at the 2nd Platoon that no one was firing at them and to start moving.[6]

As the company started moving again, the Germans were firing artillery and mortars at them, but the men kept going. Sergeant Robert Pavlowski, squad leader, was hit in the face by machine gun fire. As the medic went to his aid, he was also shot. Pavlowski died before the medics were able to evacuate him.

As the men went about 150 yards, they came to an open space which was not on the map. There were some logs lying along the edge of the clearing and Captain Whitetree, A Company commander, had the 1st and 2nd platoons establish a base of fire with their light machine guns. Whitetree contacted the 3rd Platoon and sent them around to the left of the clearing. They used a firebreak as the left boundary and advanced about 500 yards. Whitetree halted the 3rd Platoon, then called Lieutenant Leo on the SCR-536 hand-held radio and brought the other platoon up. The company bypassed the Germans and they later pulled out.

By this time, the 1st and 2nd platoons had lost a lot of men from mortar and machine gun fire. The Germans seemed to know exactly where the 109th men were at all times. When the two platoons came together, Whitetree realized they were under strength and combined the remaining twenty-five men under Lieutenant Leo's command.[7]

In this small action, A Company had lost thirty men and captured seventy prisoners. The woods were so thick in this sector that in many cases they were using hand grenades, which were more effective then rifle fire. At this point, the company had to make a turning movement to the right. It began with the combined platoon on the right and the 3rd Platoon on the left. After moving about 100 yards, the 3rd Platoon encountered machine gun fire and bursts from MP40 submachine guns (burp guns). The combined platoon went about 200 yards and held up until the 3rd Platoon came up on line.

At this point, two squad leaders and a platoon leader had been killed. Sergeant Harry Dahn took charge of the 2nd Squad, 3rd Platoon, and Technical Sergeant Cliff Wolff took charge of the platoon. Sergeant Dahn led his squad around to the right and closed in on the German machine gun crew and forced them to surrender by tossing a hand grenade into their position, killing one and wounding one. As a result of this, the platoon was able to advance.[8]

While the combined platoon was waiting for the 3rd Platoon to come up on line, Lieutenant Leo set up a defense with light machine guns and M1918 BARs. A platoon of Germans, marching in a column of two, came toward the company. When they were within 25 yards, the BARs and machine guns opened up, killing all the Germans, except one, who was taken prisoner and told them there were forty men in this group. Right after this, 3rd Platoon moved up and the company moved on about 500 yards to the battalion objective, arriving at 1:45 PM.[9]

The men realized that as soon as the Germans knew they were there, artillery and mortar fire would rain in. They pulled back about 25 yards from the edge of the woods and started digging in. Artillery and mortar fire started at about 3:30 PM, and the company had casualties, as some men had not had time to cover their holes.

About 4:00 PM, a German messenger came down the road on a bicycle. The messenger was shot and his pouch was sent back to the Battalion S-2 Section for analysis. Shortly after this, a horse-drawn wagon containing cabbage and tea came along and the men captured it.

About thirty minutes later, a horse-drawn ammunition wagon came along. The men shot at it, killing the horse and the driver. One man had fired a rifle grenade and knocked one of the wheels off.

About twenty minutes later, a platoon of Germans came down the road, but one of the A Company men fired too soon, killing two men, but giving the Germans a chance to get away.[10]

The rest of the 1st Battalion reached the objective about 2:30 PM and started to dig in. At this time there was a very heavy German artillery barrage, and the S-3 and two company commanders and several enlisted men were killed. It was rather quiet that night with very little artillery firing.

The 3rd Battalion ran into wire and minefields covered by machine gun and small arms fire and were able to advance only 500 yards. One platoon of the reserve company and one platoon of engineers were to clear the main road into Hürtgen of mines. K Company was on the right of the road and I Company, following L Company, was on the left of the road. L Company swung over to the right of the road to follow K Company, and at that point ran into a minefield and barbed wire, covered by machine gun fire. The mines could not be lifted by the engineers due to booby traps and machine gun fire. The battalion commander attempted to put one company to the left of the minefield in hope that it would clear the minefield, but was unsuccessful.

By nightfall the 3rd Battalion had gained little ground, and they were ordered to dig in for the night. The 2nd Battalion had moved forward to protect the left flank of the regiment and was attempting to make contact with C Company, but was unsuccessful. The 1st Battalion dug in on the left of the road.[11]

On November 3 at 7:00 AM, the 3rd Battalion continued the attack. The 1st Battalion was ordered to hold its position, and the 2nd Battalion was ordered to move F Company into position on the left flank and G Company into position on the right flank and tie in with the companies of the 1st Battalion. At 6:45 AM, the Germans shelled the 1st Battalion for about forty minutes. Then, at 7:30 AM, roughly 250 German soldiers, advancing closely behind the barrage, began suffering casualties from their own fire. They hit on the left flank of B Company but were repelled. Then, the Germans hit in C Company's area.

Major Ford had the forward observer bring down artillery about 100 yards in front of the positions and the attack was broken up. The rest of the Germans kept going around on the left and got in the rear of the battalion and captured the observation post. The 1st Battalion captured 100 Germans. Some men were killed from the barrage as the rounds burst in the treetops.[12]

The trees at this location were so thick that it was impossible to see more than 30 yards in any one direction. In many places they were not over 4 feet apart. With German artillery knocking the tops off, the treetops were piling up and making it more difficult to move or to see any distance from a given position. During this morning attack, the battalion's machine guns did not open fire until the Germans were right on top of them. By waiting, they killed many more than usual, as the Germans were unable to see the American positions and walked right into the face of the guns. Some fell within 6 feet of the position and the gun crew had to move the bodies to continue firing.[13]

Technical Sergeant Gary M. Dix, M Company, 109th Infantry was awarded the Silver Star for his actions on November 3. He was left in command of his section when his platoon leader went forward to re-establish contact with his company. During an attack of German artillery and mortar fire, Sergeant Dix was seriously wounded by a shell fragment which completely pierced his body. When the artillery and mortar fire ceased, a force of approximately fifty Germans attacked his weapons platoon and heavy machine gun section. Sergeant Dix, though suffering with pain, and weakened from shock and loss of blood, directed the placement of machine guns and deployed his men. Moving about with an ammunition belt tightened around his stomach to contain the bandages he had applied, he gave the necessary fire orders. Dix refused to be evacuated until the hostile force had been completely dispersed, leaving behind many German casualties.[14]

Around dusk, a Volkswagen with its headlights on came down the road and everyone opened fire, including heavy machine guns, light machine guns, and rifles. The car turned over and two Germans ran away. There were three more Germans around the car, so A Company sent a patrol of six men out to find them. Sergeant Louis Schwieger acted as the scout. As he got to the car, he made a dive into the ditch and two Germans came out with their hands up. They said there were two more, so Sergeant Schwieger and Sergeant Balleger went out over the open field and found a wounded German artillery captain and his messenger. The officer had an overlay of the entire German positions, giving the location of their guns, and location of their battalion and regimental command posts. This map was later used for air bombardments.[15]

During the night of the 3rd, the enemy action was confined to artillery and mortar fire. One of the biggest problems was bringing supplies up. Carrying parties were used and several men were lost as they had to fight their way to the front-line troops. During the night, wounded were carried out by volunteer parties. A German tank came down the road from Hürtgen and flashed his lights off and on and then went back. Lieutenant Leo was trying to get bazookas and grenades together, but before he could, the tank left. Some mines were placed on the road where the tank had come down. German patrols were all along the supply route and in the rear of the men. It was impossible to tell just when they would attack.[16]

The 3rd Battalion made very little progress during the morning. At 2:00 PM, the Battalion Commander reported having completed his mission. Upon investigation it was found that he had moved L Company into position on the left flank of the 1st Battalion and closed the gap between C Company and F Company. This was not the battalion commander's mission, but was interpreted to be that sent by radio to the battalion commander.

During this attack of the 2nd and 3rd battalions, the engineers attempted to establish a roadblock on the regiment's left flank on line with the leading companies. They met strong resistance and were unable to establish the roadblock. On the right flank of the regiment, the 112th Infantry had taken Vossenack and the gap between the 109th's 3rd Battalion and the 112th was covered by patrols.

On November 4, plans were made for E and G companies of the 2nd Battalion to pass through I Company and continue the attack to the initial objective of the 3rd Battalion. All other companies were to remain in place and K Company on the right flank was to put on a firing demonstration.

The two companies jumped off at 7:00 AM and met stubborn resistance. By the end of the day, G Company had two platoons across the Hürtgen-Germeter road and E Company was held up at the road by an anti-personnel minefield which was covered by small arms and machine gun fire. One platoon of E Company covered the road but suffered heavy losses in the minefield on that side of the road, and, as such, was lost.[17]

The engineers were again unsuccessful in establishing the roadblock on the regiment's left. An undetermined force remained in the draw on the immediate left of the regiment and a special task force from the anti-tank company, tank destroyer company, and engineers was organized and given the mission of establishing a roadblock about 1,000 yards north from the regimental main supply route.

They were unsuccessful, as the Germans were well dug in and had an estimated eight machine guns covering the approach up the draw. Contact with the 112th Infantry Regiment on the right was still maintained by visiting patrols. The regiment was ordered to assist in the capture of the roadblock which the engineers had been unable to take. Plans were completed to make a coordinated attack with the engineers at 8:00 AM on November 5. However, at 11:30 PM the division ordered the attack postponed. Plans were cancelled on November 6.

November 5 was a day spent by the front line companies in improving their positions. At 7:30 AM, they discovered a German patrol in the area trying to get out. Air support was very active as several P-47s came over, but no damage to the enemy was done. About 800 yards in front of the American positions were some German mortars, which were active throughout the day. When the men heard the mortars fire, they would dive for their holes.

Two small counterattacks were repulsed. Infiltrations of the Germans along the supply route to the 1st Battalion became so bad that it was necessary to patrol the route at all times. Attempts were made to talk the Germans in the draw on the regiment's left into surrendering. A truce was arranged and German officers met and talked with officers of the regiment, but the Germans refused to surrender. The 112th Infantry on the regiment's right was counterattacked in Vossenack and in Schmidt. Contact was maintained by patrols.[18]

After receipt of orders from the division to cancel plans to attack and capture the roadblock, on November 6, the regiment was ordered to take aggressive action with the view of occupying German positions and improving regiment positions. Plans were made to attack at 9:00 AM. F, L, and C companies were to advance in their sectors in order to cover the draw on the left with fire and to completely cover the road junction in the zone of C Company.

The companies attacked at 9:00 AM but made only slight progress. C Company was heavily shelled by mortar and artillery fire. F and L companies met strong small arms and machine gun opposition. The Germans were able to deliver flanking fire from the left of F Company. No appreciable progress was made.

By mid-afternoon on November 6, a pattern had developed where engineers were being committed as riflemen, despite some conflicting orders and a lack of communication between General Davis and the engineer commander, Colonel Daley. Into Vossenack went the 146th Engineer Combat Battalion (minus a company on detached service). To the Kall Gorge went the remnants of the 20th Engineers and two companies of the 1340th Engineer Combat Battalion. A third company of the 1340th Engineers remained in support of the 110th Infantry.[19]

In the Kall Gorge the engineers happily discovered that the Germans had gone. By nightfall a company of the 1340th Engineers was digging in at the Kall Bridge, while another company and most of what was left of the 20th Engineers took over Captain Doherty's former positions at the western entrance to the trail leading into the Kall Woods. In Vossenack the two companies of the 146th Engineers were committed so quickly that the men were still wearing the hip boots they had been using on road repair work. They moved immediately to take responsibility for the thin infantry line near the church.

The crisis in Vossenack had repercussions all the way back to V Corps headquarters. Upon first news of the catastrophe, General Gerow hurriedly alerted the 4th Division's 12th Infantry. Beginning that night, the 12th Infantry was to relieve Colonel Strickler's 109th Infantry on the wooded plateau north of Germeter. Upon relief, the 109th Infantry was to be employed only as approved by General Gerow. Even though this regiment had been mutilated in the fight in the woods, freeing it would somewhat decrease the apprehension over the recurring crises within the 28th Division. General Gerow must have recognized that, should the Germans push on from Vossenack past Germeter, they would need only a shallow penetration to disrupt the First Army's plans for the main drive to the Roer by VII Corps.[20]

During the night of November 6, both the American 146th Engineers and the German 156th Panzer Grenadier Regiment made plans for driving the other out of Vossenack. Both attacks were to begin at about 8:00 AM. As daylight came the Americans started their preparatory artillery barrage first. When the barrage had ended and the two engineer companies moved into the open to attack, German fire began. Although this shelling hit one of the companies severely, both charged forward, one on either side of the village's main street. They had beaten the Germans to the draw.

At 2:10 PM on November 6, Combat Team 12 (12th RCT, 4th Infantry Division) was notified to move at once to the vicinity of Zweifall, Germany—a distance of 45 miles. Despite the short notice, by 5:45 PM, the 12th was on the march. The entire march was made during the hours of darkness. The night was intensely dark and very rainy. The first order stated that the 12th Infantry would be attached to the 28th Division, and that initially it would go into an assembly area as division reserve. However, late that night, while the entire regiment was still moving on the road, a change of orders was delivered verbally to the column commander. It stated that the 12th Infantry will relieve the 109th Infantry in the front lines tonight without prior reconnaissance. Word had passed along the column by runner, since there was radio silence.

The change in plans was made on the march. Muddy, narrow roads caused vehicles to slide into ditches. The blackness of the night hampered operations. Finally, at about 2:00 AM, the column arrived at a de-trucking point behind the front lines. Guides met the troops. A quick decision was made. They would relieve the 109th Infantry in place unit for unit. All during this time, patrols were sent out to the rear areas and supply lines to clear the Germans patrols out. The 12th Infantry troops then marched on foot up to the front.

In spite of the many difficulties, by 12:50 AM on November 7, the regiment had completely relieved the 109th Infantry Regiment in the sector of the Hürtgen Forest 1,000 meters west of Hürtgen, running generally south to Germeter.[21]

As relief progressed, the 109th battalions moved into assembly areas west of Germeter with orders to re-organize and await further orders. At 12:00 AM the regiment received orders that 1st Battalion was to be part of a task force commanded by Assistant Division Commander Brigadier General George Davis. Orders called on them to prepare to advance through elements of the division at Kommerscheidt and recapture Schmidt. The 1st Battalion was to re-capture the forward position of Vossenack, which had fallen under German attacks, and relieve the 2nd Battalion of the 112th Infantry. The 2nd Battalion was to move to the vicinity of Kommerscheidt and keep open the supply routes of the 112th battalions located there.

At 3:00 PM, the planned mission of the 1st Battalion as part of the division task force was changed; instead, the 3rd Battalion would be moved to occupy positions north of Kommerscheidt. The battalion was guided by the acting battalion S-3. They became lost, and when darkness came, it was in the woods to the rear of the 1st Battalion, 110th Infantry. They remained there during the night of November 7. At 6:30 PM the 2nd Battalion moved into Vossenack and advanced to occupy the forward portion of the town and then relieve the 112th's 2nd Battalion. The 1st Battalion remained in position near Germeter.[22]

At 3:00 AM the next day, the 3rd Battalion was ordered to go with the assistant division commander to aid in the relief of Task Force Ripple, comprised of elements of the 110th Infantry, 112th Infantry, tanks, and engineer units, which were in serious trouble near Kommerscheidt. The battalion did not join Task Force Ripple, but took up positions near Kommerscheidt, protecting the supply route to Schmidt. This action relieved the pressure on Kommerscheidt considerably, and the task force was able to withdraw back to the assembly areas west of Germeter.

Major Howard L. Topping, commander of the 3rd Battalion, 109th Infantry, was assigned the mission of moving his battalion from the vicinity of Germeter to a position about 2 miles away on November 8. His troops were given the task of defending a road and heavily wooded draw from German infiltration, which would block the remnants of the 3rd Battalion's regiment, 112th Infantry, from an untenable position on high ground. With a small reconnaissance party, Major Topping moved out at the head.

The nearest route to his destination led across an open field under German artillery fire. During the trip, the party was twice fired upon by German artillery. Reaching the woods on the opposite side of the field near his objective, Major Topping observed a five-man German patrol moving toward him. When they were about 100 yards away, he opened fire on the Germans with his M-1 rifle, mortally wounding two of them. Continuing to his objective, he observed another German patrol about 200 yards away. Again opening fire, he killed one of them and forced the others to flee. Despite a German mortar barrage, he remained at his position until he was thoroughly familiar with the ground he was to occupy.

When he was about to leave, a German sniper from across the draw shot him through the left wrist. He returned to his battalion but refused to be evacuated until after he had led his men to their new positions. His action permitted the remnants of the 3rd Battalion, 112th to safely withdraw. Major Howard Topping was awarded the Silver Star for his actions.[23]

The 2nd Battalion continued the occupation of Vossenack and consolidated and improved their positions. The 1st Battalion was ordered to take up positions along the Germeter road, moving one company into the west end of Vossenack, and to occupy positions along the road. Major Ford, 1st Battalion commanding officer, was killed in Vossenack while attempting to reach the 2nd Battalion command post. Starting at 6:00 PM, the 2nd Battalion moved to positions further east of the town, and B Company occupied the west of the town. The 12th Combat Team was on the regiment's left and was trying to improve its positions, while the 110th Infantry was on the right. Contact with both units was maintained by patrols.[24]

On November 8, Private Elliott R. Corbett II of B Company, 109th Infantry, wrote a letter to his wife, Sudie:

> I might say with little or no compulsion that I miss you hellishly and I've had enough of humping around Europe. I see nothing in Germany to warrant fighting for any of it and being naturally a peaceful character, I look forward to a long life of security and freedom from the elements which are beginning to pall.[25]

On November 19, Corbett was captured after being seriously injured. He died of his wounds two days later.

Positions remained unchanged on November 9. Lieutenant Colonel Williams reported for duty and was assigned as the commander of the 1st Battalion. The division notified the regiment that the 12th Combat Team was to attack the following day and the 109th's 1st Battalion would support the attack by fire and at 11:00 AM the 2nd Battalion, 112th Infantry would pass through the 109th's 1st Battalion and seize the high roads and high ground to the left, north of Vossenack and south of Hürtgen.[26]

An excerpt from the diary of Thomas W. Hickman, I Company, 1st Battalion of the 109th Infantry, offers a picture of the situation facing the soldiers:

> 11/5—This place is just one big hell hole. You can't move. Death and devastation everywhere. By far this is the worse place we have been in. Our casualties are terrific. These Jerries [Germans] are pure SS.
> 11/6—Attacked at 6:00 AM and took battalion objective—Germeter. Replacements pouring in. Casualties pouring out.
> 11/7—Attacked at 6:00 AM and took the first of our division's objectives—a crossroad on Cologne-Aachen highway at Vossenack. We are really beat up now. Don't see how we can possibly hold this ground. Replacements come in and leave within an hour—either as litter cases or basket cases. We don't even have a chance to assign them to platoons or squads. The poor guys don't even know what division they are in.
> 11/8—Vossenack is leveled. Not a building standing. Wish I could get out of this place.
> 11/9—From 10:00 AM to 6:00 PM, holding. Counted four thousand rounds coming in. Our dead are all over the place. Can't waste time with them—too many casualties that need help. No possible way to get them out unless you want to join them. Everyone has trench foot. Been snowing for more than a week now. Holes are full of ice and mud. Can't help but remain saturated. Have a bad case myself. Feet hurt. We only have shoes. I even lost my leggings.[27]

On November 20 at 7:00 AM, the 12th Combat Team attacked, with the 109th's 1st Battalion supporting. At 9:00 AM, plans changed and the 1st Battalion was ordered to leave their positions and attack north of Vossenack over open ground to an objective within the woods. The 2nd Battalion, 112th Infantry, attached to the 109th Infantry, was to occupy the positions vacated by the 1st Battalion. The attack started at 11:00 AM, with B Company leading, followed by A and C Companies. German resistance consisted primarily of mortar and artillery fire, and units were reported on their objective by 3:30 PM. Communication was poor, with the 1st Battalion and the position and situation was not clear. At 12:00 AM, the 1st Battalion commanding officer was with B Company.

The 109th Regiment executive officer led a patrol to the 1st Battalion to ascertain their positions and situation. He located the various elements, established them on their objectives, and then reorganized and supplied them. On November 11–13, positions were consolidated and communications were maintained with patrols, with 1st Battalion on the left and 3rd Battalion on the right of 2nd Battalion.

Heavy German artillery fire was received throughout the day in the Vossenack-Germeter area. Getting supplies to the 1st Battalion over open ground and along the main supply route became considerably difficult as the German patrols interrupted their efforts.[28]

On November 14, orders were received that the 2nd Ranger Battalion would arrive sometime during the day and was to relieve the 2nd Battalion, 112th Infantry. The rangers were to be attached to the 109th Infantry. The other battalions of the regiment were to remain in position.

Rangers arrived in their assembly area at 5:30 PM; relief began at once and was completed by 7:00 PM. The 2nd Battalion, 112th Infantry then reverted to control of the 112th Infantry Regiment. Combat Team 12, on the regiment's left, was still trying to improve its positions but was meeting strong resistance from the Germans. The 110th Infantry, on the regiment's right, continued local attacks. Contact with both units was maintained by patrols.[29]

On November 15–17, the regiment continued with their defense of the sector, aggressively patrolling and maintaining contact with units on the left and right. Plans were made for the relief of the 109th Infantry Regiment by the 28th Infantry of the 8th Infantry Division. Major Harrison, executive officer of the 1st Battalion, was killed by a sniper while leading a patrol against Germans that had infiltrated elements of the battalion.

On November 18–19, plans were completed for the relief of the 109th Infantry by the 28th Infantry. The 2nd and 3rd battalions were to be relieved the night of November 18 and the 1st Battalion was to be relieved the following night. Upon relief, the units were to move to a rear assembly and bivouac for the night.

They boarded trucks the following morning. An advance party left for the new area at 6:00 AM, and Service Company kitchens were left with instructions to have a hot meal ready for the men when they arrived at the new area.

The relief of the 2nd and 3rd battalions and separate companies was accomplished the night of November 18, and all units moved to their assembly areas. One F Company platoon suffered casualties from artillery fire during the relief. The other units suffered no casualties.

At 8:30 AM on November 19, units boarded trucks for their new area in the vicinity of Medernach, Luxembourg. The men traveled through Roetgen, Eupen, St. Vith, Malmédy, Wiltz, and Ettelbruck.

The first units arrived at the new area at 3:00 PM and were fed, before effecting relief of units of the 121st Infantry of the 8th Infantry Division. The last units arrived in the new area at 5:00 PM and relief was completed as of 12:00 AM, when the 109th Infantry assumed full responsibility for the defense of the sector.

The 1st Battalion was relieved on the night of November 18, moved to an assembly area in the woods north of Vossenack until dark, and then moved back through Vossenack to an assembly area west of Germeter. The battalion then boarded trucks at 8:30 AM on November 19 and followed the same route of the other units to the town of Diekirch.[30]

After the extremely rigorous, active and costly series of actions against the Germans in the Hürtgen Forest, all personnel were fatigued. Immersion foot (trench foot) was prevalent among front-line troops. The organization and efficiency of units down to and including squads had depreciated due to high losses in leaders of all grades and rank. Losses were caused by both battle and non-battle casualties.

While in the Hürtgen Forest, the 109th Infantry Regiment succeeded in the accomplishment of all six missions which it was given:

> To capture and hold an objective southwest of the town of Hürtgen, and to thereby protect the left flank of the 28th Infantry Division.
> To advance through Vossenack, retake and hold the enemy forward position of the town recaptured by the Germans as a result of a counterattack, and to relieve the 2nd Battalion, 112th Infantry.
> To clear and occupy a position south of Vossenack and to assist in withdrawal from the area near Kommerscheidt of Task Force Ripple, comprised of elements of the 110th, 112th, tanks, and engineer units.
> To defend the town of Vossenack at all costs.
> To capture and hold an objective in the forest north of Vossenack.
> To displace approximately 85 miles south, relieve the 121st Infantry and take over the defense of the area previously occupied by that regiment.[31]

At the beginning of the Hürtgen Forest period (November 1–19), regimental strength was 150 officers, five warrant officers, and 2,987 enlisted soldiers. The strength at the end of the period was 145 officers, five warrant officers, and 2,817 enlisted soldiers. During fighting, the regiment received replacements in the form of sixty-nine officers and 1,277 enlisted soldiers. Casualties included: six officers and 106 enlisted killed, forty-nine officers and 752 enlisted wounded, ninety-four enlisted missing, twenty officers and 332 enlisted non-battle casualties, and ten enlisted soldiers captured. The regiment had captured 452 German soldiers during the period.

The 109th Infantry was opposed by some elements of the following German units:

11 GAF Fortress Battalion
60th *Grenadier* Regiment (116th Panzer Division)
984th Infantry Regiment
985th Infantry Regiment (353rd Division)
Combat Team Trier
20th GAF Fortress Battalion
156th *Grenadier* Regiment
Seventh Army Reconnaissance Troop[32]

While in the Hürtgen Forest, adverse weather conditions made all roads difficult to negotiate. Rain and snowstorms helped to make roads muddy and rutted, especially those leading to installations. In many instances, muddy roads had to be paved with logs in order that vehicles could enter kitchen areas. Many roads were mined, especially jeep trails leading off main highways. In forward areas, roads were non-existent, and M29 Weasels were used to haul supplies. In the regimental rear area, traffic was one way with deep muddy ditches on either side of the roads.

During their time in the Hürtgen Forest, the 109th Infantry gained considerable experience in the methods of fighting in forests and in using roads and trails for supply. They learned that a coordinated attack in a forest can be successfully launched by using organic firepower together with the firepower of attached and supporting units prior to and during the attack. It also learned that large minefields protected by wire and strongly built enemy emplacements cannot be knocked out by rifle units. The slower process of using engineers and assault teams must be used. It was found that the use of replacements just prior to or during an attack resulted in increased casualties and loss of control among units. Forest fighting proved again and again the necessity for the use of all means of communication.

The excessive number of non-battle casualties was caused by the inability to obtain a sufficient supply of arctics and overshoes in the initial engagements. The snow and wet, rain-soaked conditions of the forest led to many cases of immersion foot in many units. Leaders who were insufficiently trained and inexperienced proved a serious handicap to the unit's combat operations. These lessons were not lost on the leaders of the 109th Infantry Regiment as they rested, received replacements, and trained in the quiet sector in Luxembourg. They were soon to find out that their sector would not be quiet for long.[33]

5

110th Infantry Operations

On November 1, 1944, the regiment was positioned in the line southeast of Vossenack. Plans were completed for an attack. The day of attack was announced as November 2. On that day, the 2nd and 3rd battalions crossed the line of departure (LD) at 12:00 PM. The 1st Battalion remained in division reserve. During the attack the assault battalions received heavy mortar and artillery fire, encountered heavily booby-trapped defensive positions, pillboxes, dug-in wooden bunkers, and other prepared defensive positions. They were able to advance about 200 yards. During the night of November 2–3, German patrols tried to infiltrate and flank the lines. They met with no success.

On the morning of November 3, the 2nd and 3rd battalions again launched an attack. The 1st Battalion moved from their assembly area positions in the positions formerly held by the 3rd Battalion. The entire front received heavy mortar and artillery fire, slowing the advance. In the afternoon the 1st Battalion received orders and made plans for an enveloping movement around the enemy's right flank, to the north. A task force composed of a platoon of raiders, the mine platoon of the antitank company, and the intelligence and reconnaissance platoon of the Regimental Headquarters Company was organized under the command of 1st Lieutenant Virgil R. Lacy and given the mission of occupying the ground which would be left open by the moving of the 1st Battalion. The task force became known as Task Force Lacy.[1]

On the morning of November 4, the 1st Battalion left their positions to move to the LD for the operation. By 5:10 AM, they had arrived at the LD without incident. At 7:00 AM, the 1st Battalion crossed the LD, which was the road running east and west through Vossenack. The 2nd and 3rd battalions put into effect a fire plan and in return received heavy German mortar and artillery. There was no movement by the 2nd and 3rd battalions.

By 9:07 AM, the 1st Battalion had reached its objectives, the most southern being the town of Simonskall. At 10:00 AM, the 2nd and 3rd battalions sent out reconnaissance patrols, which received heavy mortar and small arms fire. At 1:45 PM, C Company was ordered to clean out the pocket left by the envelopment. E Company was ordered to assist.

At dark, C Company buttoned up for the night on its way to completing its mission. During the night plans were laid for the cleaning out of the pocket using C and E companies in a coordinated drive. They were attached to the 1st Battalion for control.[2]

Private George Nikola, a scout in the 1st Platoon, G Company, ran along a firebreak toward a shallow dip in the ground he thought might serve as a good field of fire for use against a pillbox. He carried a light machine gun. As he reached the hollow, he dropped to the ground and set the gun down beside him. As it touched the earth it depressed a hidden plunger on a buried mine that then exploded, destroying the barrel of the machine gun and wounding Nickola in the face. Thrashing with pain, his right foot struck a booby trap, setting it off and injuring the limb. Refusing to crawl back to safety, he remained where he was for an hour in order to shout warnings to his buddies not to venture into the area traps. When asked later why he would not withdraw Nickola said, "I came here to fight the Germans in their country and that is what he was going to do." Private George Nikola was awarded the Silver Star for his actions.[3]

On November 5, early in the morning, A Company received a small counterattack, which was driven off. C and E companies moved off and by 10:30 AM had taken three pillboxes and captured thirty prisoners. At 12:30 PM, the regimental commander received orders to have the 3rd Battalion ready to move by 4:00 PM under division control. Task Force Lacy was ordered to move to the position held by B Company, and B Company was ordered to move halfway from their present position to Simonskall. The front lines of the regiment front received heavy mortar and artillery fire.

After capturing the pillboxes, C and E companies resumed their advance, but became lost in the deep woods and did not accomplish their mission. Plans were made for C and E companies to work under control of 2nd Battalion the next day to complete their mission.

On November 6 at 2:00 AM, the 3rd Battalion, under division control, moved out to go to the assistance of the 112th Infantry in the town of Schmidt. At 8:00 AM, C and E companies moved off on their assigned missions. By 2:15 PM, C Company was tied in with A Company with about a 200-yard gap between E and G companies.[4]

On November 7 at 6:30 AM, E Company moved to close the gap between their flank and G Company, and to further clean out the enemy to their front. E Company moved about 200 yards forward and contacted G Company. C Company did not have much success in their attempt to move forward, encountering heavy small arms fire, most of which came from automatic weapons in dug-in positions. The enemy tried several times, by counterattack, to break through American lines at various points, but failed. The battalions buttoned up for the night at about 5:00 PM.

On November 8 at 1:30 PM, the 2nd Battalion, about to launch an attack, received a counterattack directed at G Company. The attack was by a force of approximately platoon strength, supported by heavy mortar and artillery fire. Some prisoners were taken, while others were killed and a few escaped.

On November 9 at 2:00 AM, members of the 3rd Battalion started to infiltrate back to the regiment, having been greatly disorganized during their engagement near Schmidt. At 10:00 AM, the executive officer of the 2nd Battalion and the S-3 of the 1st Battalion coordinated plans to close the gap between the 1st and 2nd battalions. The gap had become about 500 yards long. By 6:00 PM, the battalions were tied in with a small gap between A Company and C Company. This gap was to be covered by patrols. Both the 1st and 2nd battalions received heavy mortar and artillery fire during the day.[5]

On November 10 at 7:00 AM, the 1st and 2nd battalions commenced an attack. By 7:50 AM, F Company had captured one pillbox and had taken some prisoners. I Company was ordered to take over positions held by B Company, leaving B Company free to enter the attack.

At about 9:00 AM, both C and G companies ran into heavy fire from a house and pillbox at Raffelsbrand. F Company had taken many prisoners. By 10:20 AM, I Company had taken over B Company positions. At 11:30 AM, G Company received a small counterattack on its left flank. The counterattack was repulsed. By 12:30 PM, B Company had moved into position in the rear of C Company.

B Company was to pass through C Company and continue the attack. K Company was ordered to replace Task Force Lacy which was to move northeast and protect the left flank of the regiment and coordinate with the 109th Infantry. L Company was to occupy the position held by A Company, allowing A Company to move into position behind B Company.

At 5:00 PM, B Company had reached their objective, but were driven off by a counterattack. B Company consolidated with C Company and prepared for the night.[6]

At 7:00 AM on November 11, the 1st Battalion attacked, their mission being to clean out the enemy by an attack from the east. The 2nd Battalion was to support the attack by fire. The 1st Battalion was to attack in a column of companies. At 10:00 AM, they were still engaged with the first pillbox they had encountered. From 9:00 AM to 10:30 AM, the 1st and 2nd battalions received heavy mortar and artillery fire. At 1:00 PM, C Company started an enveloping movement around the left flank.

By 2:00 PM, C Company had been successful and was digging in. At 3:15 PM, A and B companies tied in with C Company's position, with B and C companies being consolidated due to depleted personnel.[7]

On November 12 at 10 minutes after midnight, the 1st Battalion received a small counterattack. The attack was repulsed. At 7:00 AM, A Company launched an attack to drive the Germans from their positions. One platoon of self-propelled tank destroyers was attached to the regiment and at 9:00 AM fired directly into the pillboxes from positions in F Company's area. No progress was made, as enemy mortar and artillery fire was extremely heavy. The strength of the units was greatly depleted as casualties mounted.

At 11:30 AM, the units were ordered to dig in and hold their ground. At about 4:00 PM, the 1st Battalion received an attack, which drove A Company from its position. At the same time, Captain James H. Burns, 1st Battalion S-3, was moving about 100 replacements forward. He organized them into a provisional company. The company counterattacked and reestablished the line. The 1st Battalion was very disorganized. Positions were being held by small, organized groups and not by platoons or companies.

At about 10:00 PM, the 1st and 2nd battalions received heavy mortar fire. An attack was planned for the following day, but the battalions' depleted strength forced the cancellation of the movement plan. The artillery fire plan, however, was carried out.[8]

During the night of November 12, 1st Battalion staff and Lieutenant Colonel Mather, the regimental executive officer, went to the front lines of the 1st Battalion to determine the exact strength and status of the battalion. It seemed to be in a bad way, with the men's strength, physical condition, and morale depleted. All battalions received heavy mortar and artillery fire throughout the night.

In the morning, an attempt was made to organize the 1st Battalion so that each group would have a definite leader. It was impossible to organize into platoons and companies, but all groups were organized into teams with leaders. When the 1st Battalion got underway to move to more tactical ground, they received heavy mortar and artillery fire and again became disorganized. At 9:30 AM, the 1st Battalion received an attack. All available mortar and artillery was put into action against the Germans and the attack was stopped.[9]

At 4:00 PM, the 1st Battalion started to withdraw to an assembly area in the vicinity of the battalion command post. One platoon from I Company was put in position to take over the protection of the left flank of the 2nd Battalion. It partially occupied the ground given up by the 1st Battalion. By 5:00 PM, the regiment was dug in and prepared for the night. Special emphasis was placed on supporting fire for the night, as the regiment was not in a good position to repulse a strong counterattack.

During the day and night, the Germans received reinforcements, causing its artillery and mortar fire to greatly increase. At 9:30 PM, the enemy attacked against G Company, supported by heavy mortar and light artillery fire.

The German 75mm self-propelled guns became very active against the 2nd and 3rd battalions.

Russell Arford of G Company, 110th Infantry, wrote how concern for a job finally brought him to the Hürtgen Forest. "I signed up in February 1941," he said, "figuring I would get my year of service over with and get out. By 1942, I thought jobs would be plentiful. They were, but I didn't get any of them. I sure chose the wrong time to go in, for I was immediately federalized and in the army until the end of the war." In the Kall Valley he often wondered if he would ever live long enough to work at any of those jobs. His job now was to fight for the people back home to have jobs.[10]

On November 14 at 4:00 AM, the 110th Regiment received orders to have a quartering party alerted to move by 9:00 AM. At 10:00 AM, a notice was received to be prepared to meet representatives of Combat Team 13 from the 8th Infantry Division who had been ordered to relieve the 110th Infantry.[11]

On November 15, officers and guides from Combat Team 13 arrived at the regimental command post. They were met by officers from the regiment and oriented on the positions they would occupy. During the afternoon and night, the relief took place, and the 110th moved into a rear assembly area in preparation for movement to locations in Luxembourg.

The results of operations of the 110th Infantry Regiment in the Hürtgen Forest:

> During the 15-day period of fighting, the Regiment contained the Germans on a 3,000 yard front.
> The Regiment gained 3,000 square yards of enemy territory.
> One German battalion was annihilated.
> One 110th battalion was sent to Schmidt to assist forces fighting there.[12]

The strength of the 110th Infantry Regiment at the end of November was 141 officers, five warrant officers, 2,829 enlisted men. Casualties included nine officers and fifty-six enlisted men killed, forty officers and 809 enlisted men wounded, five officers and 282 enlisted men missing in action, three enlisted men captured. Non-battle casualties included twenty-three officers and 867 enlisted men.

The 110th Infantry Regiment was opposed by some elements of the following German units:

328th Training Battalion, 89th Division
275th Division
2nd Battalion, 983rd Regiment,
6th Battery, 275th Artillery Regiment
982nd Regiment
26th Volksgrenadier Division

77th Infantry Regiment
78th Infantry Regiment
26th Reconnaissance Squadron
3rd Battalion, 26th Artillery Regiment
11th GAF Fortress Battalion
3rd Battalion, 1056th Regiment
353rd Division
941st Regiment
942nd Regiment[13]

6

112th Infantry Operations

With the three infantry regiments on line, the mission of the 112th Infantry Regiment was to attack east to capture Vossenack, after which time the regiment would change its direction of attack to the southeast on the Vossenack-Kommerscheidt-Schmidt line and capture and secure Schmidt.

Private First Class Albert Drapeau, K Company, 3rd Battalion, 112th Infantry Regiment recalled, "Approaching Germeter, we were brought into the grim reality of what may lie ahead. Dozens of vehicles were approaching us en route to the rear. They were loaded with dead and wounded."[1]

At 9:00 AM on November 2, after an artillery preparation which lasted one hour, the 2nd Battalion, with D Company, 707th Tank Battalion attached, crossed the line of departure and attacked through Germeter to Vossenack. Vossenack was held by another weak battalion of German Infantry Regiment 983, with a strength of around 150 men, the company strength of which was around 30–50 men. At the same time, the 1st Division in the north half of VII Corps sector attempted to feint the enemy into thinking the attack might be along the entire front by demonstrating with mortars, artillery, and strong patrols, but no advance was made.[2]

First Lieutenant Eldeen H. Kauffman, F Company, 112th Infantry was awarded the Distinguished Service Cross for his actions on November 2. While advancing through Vossenack, Lieutenant Kauffman personally directed fire of a tank in support of two platoons of infantry that had suffered many casualties, the advance of which was being slowed by strong German resistance. Then, armed with a pistol, he stepped into the street, firing as he went and urging his men forward. He entered several houses and assaulted Germans with his pistol, causing twelve of them to surrender and thus clearing the German stronghold. Inspired by his actions, the company moved ahead to accomplish the mission they came for.[3]

Private First Class Raymond Carpenter of M Company, 3rd Battalion spoke for many of his buddies, "I never saw a wood so thick with trees as the Hürtgen.

It turned out to be the worst place of any."[4] He could only blame himself for being there. In earlier service with the 45th Infantry Division, an Oklahoma Army National Guard outfit, Carpenter received a foot injury. After recovering, he received assignment to a quartermaster service battalion, a relatively safe rear-area job. "But I still wanted to fight for our right to be free and be of service to my nation, so in Wales I requested transfer to M Company, 3rd Battalion, 112th Infantry Regiment, 28th Infantry Division—America's oldest division."[4]

That same day, the action of Technical Sergeant Jacob Welc won him a battlefield commission. The soldiers were taking a beating at Vossenack. The roads had been converted into rivers and mud due to all the rain and snow. German artillery pummeled all routes to the advancing units. The use of vehicles was limited. Hampered by these conditions, the wounded were only brought back as far as the most advanced aid station. Further evacuation to the rear appeared impossible.

Without orders, Sergeant Welc drove one of his trucks through the mud-choked roads in the dead of night. In the battered town of Vossenack, German artillery rained in constantly. Despite the incessant shelling, he brought his vehicle into the town, helped load the wounded, and then drove over the treacherous road to the rear medical station.[5]

The 2nd Battalion of the 112th initially suffered losses primarily from German artillery, mortars, and poorly marked minefields, both German and friendly, before reaching the northeast section of Vossenack by early afternoon. The two attacking companies set up a defensive position on the forward slope of the ridge, while the reserve company mopped up the stragglers and snipers that had been bypassed.

The German well-observed artillery fire took a heavy toll on the companies, reducing them considerably. It was already evident that the artillery was unable to effectively neutralize the German observation posts and positions on the commanding ridges because the shells were coming into the town from three major points of the compass. The attacking elements reported enemy armor in the town of Schmidt, but when the report was forwarded, the G-2 promptly stated that only ten tanks were in the vicinity and they were 50 miles away.

As the 2nd Battalion initiated its attack, the 1st and 3rd battalions moved into positions to the rear of the LD and made preparations to move to the aid of the attacking battalion should it be counterattacked. The commanders also performed reconnaissance as far forward as the front line for routes of advance, thus enabling them to further refine their attack plans the following day.

To the north, the 109th Infantry had made good progress in their coordinated attack with the 112th Infantry and had succeeded in knocking out fifteen pillboxes and in capturing 200 prisoners. The 1st Battalion had advanced 2,700 yards in a drive to the northeast toward the town of Hürtgen. However, the other assault battalion attacking in the same direction could only gain 500 yards due to

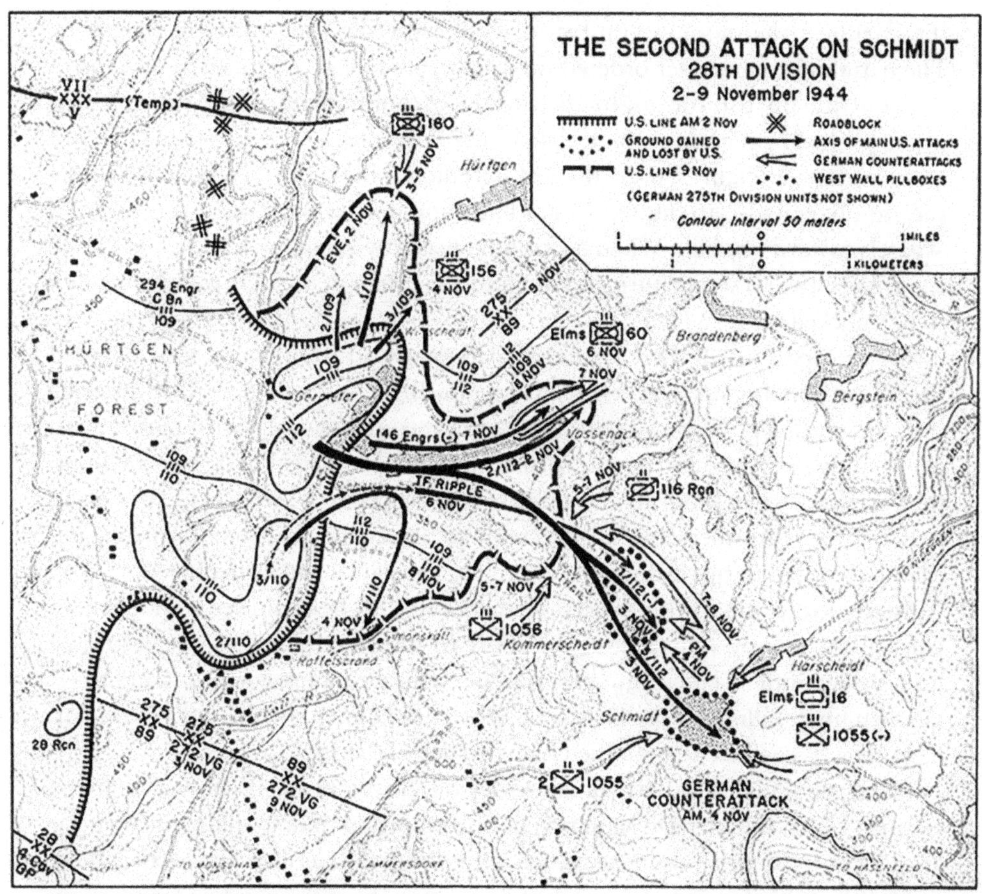

The Second Attack on Schmidt, 1944. (*US Army Center of Military History*)

the thick minefields and wire obstacles that were covered by bands of grazing fire from automatic weapons.

In the south, the 110th Infantry attacked at 12:00 PM but immediately encountered heavy artillery and mortar fire along a strong defensive position consisting of concrete pillboxes, log bunkers, and bands of defensive wire covered with machine guns. Even after the area had been saturated with artillery and mortar fire, the 110th assault battalions were unable to breach the positions.[6]

At 7:00 AM on November 3, the 3rd Battalion of the 112th Infantry launched its attack across the Kall River, and with practically no difficulty, the town of Kommerscheidt fell to K Company. The battalion then pushed into Schmidt and by evening, the three rifle companies were in the north end of the town. Only a small section of the town had been cleared of Germans by night.

Since reconnaissance had been scheduled for the night of November 2–3, several tanks immediately drove onto mines and were knocked out. Due to the darkness the mopping-up teams were engaging each other in firefights. The battalion commander ordered the companies to stop all forward movement and button up for the night. Resupply of ammunition and rations was accomplished by the use of full-tracked M29 Weasels.

Lieutenant William George, the 3rd Battalion motor officer, who was leading the supply convoy, attempted to get battalion anti-tank guns towed by M29 Weasels toward Schmidt. When his column was traversing the Kall Valley, one of the drivers made a wrong turn and ran into a German roadblock, causing the gun to be knocked out.

Private First Class Robert J. Esterly, I Company, 112th Infantry, was awarded the Silver Star for his actions. He carried a BAR and was picked to provide the chief means of firepower for a five-man reconnaissance patrol tasked with penetrating deep into German territory at night. The patrol had gone well into the Nazi lines when suddenly the stillness was broken by a German guard's order to halt. When the Americans failed to reply to the second challenge, burp gun and rifle slugs began to rip through the darkness. The patrol hastily deployed.

Esterly lost contact with the rest of the patrol. All he could see were German gun flashes. Instead of retreating, he chose to stay and fight. Crouching low, he held his fire until he had spotted the muzzle flashes from ten burp guns and rifles. He then fired, killing all the Germans. When asked later why he did not retreat, he said he "came here to fight the Germans, not to retreat."[7]

The Americans' rapid attack successes on November 2–3 showed that the German 275th Infantry Division was not in a position to hold out on its own for any longer, let alone to clear the breach itself. From the German perspective, there was a risk of the Rur dams being taken away, with the corresponding far-reaching consequences for further defense west of the Rur. During the night of November 2–3, the alert troops of the German 116th Panzer Division, the reinforced Panzergrenadier Regiment 156, were deployed to the Hürtgen area. The bulk of the 116th Panzer Division was to advance during the night of November 3–4 and begin the counterattack on November 4, the decision being made during the course of November 3.

Initially, a thrust was planned along the Hürtgen-Germeter high road in order to cut off all US forces stationed in the Vossenack area. Consequently, Panzergrenadier regiments 156 and 60 were deployed against the enemy in the Hürtgen-Vossenack area, while Anti-Aircraft 116 was ordered to advance from Zweifallshammer (south of Brandenberg) along the Kall Valley in order to separate the US units stationed in Schmidt and Vossenack.[8]

Private First Class Albert E. Drapeau wrote in his journal:

> The 2nd platoon was dug in on a forward slope facing east with the town of Schmidt being directly to our rear. Through an early morning haze, I discerned

what appeared to be about fifty enemy coming over a rise about 600 yards to our front. [...] A rising crescendo of yelling and cussing was enveloping our rear, along with increasing enemy fire. K Company was breaking, some units fleeing to our rear through Schmidt and toward Kommerscheidt. Orders to hold were being refused. I personally shouted and cussed some of these men. We came here to fight and defeat the Germans, not to run.[9]

While the assault of Schmidt was in progress, the 2nd Battalion improved their defensive positions east of Vossenack. German artillery fire on the battalion's positions inflicted heavy casualties and cut the strength of the already depleted companies to a point when they would have to have replacements or be replaced. In the end, as the reinforcements arrived, they had to be integrated into the line during the action.[10]

In the meantime, Regimental Commander Lieutenant Colonel Carl L. Peterson ordered the 1st Battalion to move into Kommerscheidt. Their mission was to secure the town and to prepare to assist the 3rd Battalion in Schmidt should they be attacked. The regimental commander knew that this movement would be the only way he could plug the gap that existed between the 2nd and 3rd battalions. The 1st Battalion was in the process of preparing their defensive position when B Company, on the south edge of the town, became engaged by an enemy force of underdetermined strength.[11]

Robert W. Meyer, B Company, 112th Infantry Regiment remembered his first night with B Company:

Light rain had started to fall and I thought, Good grief, what a miserable existence. The Hürtgen Forest was a bloody battlefield of survival. It was a kill-or-be-killed situation. Military trash was everywhere—discarded C-rations, bandoliers, empty ammo crates, unexploded shells, mess gear, helmets, abandoned stretchers, bloody bandages, and corpses were on the ground, stuck to the bushes, and in the trees.[12]

The 28th Division plan gave a battalion of combat engineers the mission of making the trail from Vossenack to Kommerscheidt passable to tanks and other supporting vehicles. This trail was nothing more than wagon tracks, so narrow and filled with sharp turns that it was almost unusable to anything but light vehicles, which were bogging down in the mud. This project was very slow developing; consequently only three tanks of the 707th Tank Battalion were able to cross the valley.[13]

On November 4, the 112th Regiment received orders to hold their present positions, so as to protect the east flank of the division. At 6:00 AM a German counterattack started with severe shelling on Kommerscheidt and Schmidt, the emphasis being on Kommerscheidt. At 8:00 AM, the enemy attacked with an estimated force of one battalion of infantry supported by ten tanks, but the attack was repulsed. At 10:00 AM, a second German attack of approximately the same strength struck at the position from the northeast and southeast.

But the defenders of Schmidt were unable to hold, and the battalion was forced to withdraw under pressure back to Kommerscheidt. Entire platoons of K and L companies were cut off, and although a few of these units got back to Kommerscheidt, the majority of them were reduced into small groups and forced to surrender.

Three tanks of the 707th Tank Battalion arrived at Kommerscheidt just as the 3rd Battalion started its withdrawal. But too late to save Schmidt. Orders to recapture Schmidt, with the time of the attack set at 3:00 PM, had to be cancelled when it was realized that the German attack had not been contained. At 3:30 PM, the enemy attack persisted but was halted before reaching Kommerscheidt through coordinated artillery, tank, infantry, and air support. The three tanks of the 707th Tank Battalion engaged German armor supporting the attack and drove them back to the cover of Schmidt. The fighter-bombers on this mission claimed credit for destroying three enemy tanks.

Later information indicated that the German 1055th Regiment had been moving through Schmidt on its way to a rest area at Duren just prior to the attack. It was halted and ordered to counterattack at Schmidt. When weapons supporting the 3rd Battalion arrived, eight tanks and four self-propelled guns, the attack was started. The 3rd Battalion, followed by the 2nd Battalion, attacked Schmidt. Both units received heavy losses.

Because of the deep stream valleys around Vossenack, it was clear that tanks could only be used effectively on the Schmidt plateau. The German 89th Infantry Division was reinforced with the Sturmgeschütz Brigade 341 and, at least initially, with parts of the Panzer Regiment 16 from the 116th Division for the counterattack on November 4. The latter, however, could not be made available before the afternoon of November 4. The German 1056th Grenadier Regiment was to be replaced quickly by parts of the 272nd Volksgrenadier Division. The German LXXIV Corps was reinforced primarily by additional artillery units, and the 275th Infantry Division by Luftwaffe fortress units.[14]

During the morning of November 4, the 112th regimental headquarters company commander came under two hours of enemy artillery fire while on a reconnaissance patrol. He recommended that, since the Germans were capable of delivering heavy artillery fire on Vossenack, it would be prudent to remain at the current command post in the pillbox 800 yards west of Germeter, or to relocate to the southeast side of the Kall River, where the Germans lacked direct observation. In the event, the regimental commander decided that the command post would remain in the pillbox, but a small operational group would be organized and move to the east side of the Kall River. The operational group was formed and in the afternoon moved by M29 Weasels to a hunting lodge on the southeast side of the draw. However, it remained there only a short time because enemy patrol activity became very aggressive and there was insufficient personnel to provide adequate security. The regimental commander moved part of this group to the 1st Battalion command post in Kommerscheidt until adequate shelter could be set up in the woods. While the command post was operating in the hunting lodge, Lieutenant Colonel Albert Flood, 3rd Battalion Commander, was wounded.[15]

In the afternoon, prior to the moving of the command post, Lieutenant Colonel Locket, regimental executive officer, while en route to a forward battalion command post, was captured by a German patrol as his party crossed the Kall River. Accompanying Lieutenant Colonel Locket were Captain Montgomery, regimental S-2, and two photographers detailed from US First Army headquarters to make a pictorial record of this action.

Captain Montgomery was wounded in the skirmish, but the patrol later abandoned him in one of the many log bunkers in the area. Later he managed to work his way to the road, where he was picked up and evacuated. The 2nd Battalion in the meantime continued to hold its positions in Vossenack in the face of the precision fire from enemy artillerymen. A counterattack at 2:30 PM was beaten back with no loss of ground.

The unstable situation on November 4 was only slightly improved the next day when eight medium tanks and seven tank-destroyers traversed the Kall Valley. During the day, the depleted remnants of the 1st and 3rd battalions improved and consolidated their positions when they were not warding off small, localized attacks or sweating out the numerous heavy artillery concentrations. The newly arrived armor knocked out several enemy tanks. It was evident that Kommerscheidt, being commanded by high ground on three sides, was not a good defensive position. In addition the enemy had infiltrated down the Kall Valley and was constantly threatening the only supply route, which due to the rain and the snow, had become almost impassable. Three tanks had already thrown their tracks in an effort to cross the draw. The engineers spent most of their days and nights fighting off or preparing to fight off these infiltrations, consequently there was little time remaining for them to repair or improve the trail.[16]

Late in the afternoon of November 5, General Cota, commanding general of the 28th Infantry Division, ordered that Task Force Ripple, under the command of Lieutenant Colonel Richard W. Ripple, be organized and given the mission of attacking through the 112th Infantry and retaking Schmidt on November 6. Upon recapturing Schmidt, the task force would set up roadblocks and prepare to hold the town until the 112th could relieve them. The task force upon relief would then prepare to attack in the direction of Steckenborn. Task Force Ripple was composed of the 3rd Battalion of the 110th Infantry (approximately 350 men), A and C companies with one platoon of B Company of the 707th Tank Battalion, and a detachment of the 893rd Tank-Destroyer Battalion.

The 2nd Battalion in Vossenack shook off two enemy counterattacks as it was slowly being gnawed away by artillery fire. The forward echelon of the regimental command post was dug in about 800 yards northwest of Kommerscheidt, in the area of C Company, which was in 1st Battalion reserve.[17]

The fighter-bombers of the Ninth Army Air Force strafed and bombed Schmidt where the enemy appeared to be assembling for a major attack on Kommerscheidt. On November 6 at 2:00 AM, Task Force Ripple moved from its assembly area toward the Vossenack-Kommerscheidt trail, keeping on the edge of the woods so as to avoid the artillery fire that was falling in Vossenack. Lieutenant Colonel Ripple planned to use the present front line of the company in position just west of Kommerscheidt as the LD for the attack on Schmidt.

As the task force attempted to cross the stone bridge over the Kall River, it was fired upon by infiltrated enemy and therefore had to fight its way to the positions of the 1st and 3rd battalions. The armored elements of the task force remained in the vicinity of Vossenack until the trail could be cleared. Prior to the arrival of the task force, the 1st and 3rd battalions began to receive very heavy artillery fire that was coupled with fire from self-propelled guns and small arms on their positions. It was evident that the enemy was waiting for the task force to attack because it appeared that every gun had re-zeroed in on Kommerscheidt and every observer had his attention focused on the area and fired at anything that moved to the front of the town. The impracticability of the attack of the task force was soon realized and was called off. The task force moved into and prepared a defensive position to the right of C Company.[18]

The 2nd Battalion in Vossenack was attacked twice, but both assaults were beaten off. However, the increased volume of direct fire from self-propelled guns, added to the ever-increasing pressure of the infantry attacks, forced the battalion to withdraw to the church in the center of the town. Here the battalion was reorganized and reinforced with the 146th Engineer Battalion in the town, the 20th and 1340th engineer battalions on a line south of the town extending to the east side of the stone bridge across the Kall River, and the 2nd Battalion in positions along the north edge of the town. The 20th Engineer Battalion had the mission of trying to keep the trail across the Kall open as it was the only line of communications between the troops in Kommerscheidt and those in Vossenack. Counterattacks continued but the positions as they were reinforced held.

At this point, the situation in the 112th sector was critical. The ever increasing fury of the enemy attacks was taking a heavy toll on men and material. The armor of the 707th Tank Battalion and the 893 Tank-Destroyer Battalion was slowly being made ineffective due to the concentrated fire placed on them in the exposed positions they were forced to utilize. The road between Vossenack and Kommerscheidt, inadequate at the start of the attack, became an obstacle when soaked by the rain and snow as the prevailing weather deteriorated. The other roads were so deep in mud that traffic had to be kept to an absolute minimum.

The physical and mental condition of the men on position was anything but desirable. They were just existing: cold, soaked to the skin by rain and clinging, wet snow, and miserable. The constant threat of counterattack and the methodical pounding of their position by an ever-increasing volume of massed enemy artillery fire made sleep scarce and casualties high. Replacements joined the fight and were evacuated before the squad leaders got to know their first names.

Hardly any of the men on the ridge could understand why the Germans had spared them the familiar artillery fire that morning. The unaccustomed silence aroused suspicion. Then a short burst of rifle or machine gun fire, a shrill cry of terror—from somewhere—silence again. About half an hour later, the German guns opened fire with such intensity that the men could no longer hold their positions. Panicked, the soldiers of G Company grab their equipment and rush back headlong. Impressed by the flight of their left-hand neighbor, the company commander orders F Company to return to the reserve company's position. But the urge to run is contagious. As soon as the men start moving, nothing can stop them. The reserve company also begins to falter. Although no one can claim to have seen a single enemy soldier, hardly anyone doubts that they were literally on their heels.

Pushing each other, shoving over each other, the soldiers race through Vossenack with wild eyes, throwing their equipment wildly from them. Circumstances have brought to the surface one of the most effective forces in war, the one that turns brave men into cowards. Rushing out of the command post near the church, the soldiers of the battalion headquarters desperately try to resist flight. It is an impossible task. Most men only think of an unspecified place that means safety—the rear positions. At around 10:30 AM the officers have managed to form a thin line of support across the town, roughly at the height of the church. But this 'line' comprises no more than seventy men.

During the day a German self-propelled gun that was located somewhere near Brandenberg had laterally bracketed the shallow dugout that served as the forward regimental command post. The crew had fired all but one round when a P-38, armed with a Blaze Bomb, dive-bombed the enemy position and silenced the gun. Many drawn and weary faces who had heard the aircraft go into its dive and watched the effect of the bomb took another glance at the plane and mutely blessed and thanked this unknown pilot for taking a thorn out of their backs. The P-47s bombed and strafed Schmidt in an effort to disrupt the assembly of troops preparing for the attack on Kommerscheidt.[19]

In the north, the 109th Infantry made little progress in its attack, meeting the usual murderous curtain of fire that the enemy laid down in front of their barbed wire and minefields. At 3:00 PM the 12th Regimental Combat Team of the 4th Infantry Division was attached to the 28th Division, and plans were made for the relief of the 109th Infantry on November 7. V Corps' artillery had fired 15,000 rounds and the tank-destroyers had fired 1,650 rounds, equivalent to over ten rounds per minute, for this 24-hour period.

The November 7 attack was initiated at 8:00 AM by the 146th Engineer Battalion attacking toward the east end of Vossenack in an effort to regain the ground that had been lost the day before. The attack was supported by tanks and artillery, and as was the usual case in this German artillery impact area, the enemy laid a blanket of shells on the attackers. The attack was successful and most of the ground was regained. The 2nd Battalion of the 109th Infantry was ordered to relieve the 2nd Battalion of the 112th Infantry in Vossenack, which it completed by 8:40 PM. The badly mauled 2nd Battalion retired to an assembly area west of Germeter, where it was to be rehabilitated.

The morning of November 7 also brought the much-anticipated attack on Kommerscheidt. Although the first attempt to seize the town was heavily supported by tanks and artillery fire, it failed to accomplish its mission. It was a different ending when the enemy attacked at 2:30 PM behind a heavy curtain of artillery fire and supported by fifteen to twenty tanks; the fight that ensued was bitterly fought, but the overwhelming odds could not be surmounted.

The fragments of the two battalions withdrew after their positions became untenable to the line held by C Company and Task Force Ripple. Prior to the loss of Kommerscheidt, the division issued orders to form another task force with Brigadier General George A. Davis, assistant division commander, in command. This task force would incorporate Task Force Ripple and would have the mission of recapturing Schmidt.

Before Task Force Davis could be fully organized, the corps commander ordered that, due to their precarious position on the south side of the Kall River, the troops would be withdrawn. Task Force Davis was given the mission of protecting the withdrawal of these troops on the night of November 8–9. The tank-destroyers were credited with knocking out five enemy tanks, but of the armor that had traversed the Kall Valley, only one tank and two tank-destroyers remained operational. One of the tank-destroyers was lost when a mortar shell hit inside the open turret.

The aid station which had been operating in the Kall Valley was captured by German patrols once a day for the past two days. Captain Madden, the regimental chaplain, who could speak excellent German, said the patrol leader would search the aid station for weapons—then ask him if they had enough food and medical supplies. After being informed that the aid station was well supplied, the satisfied patrol leader would move his patrol down the valley and continue on his mission. Captain Madden said that within an hour an American patrol, usually consisting of engineers, would approach from the same direction and continue the way of the German patrol.

On November 8 the front was relatively quiet, with only spasmodic artillery fire to remind the alert defenders of the enemy's potential. The aggressive probing of the line had practically ceased, but since counterattack was the enemy's strongest and most likely capability, it remained a constant threat to those men still on the south side of the Kall River. Lieutenant Colonel Ripple, aided by the very capable Major Richard A. Dana, S-3 of the 112th Infantry, and a few other officers, had made a tentative plan to withdraw, which could be put into effect once the order was received.

It was at the completion of this plan that one of the men just outside the shallow log-covered hole that served as a command post was heard to exclaim, "Holy Hell, here comes a chicken colonel from the 5th Armored Division!" The unshaven, mud-caked faces of the small command group that had been ageing a year for every day that they had spent on this position suddenly came to animated life. Although nothing was said in the moment, the thoughts of the men present were unanimous: this meant that help was on its way.

The colonel introduced himself as Colonel Gustav M. Nelson and stated that he was assuming command of the 112th Infantry. The colonel had led a patrol through the draw so as to take command of the withdrawal of his regiment. When asked as to the strength of the task force, Colonel Ripple told him there were approximately 350 effectives and about fifty wounded, of which twenty could walk. Informed of the plan for withdrawal, Colonel Nelson approved, and the plan was put into action.[20]

Private Clarence Skains remembered that he and Private Nathaniel Quentin, both of M Company, 112th Infantry were in Kommerscheidt, when a general withdrawal was ordered. No one told them of the order, so they remained in town, while around them other members of their squad lay dead in their foxholes. Quentin noticed a platoon of enemy soldiers crawling toward him, their uniforms blending with the saturated ground now covered by falling snow. He allowed them to advance within 25 yards and then opened fire with his BAR, killing twenty and forcing the others to retreat.

The Germans attacked again, in one- and two-man rushes, running through a turnip patch toward Quentin and Skains. The men held their ground and fired steadily, and the Germans retreated. Skains wrote that there was no way they were going to withdraw, even if they had received the order to. They came to defeat the Germans, and that is what they were going to do.[21]

Private Kensler made another entry in his diary on November 8, recording what he wrote to his wife that day:

> During the night it snowed. It was damp and cold. I pray God that this may soon end and stop the killing and suffering. To me war is murder. Maybe others would not agree, but that's one nice thing about being an American, everyone can have his own thoughts and ideas. Thank God for that. This is why we are here. Good night, my darling.

He also recalled:

> The forest was a helluva eerie place to fight. You can't get all of the dead, because you can't find them, and they stay there to remind the guys advancing as to what might hit them. You can't get protection. You can't see. You can't get fields of fire. Artillery slashes the trees like a scythe. Everything is tangled. You can scarcely walk. Everybody is cold and wet, and the mixture of cold rain and sleet keeps falling. Then they jump off again, and soon there is only a handful of the old men left.[22]

Staff Sergeant Conrad W. Johnson was with D Company, 1st Battalion, 112th Infantry. In an interview by the 28th Infantry Division Public Relations Section on September 28, 1945, he recalled that after a few days rest from the fighting at the Siegfried Line, he was back in the fighting in the Hürtgen Forest.

The fighting was tough because the land was hilly and there were thick woods. It was there that his unit was surrounded. Some of the men were able to escape, but he was one of the ones taken prisoner by the Germans. He helped carry some of the wounded to a German aid station for treatment.

After marching for several days, the group came to Bonn, Germany. There they were loaded into boxcars and sent to Stalag XII-A in Limburg, Germany. Even though he was captured, Johnson latter wrote home that he did his best trying to stop the Germans. He knew that his side would eventually win.[23]

The 112th Infantry Regiment was opposed by some elements of the following German units:

275th Infantry Division
    141st Fortress Battalion
20th GAF *Fusilier* Battalion
Kampfgruppe Wegelein
275th *Fusilier* Battalion
1412th Infantry Battalion
89th Division
89th *Fusilier* Battalion
1055th Regiment
116th Panzer Division

60th Panzer *Grenadier* Regiment
156th Panzer *Grenadier* Regiment

Kampfgruppe Trier

Reserves Identified:

Kampfgruppe Brandes
Kampfgruppe Feind
73rd Engineer Battalion
275th Engineer Battalion[24]

7
707th Tank Battalion

The objective assigned to the 28th Infantry Division by V Corps was the Vossenack-Strauch-Schmidt area. Schmidt was an important communications center located astride an east-west road which the First Army wanted for an MSR, and in addition was on a ridge overlooking the Schwammenauel Dam, one of the vital Roer dams. East of the division and in the center of its sector lay the town of Vossenack atop an east-west ridge surrounded by woods. To the north lay the Hürtgen-Brandenberg-Bergstein ridge, which dominated the Vossenack ridge, similarly to the ridge on which lay the towns of Schmidt and Kommerscheidt. The 707th Tank Battalion was assigned to support the 28th Infantry Division in this effort.[1]

The 28th Infantry Division plan of attack provided for the 109th Infantry Regiment to be committed on the north flank in the direction of the town of Hürtgen, the 110th Infantry Regiment on the south flank toward Simonskall, and the 112th Infantry Regiment in the center to take, in turn, the towns of Vossenack, Kommerscheidt, and Schmidt. The 707th Tank Battalion, commanded by Lieutenant Colonel Richard Ripple was to support the attack. This battalion had joined the 28th Infantry Division on October 6, and up to the time of the Hürtgen operation had seen very little combat. In this operation, the 707th Tank Battalion would fight mostly in support of the center regiment.

In front of the division on both north and south were dense forests cut by deep draws that hid numerous defenses such as pillboxes and antitank and anti-personnel mines, plus other types of manmade obstacles. In the center was the open ridge on which lay the town of Vossenack. Southeast of Vossenack and separating it from Schmidt was the Kall River, which ran through a steep, wooded gorge. This river was crossed only by a steep wooded trail connecting Vossenack and Kommerscheidt, which was to become the main supply route for the forces south of the Kall River.[2]

Before the attack, the 28th Division G-2 estimated that to the immediate front to the north and south the enemy had approximately 3,350 men, all fighting under the German 89th Infantry Division. The total reserve capable of rapid intervention was estimated at 2,000 not committed and 3,000 from less active fronts.[3]

The town of Vossenack, about as wide as a city block and 2,000 yards in length, lay astride a road which ran along the top of an open ridge. Near the town center, the church formed a prominent landmark and overlooked the deep draws from the surrounding woods which reached up to the outskirts of the town on the north, east, and south.

On November 2 at 9:00 AM, after an hour of artillery preparation, the 2nd Battalion, 112th Infantry jumped off from the vicinity of Germeter. Moving down the ridge, G Company was on the left, F Company on the right, with E Company following in reserve. In support of this attack was C Company, 707th Tank Battalion. The 1st Platoon, under Lieutenant William S. Quarrie, plus two tanks from the 2nd Platoon attacked with G Company. The three remaining tanks of the 2nd Platoon, with Lieutenant James J. Leming in command, attacked with F Company's Lieutenant Joseph Novak's 3rd Platoon. E Company was to assist in mopping up the objective or to come to the aid of the other tank platoons if required. The attack progressed satisfactorily and the infantry was on the objective shortly after 10:00 AM.

The tanks, however, had trouble from the start. The 1st Platoon sergeant's tank had a track blown off while moving through a gap in an American-laid protective minefield. Next, Lieutenant Quarrie's tank became mired in the soft ground. Captain George S. West, commanding the tank company, saw the difficulty, came forward, and placed the lieutenant in his tank, and the platoon moved on. The last tank of the 2nd Platoon went too far south and was knocked out by Panzerschreck fire.

The platoon commander, Lieutenant Leming, who was having trouble with his tank gun, radioed the 3rd Platoon for assistance. One section came forward and was sent toward the eastern end of town. After bringing his gun into action, Leming moved forward, only to have his tank immobilized by a German mine. Meanwhile, Captain West left his own tank to Lieutenant Quarrie and commandeered a 3rd Platoon tank, which struck a mine in Vossenack shortly afterward and was put out of action. He then boarded a battalion headquarters tank in the town, which was serving as a forward observation platform for the battalion's assault gun platoon. The difficulties of command under the conditions which faced Captain West can be appreciated. His platoons were in support of three different infantry companies; he could only act as an expediter and to do this he required both transportation and communication.[4]

A tank retriever which came into the town to evacuate Lieutenant Leming's tank was hit and immobilized by German artillery fire. Thus, by 1:00 PM, five tanks and one retriever were out of action, which reduced the effective strength of the company by roughly one-third. Most of those tanks were recoverable but were of no immediate value to the infantry they were supporting. At 4:00 PM, the company returned to an area within 400 yards of Germeter, where they spent the night, remaining on call from the infantry.

At about 5:00 AM the next day, the tank company moved forward and occupied supporting positions on the north and east edges of Vossenack. The company remained in these positions, encountering no enemy activity until heavy artillery began to land about 12:00 PM. All tanks except three were ordered back into Germeter. The three remaining were the command tanks of the 1st and 2nd Platoons, and that of the battalion headquarters, which had been ordered to stay in the town for communication purposes. The command tank of the 1st Platoon was still immobilized but could be used in this capacity. At about 12:30 PM, hostile artillery fire came down on the battalion headquarters tank, knocking it out, and at 3:30 PM, the only operative tank in Vossenack was ordered back.[5]

No further tank action occurred until the following morning, when the 2nd Platoon was used in a fire support role for one of the battalions of the 110th Infantry Regiment to the south. The mission was completed by 7:05 AM, and the platoon returned to company control. At 10:30 AM, on the request of the infantry commander in Vossenack, the four tanks of the 1st Platoon went forward to neutralize small arms and machine gun fire coming from the woods north of the town. The tanks moved in and fired high explosive shells at ranges of 150–200 yards, neutralized the enemy fire, and returned to Germeter at 11:00 AM.

Again, at the request of the infantry, one section of the 2nd Platoon plus the company commander in his tank went back into Vossenack, where the 2nd Battalion, 112th Infantry was still holding at considerable cost. The eastern end of the town and the eastern slope of the ridge where the infantry had dug in was being continuously battered by artillery, which took its toll in casualties and undermined the morale of the defenders. The western end of the town was relatively quiet, except for troops passing through en route to Kommerscheidt. Medical and other vehicles continued to use the route through Vossenack to the south.

While the three tanks were engaged in counteracting small arms fire at the direction of the infantry, Captain West's tank backed into a crater and broke a drive shaft. He ordered the other tanks back and stayed with his own until he was towed back by company maintenance. At 6:15 PM, Lieutenant

Quarrie with three tanks of the 1st Platoon moved to the position occupied by F Company. He spotted tracer fire coming from a draw east of the town and radioed the position to the battalion assault guns, which fired into this draw until divisional artillery took over. A German POW later stated that this fire broke up a counterattack which was forming in the draw, indicating the advantage of having an assault gun platoon organic to the tank battalion.[6] Lieutenant Quarrie remained with F Company all night while the balance of the tanks was in Germeter.

At 7:00 AM on November 5, Captain West moved with Lieutenant Leming's three tanks to positions from which they could fire into the woods north of Vossenack on mortar and enemy small arms locations. Here one tank received a direct high explosive hit which killed the driver and destroyed the 75mm gun. The other tanks returned to Germeter at about 10:00 AM. At 2:00 PM, Lieutenant Leming went forward with his platoon in order to repel a reported counterattack. Captain West accompanied this platoon, which moved forward to support Lieutenant Quarrie's G Company unit and continued to provide support to E Company. The entire eastern end of the ridge came under intense heavy artillery fire, and by 3:00 PM, both platoons were receiving heavy fire and withdrew to Germeter, apparently without orders. Captain West, in his tanks, remained in turret defilade behind G Company. At 5:30 PM, Lieutenant Quarrie again reported to F Company with an extra tank borrowed from the 2nd Platoon. He remained with them all night, returning to Germeter early the next morning.[7]

After Lieutenant Quarrie reported back, Lieutenant Colonel Ripple received orders to get all available armor into Vossenack to stop an enemy counterattack; B and C companies, 707th Tank Battalion were committed. B Company initially sent its 1st Platoon, under Lieutenant Carl A. Anderson, into town. This platoon was soon followed by Captain George S. Granger, the company commander, and the 3rd Platoon, under Lieutenant Danforth Sherman. C Company, with its eight tanks, came last.

The situation described by the tankers was one of complete confusion. Many of the infantry were running to the rear out of town. None of the tankers know where the front lines were or where the counterattacking enemy was located.

The 1st Platoon, C Company occupied a position northeast of Vossenack and fired to the north until about 9:00 AM, when it pulled back to Germeter. Meanwhile, in B Company Lieutenant Anderson evacuated the crew of a damaged C Company tank by placing one man from the crew in each of his tanks and returning with his entire platoon to the LD. Although he had asked for and received permission from Captain Granger to make this evacuation, there seems to be no sound reason for taking all of those tanks out of action at a time when presumably they were badly needed. He soon returned to Vossenack, however, and relieved the 2nd Platoon, C Company by 9:30 AM.

When the company's three tanks first entered Vossenack, they knew nothing of the terrain and even less about the situation. As a result they fired first into buildings occupied by friendly infantry, causing some casualties. They also fired perilously close to the 3rd Platoon of C Company and some tank destroyers which were in the town. During all of this time, Captain Granger was trying to locate the infantry battalion commander to get an intelligent picture of what was happening.

Whether or not there was a German counterattack is uncertain from the available accounts. Lieutenant Novak's C Company, 3rd Platoon is credited with stopping some German infantry approaching the town from the east and southeast. The one fact that can definitely be reconstructed is that the American infantry defenders, having been subjected to unceasing artillery and mortar fire for five days, had reached the limit of their endurance. When the first shouts of counterattack went up, panic spread like wildfire and the men left their holes and ran to the rear. When Captain Granger located the infantry battalion command post, he found that the battalion commander, though present, was a combat fatigue casualty and that a captain on his staff was in actual command.

In the initial action of B Company in Vossenack, it is of interest to note that requests and orders sent to B Company came from Captain West's C Company, rather than from their own tank or infantry battalion commander. Captain West was in town at the time B Company was committed, but accounts indicate that even he did not know the infantry situation. Captain West was killed at about 9:00 AM by an enemy shell which landed in the turret of his tank. Captain Granger took command of the tanks of both companies and kept his 1st and 3rd platoons in the vicinity of Vossenack for the remainder of the day. Artillery fire knocked out three tanks, and the only direct action against the enemy was the destruction of a small infantry counterattack. At 9:00 AM, Lieutenant Quarrie, C Company came forward and relieved the tanks of B Company for the night.[8]

This day's action at Vossenack is a graphic illustration of the dangers attending such vague orders as those that sent tanks into the town. The communication and coordination necessary between the tanks and infantry had completely broken down. At the time of Captain West's death, the remaining tanks were under the command of Captain Granger, who was not familiar with the terrain and was also occupied trying to establish contact with local infantry defenders.

By this time the foot troops in Vossenack consisted largely of engineers of the 1171st Engineer Combat Group, with two battalions supporting the 28th Infantry Division. During the night, General George A. Davis, assistant division commander, visited the town and ordered the engineers to retake the eastern end, which had been abandoned by the infantry and reoccupied by Germans in undetermined strength.

About 3:00 AM the following day, Lieutenant Quarrie's tank was disabled by a direct hit on the turret while another tank of his platoon was hit in the engine compartment. Lieutenant Quarrie was not injured, however, and at 5:00 AM he was called to the engineer command post for his recommendations as to the employment of tanks in the 1171st Engineer counterattack to take place that morning. He explained that he was to be relieved by Lieutenant Johnson of B Company but recommended that tanks not be used on the left (north) flank of the town because of its vulnerability from the high ground at Hürtgen and Brandenberg.

At 7:30 AM, Lieutenant Johnson, accompanied by Lieutenant Anderson and Captain Granger arrived. Lieutenant Anderson led Quarrie's platoon back to Germeter, and after orienting Johnson on the engineer plan, Quarrie followed with Captain Granger. At this time the engineers held a north-south line through Vossenack at about the center of the town. Lieutenant Johnson's platoon was to move up the right (south) flank of the town immediately after the artillery barrage which heralded the engineer attack. One company of engineers was to attack from house to house up the main road of the town, with Lieutenant Johnson's tank firing two rounds into each house before the assault. This plan succeeded and the engineers were able to retake the entire town.[9]

Despite facing direct and indirect artillery fire, as well as bombing and strafing from friendly aircraft, tank casualties were primarily caused by other factors. One was immobilized by a mine, another became bogged in a shell hole, while a third became inoperative because of a broken gas line.

An incident occurred here which emphasizes the necessity for dependable communications. A garbled radio message caused the engineers to withdraw from the eastern end of the town under the impression that they were being ordered to hold a north-south line through the church. They did this without notifying the tanks and then called on artillery and mortar fire on the eastern end of the town. This fire fell around Lieutenant Johnson and his tanks until he succeeded in getting it moved further east.

The vacant part of the town was again occupied by friendly troops, and the tank platoon remained in position until relieved by Lieutenant Anderson and his platoon at 6:00 PM. This platoon immediately received direct artillery fire from its right front, and Lieutenant Anderson ordered his tanks to move back, intending only that they back out of the line of fire. However, when his radio failed, he lost contact with the rest of his platoon, as a result of which they retreated all the way to Germeter. He started back after his platoon, but en route he met Lieutenant Colonel Henbest, commanding the 2nd Battalion, 109th Infantry Regiment, which had been ordered to relieve the engineers of the defense of Vossenack. The colonel told him that he and Captain Granger had decided to keep the tanks in Germeter, since they could move up easily when desired, and their presence only drew unwelcome artillery fire.[10]

At about 5:00 AM on November 8, Lieutenant Colonel Henbest called for tanks, and at 6:00 AM Lieutenant Anderson, with four tanks, moved into Vossenack and occupied positions at the western end of the town. His platoon moved in and around the town for the rest of the day except between 12:00 PM and 2:00 PM, when he returned for resupply. He was relieved at 12:00 PM by Lieutenant Novak of C Company, who remained in the town after Anderson's platoon returned.

Anderson's main action during the day consisted of firing his tanks and adjusting artillery fire on moving targets and gun flashes. He also called and received an air strike on some enemy tanks which had been sighted. After dark, both platoons returned to Germeter; Lieutenant Novak came back on foot ahead of his platoon suffering from severe shoulder and leg wounds.

November 8 marked the last of action for C Company in Vossenack. During the fighting here, it had tried to keep one platoon in town with the infantry at all times. This effort was not a typical response to specific requests for armor on particular missions, but rather an attempt to provide continuous armored support. At 6:30 AM on November 9, the 2nd Platoon from B Company, numbering three tanks, moved into Vossenack. By now it was snowing and visibility was zero. At 9:00 AM, one of the sergeant tank commanders asked permission of Lieutenant Johnson to return to Germeter. His gunner was almost hysterical from battle exhaustion and needed a rest.[11] Permission was granted, and two tanks were left in the town. Later that morning, an officer from the artillery walked over and asked the tanks to leave town. They did so, apparently without questioning the authority of the order. This concluded active participation of B Company, 707th Tank Battalion in Vossenack, although it remained on alert status in Germeter during November 9 and 10.

The action of the 707th Tank Battalion at Vossenack is a perfect illustration of three things. One is the unnecessary loss of lives and material occasioned by lack of mutual understanding between the armor and infantry arms. The second is the lack of efficient communication between these two arms or the failure to use the means available. The third is the lack of exchange of tactical information between those arms at lower levels.

It was vital to the 28th Infantry Division to hold Vossenack, since the division's main supply route to Schmidt passed through this town. Perhaps if the tanks had been used as a mobile reserve and given complete, clear, and concise orders when committed, the losses both to the armor and the infantry would have been less. The role of the engineers in this action should not be overlooked. Their mine reconnaissance and mine clearing activities did little to prevent the loss of tanks from mine damage. At a minimum, routes of counterattack should have been cleared early in the action in order for the infantry to receive maximum benefit from the armor in the mobile reserve capacity.[12]

Concurrent with the action at Vossenack, troops of the 112th Infantry became involved in fighting at Kommerscheidt and Schmidt. These two towns are accessible from Vossenack only by a tortuous, twisted trail which passes through the forest and dips into the valley of the Kall River. This trail was a distinct obstacle for medium tanks, tank destroyers, and supply and medical vehicles. It was unpaved, narrow—barely the width of a tank—and characterized by sharp turns and rock abutments which hindered the passage of vehicles. These conditions were aggravated by the frequent rainfall that occurred earlier in the month.

Schmidt, it will be remembered, was the objective of the 112th Infantry and of the 28th Infantry Division in the attack which began on November 2. Its importance lay in the control it provided over a good road net and the fact that it dominated the Schwammenauel Dam on the Roer River. Since Vossenack had been taken with comparative ease on the first day, it was decided to pass the 1st and 3rd Battalions of the 112th through the 2nd Battalion in Vossenack to attack Kommerscheidt and Schmidt, respectively. This was a slight change from the original plan which contemplated attacking through Richelskaul. However, after an abortive attempt in this direction on November 2, the plan was changed as indicated.

The new plan was successful, and by nightfall the 3rd Battalion, 112th was in Schmidt, having taken it virtually unopposed, while the 1st Battalion, 112th was in and around Kommerscheidt, also occupied with very little trouble. However, the attackers who had been so successful soon became the defenders of their respective towns without American armor forward to support them; A Company, 707th Tank Battalion was the unit committed to the support of these troops, reinforced by C Company, 893rd Tank Destroyer Battalion.

A Company, 707th Tank Battalion was located in Germeter in a reserve role. Its mission was threefold: to provide supporting fire for C Company during the infantry's attack on Vossenack; to guard against a possible counterattack from Hürtgen and the northeast; and to be prepared to support the attack on Schmidt by the 1st and 3rd battalions, 112th.

After an inactive day, Captain Bruce M. Hostrup, the company commander, was called to the regimental command post at 6:00 PM. He was told that his company was to support the attack of the 3rd Battalion, 112th Infantry, which had the mission of securing Kommerscheidt and of driving on to seize, consolidate, and establish roadblocks in Schmidt. Next he met Lieutenant Colonel Flood, commander of the 3rd Battalion, 112th Infantry, to discuss plans for the attack.

The tanks were to be employed as follows: the 2nd and 3rd tank platoons would support L and K companies, respectively, as they attacked Kommerscheidt abreast of each other, starting from the church at Vossenack, with the 1st Tank Platoon to follow at about 400 yards. The tanks with the leading companies were initially to lead the infantry and assist in cleaning out any Germans who might occupy the nose of the ridge.

Next, they planned to fire into the woods while the infantry moved forward, and then, finally, pull back to high ground, from which they could fire directly into Kommerscheidt until the infantry reached the hill immediately north of town. Although the assaulting infantry companies planned to lay wire as they advanced, the tanks' ceasefire was to be controlled solely by visual signals.[13]

The attack started at 7:00 AM on November 3, and went almost as planned. Platoon leader Lieutenant John J. Clark lost his tank to a German mine. The rest of the tanks pulled back to high ground, commenced firing into Kommerscheidt, as outlined, and lifted fire when they were able to see the infantry moving in good formation up the high ground on the other side of the Kall River. The tanks then took advantage of what defilade was available and waited for word from the engineers that the trail between Vossenack and Kommerscheidt was passable.

At about 5:00 PM, word came from Lieutenant Colonel Ripple that the engineers had reported the road clear. However, Captain Hostrup, in one of his tanks, reconnoitered the road and found it still impassable for tanks. After reporting this to Colonel Ripple, who relayed it to division headquarters, the captain was subsequently ordered to remain in place until morning. He was told engineers would work on that road to Kommerscheidt all night, which they did. Though artillery and mortar fire struck several times, they caused no material damage. By this time, however, three tanks had been rendered inoperative from other causes: one, Lieutenant Clark's, had hit a mine, a second had thrown a track, and a third had bellied up on a sharp rocky ridge. In turn, the fire received during the night prevented retrievers from coming to their aid.[14]

At daylight, A Company again tried the trail to Kommerscheidt. Lieutenant Raymond E. Fleig, leading the first platoon, started to move through the draw, but as he reached the entrance, his tank hit a mine and threw a track. This was twenty-four hours after the engineers had reported the road clear of mines. Lieutenant Fleig reported to Captain Hostrup, who told him to get his tank clear of the road because the company had to go through. Lieutenant Fleig then began a battle with the terrain which resulted in a number of disabled tanks, denying tank support to the infantry in Kommerscheidt and Schmidt. In attempting to move his second tank around the first it slipped off the left side of the road and became mired in the soft ground. At this point his platoon sergeant, using the command tank as an anchor, winched the remaining three tanks of the platoon past the command tank and removed the stuck tank.[15]

As soon as the lead tank was clear, Lieutenant Fleig took it toward the river, being forced at intervals to back and turn the tank in order to negotiate the turns in the trail. At the three switchbacks he was forced to direct the tank on foot. After crossing the stone bridge at the Kall River he led his tank on foot nearly to the top of the hill north of Kommerscheidt. He made a brief visual reconnaissance of his route, mounted his tank, and rode into town, arriving at about 7:30 AM.

There he reported to the commanding officer of the 1st Battalion, 112th Infantry, stating that he expected the rest of his company up by noon. The colonel told him that a German counterattack had driven part of the 3rd Battalion out of Schmidt and asked him to take a position from which he could support a further withdrawal. Lieutenant Fleig was joined at about 9:30 AM by his platoon sergeant with two tanks. All three tanks were placed in partial defilade covering Schmidt.

The Germans apparently no longer considered the defense at Schmidt effective and at 11:00 AM counterattacked Kommerscheidt with infantry and tanks. Lieutenant Fleig destroyed two German Mark IVs, and the other two tanks accounted for a third. Fleig then moved to his left where the defenders were giving way, engaged, and knocked out a Mark V Panther, after which he returned to the other American tanks and continued to fight with them until the attack was finally repelled at 1:00 PM.

The tanks spent the remainder of the afternoon firing at two pillboxes west of Schmidt which the enemy was trying to reoccupy. Lieutenant Fleig had been instructed not to fire into Schmidt, as part of M Company, 122nd Infantry Regiment was still there. At about 3:00 PM, these troops pulled out and Lieutenant Fleig was ordered by the regimental commanding officer to remain where he was. The colonel promised him infantry ground support, adding that he expected another counterattack. It was also his opinion that moving the tanks out of position, even for resupply, would cause the infantry on the position to leave as well. The expected night attack did not materialize, but artillery and mortar fire rained on the area.[16]

During the time Lieutenant Fleig was engaged in Kommerscheidt, Captain Hostrup was desperately trying to reach the town with the remainder of A Company. He had walked down the trail to assist the last of Lieutenant Fleig's platoon in crossing the Kall River. The last tank of the platoon threw a track and became mired at the bottom of the draw.

About this time Lieutenant Clark, in his platoon sergeant's tank, led his platoon forward. Not knowing the method which had been used to winch the 1st Platoon around the dead tank at the trail entrance, Lieutenant Clark lost his tank off the road to the left when it tried to pass. Lieutenant Clark and the sergeant dismounted to survey the situation, when artillery fire killed the sergeant and wounded Clark. The next two tanks, using the two immobilized tanks as buffers, went straight through on the road. Upon reaching the first bad curve, the tank in the lead slipped off the road to the left and threw a track. The next tank, about 150 yards behind, also slipped off the left of the road throwing both tracks. Thus there were three tanks now blocking the main supply route to Kommerscheidt, with little chance of getting maintenance vehicles near them.[17]

Captain Hostrup, later joined by personnel from his company maintenance section, worked on the vehicles and on the main supply route. The center tank of the three was of most concern to the workers; its tracks were replaced time after time, only to have it roll a few yards and lose its tracks again. The tankers in the draw also assisted the engineers in trying to dig bypasses out of the high right bank of the road to reopen it for traffic. These banks were largely stone, however, and even blasting failed to produce satisfactory results. During the day and night, the work of the tankers and engineers was continually interrupted by mortar and artillery fire. At one point, they were even delayed by the stream of infantry pouring back from Schmidt. Captain Hostrup kept Colonel Ripple abreast of the situation and received a promise of additional engineers.

By midnight, the tank battalion S-4 was on the road waiting to take a supply train through to Kommerscheidt. Finally, acting on orders from tank battalion headquarters and with daylight approaching, Captain Hostrup and his men rolled the blocking tanks into the draw, permitting the supply trains to go through. At 4:30 AM, Captain Hostrup walked back up the road to the position of his 3rd Platoon and stayed there until 6:00 AM, at which time he returned to the main supply route. He learned that the engineers had been able to get bulldozers in and that the road was now passable.

Back with the 3rd Platoon, he attached the remaining two tanks of the 2nd Platoon and followed the group toward the road entrance. Lieutenant Payne, commanding the 3rd Platoon, halted to allow nine destroyers from the 893rd Tank Destroyer Battalion to move through ahead of him. Little difficulty was experienced with the road, and Lieutenant Payne had his platoon on the hill north of Kommerscheidt by 9:00 AM. Captain Hostrup's tank developed engine trouble south of the Kall River, and he radioed Lieutenant Fleig to take command of all tanks in the area pending his arrival.[18]

Lieutenant Fleig, with his three tanks, helped the infantry beat off a small tank-infantry counterattack, which faltered after a German Mark VI Tiger had received seven direct hits from the American tanks. About 9:00 AM, the Germans counterattacked again, this time without tanks. The tank destroyers arrived in town during the second attack, which was also beaten off. Lieutenant Payne's platoon then joined the defenders, and the enemy counterattacked regularly at about four-hour intervals throughout the rest of the day. None of these attacks were successful.

At dark the tank destroyers went to the rear to resupply, but the tanks again were ordered to remain in town. Captain Hostrup's tank, again operative, was at the regimental command post, where the regimental commander wanted it for communication purposes. The division commander's orders to the regiment that night were to hold Kommerscheidt at all costs.

At about 3:30 AM, a German counterattack cut off the lightly defended main supply route, and the enemy roamed it practically at will. Part of the tank battalion's S-4 section was cut off in Kommerscheidt. The infantry regimental command post moved south into town and joined the 1st Battalion command post.[19]

At 9:00 AM, A Company's tanks, protecting the south and southeast flanks of the town, spotted another counterattack, which was then effectively broken up by artillery, tanks, and tank destroyers. The tanks remained on a forward slope all day with the dug-in infantry but were forced to move continually in the face of direct fire and artillery from the excellent German positions near Schmidt, Harscheid, and Bergstein, consuming more of their now precious gasoline. When night fell, the tanks pulled in near the buildings of the town. Two of Lieutenant Fleig's tanks were sent to the rear, having received direct hits, which jammed their turrets. Meanwhile, an unusual event was taking place.

The tank battalion commander was appointed commander of a task force to be known as Task Force Ripple consisting of: 3rd Battalion, 110th Infantry (already weakened by fighting in the south of the division sector); A Company, 707th Tank Battalion (already in Kommerscheidt); D Company (light tanks), 707th; C Company, 893rd Tank Destroyer Battalion (also in Kommerscheidt but weakened by three or four destroyers), plus one platoon of B Company, 893rd Tank Destroyer Battalion.

D Company, 707th Tank Battalion was on a screening mission to the south and actually never joined the task force, nor did the extra platoon of tank destroyers. At 2:45 AM on that cold November morning, the battered infantry battalion of Task Force Ripple crossed its Line of Departure (LD), initiating an early-morning attack despite previous losses and difficult conditions. Its mission was to pass through the embattled defenders of Kommerscheidt, pick up the remainder of the task force, and recapture Schmidt.

At daylight the weather, already cold, was made more disagreeable by rain. The 3rd Battalion, 110th Infantry Regiment, under Lieutenant Colonel Ripple, the task force commander, arrived at the wood line north of Kommerscheidt in time to witness a German counterattack on the town following a thirty-minute artillery preparation. The size of the enemy force was estimated at between one and two battalions with tank support. Estimates of hostile tank numbers varied from six to thirty, but the observers in many cases were bordering on hysteria.

The infantry dug in about the town had had fire poured into their foxholes from dominating positions for several days. The enemy tanks were engaged by American tanks, tank destroyers, and bazookas. Three tank destroyers and two of the defending tanks were knocked out. One sergeant tank commander, whose tank was shot out from under him, took over the crew of a tank destroyer which had lost its commander and fought until that too was knocked out. The defending armor began a withdrawal to the north, losing two more tanks to thrown tracks. The infantry, battered and depleted by the constant fire of the past five days, was also leaving. Finally, one- and two-tank destroyers remained and supported C Company, 112th Infantry, holding the wood line north of Kommerscheidt, where the infantry battalion of Task Force Ripple was also located. The one remaining tank was Lieutenant Fleig's.[20]

After dark, Lieutenant Payne took a patrol forward and carried back ammunition from his own immobilized tank to be used by Lieutenant Fleig. The defenders of the wood line were required to beat off another counterattack during the night. This ragged force held the wood line during the following morning, even though many of the troops had gone to the rear during the night. There was little activity on this day, but recapturing Schmidt was out of the question. About 5:00 PM, the force was ordered to withdraw north of the Kall River and to destroy the remaining tanks and tank destroyers. This terminated the action of A Company, 707th as a fighting force in the Hürtgen Forest.

The remaining men of the company were led back to Germeter by Captain Hostrup, Lieutenant Fleig, and other officers. A Company, 707th had lost fifteen of its sixteen tanks and thirty-two men were missing. The key to the failure of the forces at Kommerscheidt and Schmidt was the failure of adequate and timely armored support. Because of the terrain and road net, armored support was in turn dependent on engineer support.

We have seen that the bulk of the engineer group attached to the 28th Division was engaged in fighting in Vossenack. Even those who were assigned to make the main supply route passable for tanks were required to provide their own security, which reduced the number of men available to work on the road. The lesson learned was that, for armor to support effectively an infantry operation, it must be ensured, before the operation begins, that the armored units can reach the vital areas when needed. The loss of Schmidt was a bitter blow to the Allied cause and was not recaptured until early 1945.[21]

In spite of the inadequate road net, resupply of the 707th Tank Battalion became serious only in regard to A Company in Kommerscheidt. B and C companies withdrew their platoons regularly from Vossenack and were able to effect resupply with relative ease. During the action at Kommerscheidt, the battalion supply trains reached A Company twice, one on the night of November 4–5 and again on the following night.

The trains consisted largely of M29 Weasels which had been borrowed from the infantry, and even these versatile vehicles had difficulties with the main supply route, since they were pulling trailers. The trailers had to be unhitched and manhandled around the difficult turns of the main supply route. Two-way traffic was out of the question, even though this road was the only route for medical evacuation of troops south of the Kall River. On both nights the troops of the tank battalion in Kommerscheidt received gasoline, ammunition, rations, water, and mail.

On the second night part of the supply section, including the S-4 and the Headquarters Company commander who had accompanied him, were cut off when the Germans moved onto the main supply route. They subsequently took part in the withdrawal described in the account of A Company, 707th. From both a logistical and tactical perspective, B Company conducted sustained indirect fire missions for four days under the direction of the 28th Division. They were able to keep up their fire at a time when artillery ammunition to the division was being rationed.

Evacuation of vehicles presented an unusual problem, in that all of them had to be moved or repaired under fire. Under normal conditions the fighting would move on when the maintenance crews were conducting battlefield evacuation, but in the Hürtgen area, maintenance vehicles were vulnerable to the same enemy action that took its toll on the tanks. The situation which developed on the main supply route between Vossenack and Kommerscheidt demanded the presence of maintenance vehicles, but the condition of the road as well as hostile artillery made it almost impossible for these vehicles to be used.[22]

The 707th Tank Battalion lost thirty-one medium tanks in the Hürtgen Forest Battle; A Company fifteen, B Company seven, C Company nine. Most of these were due to mines or enemy shell fire. On the night of November 8–9, the battalion reached its lowest ebb with only nine effective medium tanks remaining. D Company, the light tank company, was not committed.

In view of the vehicular losses, the personnel casualties among the tankers seem rather light. The missing men of A Company doubtless included some dead and wounded. However, aside from these, only three men were known to be definitely killed, with one officer and six men wounded. Exact figures for B Company are not available, but after-action reports indicate that they were rather light. C Company had two killed (including the commanding officer), one man missing in action, and one officer and eleven men wounded.

From the standpoint of combat effectiveness, the above tank casualty figures are important, as is the fact that during the action many tanks were immobilized by thrown tracks or soft ground. Since the prevailing conditions prevented these tanks from being rapidly returned to action, they were just as ineffective as if they had been completely demolished. At no time during the action at either Vossenack, Kommerscheidt, or, in particular, Schmidt did the infantry have the tank support to which it was entitled.

The 707th Tank Battalion was employed entirely in support of infantry, either offensively or defensively, but never in a separate armored action. Neither the battalion nor its companies were at any time employed en masse against a given objective. This was largely precluded by the terrain rather than by tactical decision.[23]

8

630th Tank Destroyer Battalion

At the beginning of November, the 630th Tank Destroyer Battalion supported the 28th Infantry Division with six platoons that were in direct fire positions in the vicinity of Zweifall, tied in with the 28th Division Artillery. On November 2, the 28th Division began an attack to the east and northeast toward Hürtgen and Vossenack and then attacked south toward Kommerscheidt and Schmidt. A and C (-) companies supported the 109th and 112th Infantry Regiments, respectively. B Company was attached to the 110th Infantry Regiment.[1]

Due to mines and roadblocks on the majority of passable roads and trails, occupation of positions by the 630th companies was delayed. Heavy German artillery and mortar fire was received. Enemy tanks were reported at Schmidt, Hürtgen, and east of Vossenack.

From 6:00 AM to 5:00 PM on November 1, the 1st and 2nd platoons of A Company were tied in with 107th Field Artillery Battalion. A total of sixty-six missions were fired at eleven concentration points in the vicinity of Hürtgen, with 300 HE rounds and sixty-three HERC rounds expended. Eighteen rounds of HE ammunition were fired in registration.

The 3rd Platoon of A Company tied in with C Company for indirect fire. The 3rd Platoon, B Company, in an indirect fire position, was tied in with the 109th Field Artillery Battalion. They fired 194 HE and 200 HERC rounds in seventy-five missions at Schmidt and the vicinity. Twenty-two concentration points were fired upon.

C Company, tied in with 229th Field Artillery Battalion, was in indirect firing positions. Twelve concentrations, totaling 285 HE rounds, were fired at Schmidt and vicinity. The 3rd Platoon of C Company was in defense of the division command post. The 1st Reconnaissance Platoon remained in their assembly area and the battalion command post remained at Mulartshutte.[2]

During the night of November 1–2, A Company had its 1st and 2nd platoons tied in with the 107th Field Artillery Battalion. During the night, sixty-six missions at eleven concentration points were fired, with 192 HE and 72 HERC rounds expended. From 8:00 AM to 10:00 AM on November 2, seventy-six missions firing on thirty-eight concentrations were fired with 366 HE and 182 HERC rounds of ammunition expended. The targets were Hürtgen and Klenham. The 3rd Platoon, A Company tied in with C Company for indirect fire.

At 10:00 AM A Company began to move northeast in direct support of the 109th Infantry. which began an attack at 9:00 AM. Due to the prevalence of mines, the anticipated gun positions could not be occupied. The 1st Reconnaissance Platoon, supporting A Company, reconnoitered routes. One 1.4 ton vehicle of the Reconnaissance Platoon was damaged by a mine, with one man being injured. Two men from A Company were injured by German artillery shell fragments.

The 3rd Platoon of B Company, attached to the 110th Infantry Regiment, was tied in with the 109th Field Artillery Battalion and fired 138 harassing missions at the Vossenack-Schmidt area, totaling 500 HE and 199 HERC rounds of ammunition. The 2nd Reconnaissance Platoon held a screen during the firing.

During the day, the C Company command post and the 1st and 2nd platoons moved east to support the 112th Infantry but, due to mines, had to enter the assembly area near the command post. During the night, C Company fired forty-three rounds of HE harassing fire at two concentration points. The targets were in the Bergstein-Kommerscheidt area.[3]

During the night of November 2–3, A Company, supporting the 109th Infantry, was attempting to get into direct fire positions but were delayed by mines and small enemy groups on one road and by mines and roadblocks on another. During the day, the 1st Reconnaissance Platoon began moving mines from the road along the west bank of the Kall River.

At 9:00 AM enemy outposts of eight to ten men fired on the Reconnaissance Platoon and the operation was delayed. Two men were injured by booby traps. The 3rd Platoon of B Company, attached to the 110th Infantry, tied in with the 109th Field Artillery Battalion, fired 132 missions thirty-three concentration points at targets in the Schmidt-Gerstenhof area. A total of 246 HE and 254 HERC rounds were fired.

C Company, 3rd Platoon was in direct support of the 112th Infantry and spent the night in their assembly area. Although the infantry entered Vossenack without too much difficulty, mines held up the movement of tank destroyers. By 5:00 PM, the 1st and 2nd platoons were moving to positions on the south edge of Vossenack.

From 5:00 PM on November 2–3 to 6:00 AM on November 5, A Company continued in direct support of the 109th Infantry. During the day attempts were made to secure better gun positions, but due to mines, roadblocks, and enemy action, these attempts proved useless. Strong German resistance was encountered during the afternoon by the 1st Reconnaissance Platoon. A 0.25-ton vehicle was damaged by German artillery fire.

At 5:00 PM, four German mortars and one observation tower were knocked out by the 3rd Platoon, A Company with twenty rounds of HE direct fire. The 3rd Platoon, B Company, tied in with the 109th Field Artillery Battalion, fired 400 rounds of HE during the night in eighty missions, firing at twenty concentration points in the Woffelsback-Ruhrberg-Oteckenborn area. C Company, 3rd Platoon was in direct support of the 112th Infantry.

Attempts were made to occupy gun positions in Vossenack, but mines, rubble in the streets, and heavy German artillery fire prevented most of the attempts. Two men were injured by artillery fire and a 0.25-ton vehicle was damaged. During the day, operations were severely hampered by heavy enemy artillery fire in the Vossenack area. Much of the German artillery was direct and some was observed.

At 6:00 PM, German planes bombed in the vicinity of B Company, but no damage resulted. Enemy tanks were reported in Schmidt, but due to a lack of roads and bridges, nothing could be moved to the area. Other enemy tanks were reported in the vicinity of Hürtgen and east of Vossenack, but none were engaged. During the night, B Company fired 200 HE and 200 HERC rounds in direct fire.[4]

From 6:00 AM to 5:00 PM on November 5, A Company continued in direct support of the 109th Infantry. The 1st Reconnaissance Platoon formed a screen in the front and the 3rd Platoon killed one German. During the day, the 3rd Platoon fired forty-three HE rounds in the vicinity of Hürtgen and Kleiham, damaging two German tanks, a Mk IV and a Mk V.

During the afternoon, gun crews attempted to clear the area of fallen trees so better positions could be occupied. Heavy artillery fire in that area hampered operations. The 1st Platoon, B Company, tied in with the 109th Field Artillery Battalion, fired 200 HE and 200 HERC rounds in eighty-eight missions at twenty-two concentration points in the vicinity of Steckenborn-Woffelsbach. The 2nd Reconnaissance Platoon, supporting B Company, held a screen. One man from 2nd Platoon, B Company was wounded during the day by artillery fire in the Vossenack area. German tanks were reported in the Hürtgen-Kleiham area and in Schmidt.[5]

During the late afternoon of November 5, in the section of the 3rd Platoon, A Company continued direct fire on the Hürtgen-Kleiham area, knocking out one German Mk IV tank and killing twenty enemy troops. During the day, a section of the 3rd Platoon fired seventy-seven direct HE rounds at the Hürtgen-Kleiham area at a range of about 6,000 yards, destroying one enemy anti-tank gun, one workshop, one command car, one light vehicle, one observation post and two 2.5-ton trucks. Approximately thirty-eight German soldiers were killed. One man from the 1st Reconnaissance Platoon and two from A Company were injured by German artillery fire.

The 3rd Platoon, B Company, tied to the 109th Field Artillery Battalion, fired 200 HE and 400 HERC rounds in 156 missions at thirty-four concentration points in the Steckenborn and Woffelsback-Ruhrberg area. The 2nd Reconnaissance Platoon held a screen while one section of the 1st Platoon was moved to the rear for an ordnance check during the night, as both guns had been damaged by shell fragments. Heavy artillery fire was experienced during the day, particularly in the Vossenack-Germeter area. The battalion command post remained in Mulartshutte.

From 5:00 PM on November 6 to 5:00 PM on November 7, A Company continued in direct support of the 109th Infantry. The 3rd Platoon continued direct fire on the Hürtgen-Kleiham area, knocking out one 2.5-ton vehicle and killing forty-four German soldiers. During the day, a section of the 3rd Platoon fired eighty-eight direct HE rounds at the Hürtgen-Kleiham area. One section of the 1st Platoon, C Company was sent to the area for repairs.

During the early part of the night on November 7, the 801st Tank Destroyer Battalion relieved the 1st and 2nd platoons of A Company and occupied their positions. At 2:00 AM, three guns of the 1st Platoon took up a new position and fired thirty-seven HE rounds and captured ten prisoners. During the afternoon, the 2nd Platoon took up a new position and provided direct fire into the Hürtgen-Kleiham-Grosshau area. B Company, still attached to the 110th Infantry and tied in to the 109th Field Artillery Battalion, fired 299 HE and 197 HERC rounds in ninety-nine missions at thirty-three concentration points in the Steckenborn and Woffelsbach area.[6]

During the night of November 8, 3rd Platoon, A Company moved to positions at the west edge of Vossenack. The 2nd Platoon was able to fire into the Hürtgen-Kleiham area. No firing occurred on November 9 due to poor visibility, the result of snow and mist. One half-track from the 1st Platoon was hit by enemy artillery fire and destroyed. One gun from the 1st Platoon, B Company was damaged by German artillery fire and had to be sent to the area for repair.

From 5:00 PM on November 9 to 5:00 PM on November 10, A Company continued in direct support of the 109th Infantry. The 2nd Platoon fired into the Hürtgen-Kleiham area, with twenty-six HE rounds fired. One German half-track and one wheeled armored car were destroyed and approximately three Germans killed. Direct fire was placed in the woods in support of the 112th Infantry during the morning and at the Bergstein-Bradenburg area during the afternoon, with twenty-five rounds of HE fired. The 1st Reconnaissance Platoon remained in the assembly area with one man injured by artillery fire.

The 1st Platoon, B Company, in support of the 110th Infantry, occupied positions where it could place harassing fire at an area in advance of the 110th, with 337 HE and three APC rounds fired during the day. C Company, 3rd Platoon operated under 630th Tank Battalion control as the 112th Infantry was withdrawn for reorganization. The 2nd Platoon fired direct fire during the morning in support of the 112th and during the afternoon fired at the

Bergstein-Brandenburg area with ninety-three HE and forty HERC rounds. German artillery fire in the Vossenack area continued to be moderate and consisted largely of direct or observed fire.[7]

During the early evening of November 10, the fourth gun of the 1st Platoon joined the others, covering south and southeast of Vossenack. One section of the 1st Reconnaissance Platoon formed a screen for each section. During the day, both sections were moved to positions from which they could fire on the Hürtgen-Kleiham area, but poor visibility prevented firing. Prior to dusk, the guns were removed to their original positions.

The 3rd Platoon occupied positions at the west edge of Vossenack. Five prisoners were captured by the 1st Platoon in Vossenack. One section of the 1st Platoon, B Company, still supporting the 110th Infantry, occupied positions from which it could fire directly at two pillboxes. Sixteen HE rounds were fired, but the damage was undetermined. Enemy artillery fire continued to be moderate and consisted largely of direct or observed fire.[8]

On November 12, the 1st Platoon, A Company, still in direct support of the 109th Infantry, was in a position covering south and southeast of Vossenack. One prisoner was captured. The 1st Platoon of B Company occupied positions from which it fired fourteen rounds directly at enemy vehicles. The damage was undetermined.

On November 13, 1st Platoon, B Company, in direct support of the 110th Infantry, occupied positions from which it could support the 110th's attack with harassing fire along the Steckenborn-Schmidt road and on high ground. One German self-propelled gun that had been firing on the 110th was neutralized, with 886 HE rounds fired by the platoon during the day. Fire was direct at 3,000 yards but not observed due to mist and snow. C Company (-) one section, (3rd Platoon) operated under 630th Battalion control. One gun was placed to cover a road junction to the north.[9]

From 5:00 PM on November 13 to 5:00 PM on November 14, A, B, and C companies moved their guns to more favorable positions and to defend the 28th Division command post. Enemy artillery fire on Vossenack was moderate to heavy. During November 15 and 16, the companies again moved units to more favorable positions. At approximately 6:00 PM on the 15th, two men from the 3rd Platoon of C Company were injured by artillery fire. At 6:00 AM on the 16th three more men from the same platoon were injured by artillery fire. All five men were evacuated.

On November 17, elements of the 644th Tank Destroyer Battalion arrived to discuss relief. The 1st Reconnaissance Platoon moved to the new battalion area in the vicinity of Boevange, Luxembourg. During November 17–20, the battalion prepared to move to their new area. At 9:00 AM on November 20, the 630th Tank Destroyer Battalion moved to the new 28th Infantry Division area.[10]

The 630th Tank Destroyer Battalion came in contact with the following German units:

- 26th Volksgrenadier Division
    - 77th Infantry Regiment
    - 78th Infantry Regiment
    - 29th Infantry Regiment
    - 26th Artillery Regiment
- 1057 Infantry Regiment
- 3rd Troop, 21st Panzer Reconnaissance Battalion
- 9th Field Prisoner Battalion
- Elements of the 352nd Infantry Division[11]

9

893rd Tank Destroyer Battalion

The 893rd Tank Destroyer Battalion was operational from November 1 to 30. The battalion was assigned to the US First Army and attached to V Corps and 3rd Tank Destroyer Group throughout the entire period. The battalion, (-) A Company, and the attached 1st Reconnaissance Platoon was attached to the 28th Infantry Division from November 1 to 19.

Throughout the month of November, the line companies were supporting the infantry from indirect firing positions or by close-in anti-tank support in direct fire in the vicinity of Vossenack. In support of the 28th Infantry Division, both B and C companies were committed in direct support. This action was not successful in holding all of the ground first gained in the attack due to an inadequate route for supplies and reinforcements and an inability to keep that route open because of the enemy's terrific reaction to the battalion's advance. As a result the ground gained in the vicinity of Schmidt and Kommerscheidt had to be given up and much of the equipment abandoned.[1]

During the same month, B Company lost seven M10s: two were damaged by mines; one was dropped into a basement when the ground gave way; two were mired down in enemy territory; two were knocked out by enemy anti-tank fire. C Company lost eleven M10s: one to enemy mines; one, having thrown a track, was left in enemy territory; eight were destroyed by enemy anti-tank and artillery fire; one was destroyed by the crew when abandoned. The 893rd had the following casualties: thirty-eight lightly wounded; twelve seriously wounded; twenty missing in action; nine killed in action. During this time, a total of 569 rounds of HE, thirty-nine rounds of APC and three rounds of HVAL were fired in direct fire.

The results of direct fire are as follows:

6 Mark VI tanks
10 Mark V tanks

3 Mark IV tanks
1 88mm self-propelled gun
1 anti-tank gun
4 pillboxes
4 machine gun nests
1 enemy fuel dump
1 roadblock neutralized
1 building damaged and set on fire
1 supply dump destroyed
363 enemy personnel killed
75 enemy captured[2]

10

1340th Engineer Combat Battalion

The 1340th Engineer Combat Battalion operated under the 1171st Engineer Group plan, which was issued on October 30 and amended on November 1. At the start of the operation, Lieutenant Setterberg was in command of the 3rd Platoon, and was assigned originally to keep open the 110th Infantry Regiment main supply route from the road junction at map coordinates (003312) to (001315).

At the same time, 1st Lieutenant William J. McCarthey of the 2nd Platoon was assigned the mission of maintaining the main supply route between the 110th Infantry and the 112th Infantry from the road junction at map coordinates (003312) to (005320). This was the original mission of B Company. It continued until about noon of November 6.[1]

On November 5, Colonel Daley assigned the mission of sending one platoon through Vossenack and then into the draw south of Vossenack in order to reach point (033314) to sweep mines and open the road to traffic to about (019324). First Lieutenant Kelsey C. Mannin of the 1st Platoon and Lieutenant Setterberg took care of opening the road and sweeping for mines to a fire break at map coordinates (019323) to (019315).

At this point, 2nd Lieutenant Edward Vichy, serving as an additional officer with the company, was pinned down by German small arms fire while with a mine detector detail of about twelve men. After several minutes under fire, they withdrew. The 3rd Battalion, 110th Infantry commander stated that the road was not open, but they had tried to get as far ahead as possible. The engineers opened a road junction, filled two craters and cleared some trees blocking the road. The job complete, they returned to their bivouac area.

Private Doyle McDaniel, A Company, 1340th Engineer Battalion, wrote that his platoon had advanced to the crossroads by a church and were pinned down by German sniper fire. Private McDaniel climbed onto a shed roof to locate the German positions. As he jumped down, he landed beside a German soldier. Before the man could react, McDaniel shot and killed him. He wrote "I felt bad about killing the German but knew I had to. I came to Germany to protect my wife and new baby at home."[2]

On November 6, Lieutenant Mannin and his platoon went up to clear a road at (019324) to the southeast to approximately (033314). They ran into some artillery fire at a crossroad but were able to avoid it. While carrying out this mission, General Davis came up to Lieutenant Mannin at 10:00 AM and told him to send his engineer equipment back and to be prepared to go into the line as infantry. He told Mannin to wait for further orders.

At 11:30 AM, Captain Greegan received orders to alert the company for a move and was told that Mannin would return and join the company. Major John G. Auld, the battalion executive officer, was to lead the company to the Kall Bridge and contact C Company and Colonel Setliffe. They went through the draw south of Vossenack. Major Auld contacted Colonel Setliffe by SCR-300 radio. The colonel gave orders for the company to remain where it was and said that he personally would contact them. Colonel Setliffe and Major Argus arrived from the bridge and told Creegan that B Company's mission had been changed and that he was to contact the infantry commander in Vossenack with the view of offering help.[3]

The infantry commander said he had a battalion of engineers in there already (the 146th), and could not see where he needed more at the time. The infantry commander said to dig in at their current position with the remainder of A Company, 20th Infantry, which by then had twenty-eight men and three officers left. During this time, there was some German artillery fire near the 3rd Platoon area and continuous artillery fire down in the draw. In moving to join the 20th, the 1st Platoon was hit by artillery in the draw, while the Germans dropped other artillery fire over the heads of the moving troops.[4]

They dug in and remained in position until Captain Dberty of A Company received a radio message that he and Creegan were to report to the 146th Battalion command post in Vossenack. The commander of the 146th Battalion, Lieutenant Colonel Isley, told them they were to move to the east, to the forward slope of a hill below Vossenack. There was continuous artillery fire and the forward slope was in an exposed position since it was in the open.[5]

Dberty and Creegan returned at about 4:00 AM and alerted the companies to conduct a reconnaissance of the area. However, as heavy artillery file continued to rain down, they could not move out. Colonel Setliffe agreed that moving out was impractical and revised the plans to move down and reinforce C Company at the bridge. The remainder of A and B companies were to stay in position. They also received orders to set up machine guns (one .30 caliber from B Company and one from Company A, 20th Battalion) to cover the main road down as far as they could see. They placed bazookas and machine guns together to supplement each other at (042321). Another machine gun was placed to the east to guard the supply trail. During the night, six M29 Weasels and nine 2.5-ton truck brought supplies.

The First Platoon went to the bridge at about 1:00 PM on November 7. When they got into position, one man had been killed and two wounded. They dug in and the German artillery continued to pound the area. The following morning Lieutenant Setterberg and a six-man patrol left to reconnoiter the road from the bridge to the edge of the woods. Setterberg said he was supposed to go to the third bend in the road on the other side of the bridge.

He went as far as C Company, where he talked to Captain Lund. Lund told him that nine 2.5-ton trucks had gone through, but the Germans had held the bridge since. A German machine gun was covering the bridge. Setterberg decided that he did not have enough men to go across. He concluded that the road was probably open since the nine trucks had gone through. He reconnoitered from the bridge to the edge of the woods and found it clear.

On the way up, they ran into heavy artillery. The men at the aid station, which was on the left, or west, side, going toward Vossenack, in a ground log shelter, said they were under observation and that the Germans fired on them every time they moved.[6]

At about 12:00 PM, a heavy artillery concentration, probably 150mm guns, landed in the 3rd Platoon area, which was the farthest west of the edge of the woods. This action killed Captain Joseph B. Traywick, the battalion medical officer, 1st Lieutenant Emil Alcich, executive officer of A Company, 20th Battalion, one medic, Tech Sergeant Leahu, six men from the company, two men from A Company, 20th Battalion, and one man from B Company, 20th Battalion. The artillery barrage wounded thirteen.

Captain Creegan ordered the 3rd Platoon to move up to the 1st Platoon's old area on the eastern edge of the woods. The rest of the company remained where they were for the rest of the day. At 4:00 PM, Creegan received an order to move to the bridge and reinforce C Company. Fifteen minutes later the order was rescinded. Captain Creegan then left and went to the aid station with trench foot. Lieutenant Setterberg took over.[7]

At 6:30 PM, Colonel Setliffe issued an order that approximately 4,000 yards of anti-tank mines would need to be laid, and, with the infantry commander's approval, the engineers could then be relieved. Setterberg received a radio message shortly after that a carrying party with mines and bedding rolls were on their way to him. The bedding rolls, rations, and water arrived about 10:30 PM.

At 2:45 AM the next morning, 2nd Lieutenant Joseph Alter, the administrative officer of B Company, delivered a written message addressed to Colonel Setliffe saying that the minefield job was cancelled and that the battalion was to withdraw before daylight. Colonel Setliffe was at the bridge before returning to his position. At that point, the instructions were to move out at 4:45 AM.

The situation on November 7 had been highly confused. There were constant and repeated messages that said there was nothing out in front. However, battalion, company, and platoon commanders of the infantry units said that their units had been chopped up and that they were getting out. This left the engineers in a bad position.

At one point, Creegan said he ordered one lieutenant, who was accompanied by six or eight men, to dig in. The lieutenant balked at first, but since none of his men were wounded, he finally obeyed orders. They finally pulled out at 4:30 AM, saying they were going back to the vicinity of the artillery, where they would find no Germans. They were afraid of a counterattack at dawn. They had all been through a very grievous strain.

Going into positions, B Company had ninety-nine men. At the end, 1st Platoon had twenty-seven to twenty-eight men, and the 2nd Platoon had seventeen men.[8]

11

20th Engineer Combat Battalion

The 20th Engineer Combat Battalion operated under the 1171st Engineer Group plan which was issued on October 30 and amended on November 1. The amendment merely provided for the use of the engineer troops on approach roads to the LD prior to the commencement of the attack.

Before the operation commenced, the battalion commander visited the commander of the 112th Infantry Regiment and arranged for the location of the forward bivouac area. With the concurrence of the regimental commander, he arranged that the engineer battalion would follow (in column) behind the 2nd Battalion, 112th Infantry.

From the initiation of the attack on November 2, the engineer reconnaissance officer was to work in the area of the 3rd Battalion of the 112th. They were not to tie themselves down to any specific body of troops but were to follow as close behind the leading infantry as they could. They were to move from unit to unit in order to develop the essential engineer information which, in this case, concerned the route from Germeter through Vossenack to Schmidt.[1]

On November 2, the 3rd Battalion, 112th Infantry did not advance sufficiently for the engineer reconnaissance officer to develop any valuable information. The 1st Battalion advanced only some 400 yards beyond its LD and the engineer reconnaissance officer of that battalion likewise developed nothing of importance.

On November 3, the plan was for B Company, 20th Engineer Battalion to take care of any engineering work required between the LD and the river crossing and the continuation of the road into Schmidt. Company C could only be obtained by request from the group commander and was engaged in work in the rear area.

Before noon on November 3, the first report received addressed the necessity of clearing the rubble and mines out of Vossenack, which B Company was tasked with. At 9:25 AM, Captain Miller reported that elements of the 3rd Battalion, 112th Infantry had crossed the stream moving between two routes. Sometime later it was reported that one of the roads was a dirt road. At 11:40 AM,

Lieutenant Lyons was ordered to the road and confirmed this fact. About 2:30 PM, word was received that the stream was fordable but needed corduroy for the approaches and B Company was ordered to move out as fast as possible from the bivouac area to the stream.[2]

At 3:15 PM, a message was sent to B Company giving the construction of a ford priority. At 3:40 PM, word was received that the class-30 stone-arch bridge (Kall Bridge) was still in existence. Word reached the 20th Engineer Combat Battalion that the narrow road and a projecting rock ledge could pose an obstacle to traffic. The group commander called and advised sending the air compressor and a bulldozer to the scene. Arrangements were made to send both with Captain Lutz, who had returned to the battalion command post to report on the condition of the roads.

At 7:30 PM, A Company was informed that the roads must be made passable for tanks. At 10:45 PM, the commander of A Company was directed to sweep the road of mines that night and improve the bad curves. At 9:10 AM on November 4, the commander of A Company reported that the roads had been swept for mines and open for tanks. A detail was continuing to work on the narrow section of the road leading to the Kall Bridge despite heavy German artillery shelling and casualties.

At 11:35 AM, B Company reported that three tanks had successfully negotiated the defile but were now stuck with their treads thrown and that the rock shelf was falling away in places. Between 11:35 AM and 3:00 PM, constant efforts were made to obtain more information on the situation of the three wrecked tanks, but no reliable information was forthcoming on the action being taken to remedy the situation. At about 3:30 PM, General Cota called the 1171st Engineer Group commander and directed him to send a competent officer forward to take charge. The group commander himself went forward and took charge that night.[3]

The group commander directed Lieutenant Colonel Sonnefield, 20th Engineer commander, to attempt to walk an armored bulldozer across in the daylight and to take an air compressor out at night. He released C Company and ordered that the road to the bridge be made passable for M29 Weasels that night by cutting away the rock on the inside of the curves near the wrecked tanks. At 8:05 PM, a telephone message from the group commander further amplified the engineer's mission by directing that the road be cleared for passage by 5:30 AM the next day. He authorized the engineers to throw the tanks over the side if necessary. Colonel Sonnefield went forward to B Company's command post, arriving at approximately 9:40 PM. Sometime later, Colonel White, the group executive officer, joined him and spent the night, periodically checking the road.[4]

At 5:15 AM, Lieutenant Colonel Sonnefield reported that the road had been opened. By 10:54 AM, seven self-propelled tank destroyers and five tanks had gone across the bridge safely and reached the top of the far bank. In the meantime, a traffic control system had been set up using wire on the north bank and radio on the south bank to prevent vehicles meeting on the one-way road.

In the afternoon, the division engineer and the group S-3 both examined the road and made suggestions for improvements. As it was expected that C Company would have some pillboxes to blow on November 6, arrangements were made to haul explosives forward for that purpose. As 5,000 pounds of explosives were being brought forward during the night, enemy patrols started attacking. The situation for the 20th Engineers shifted from an engineering problem to a tactical one.[5]

12

146th Engineer Combat Battalion

On November 6, C Company was just in its assembly area and A Company was coming up to the top of the woods that morning, when General Davis came up in a jeep. He spoke to Major Baker, asked who they were and immediately ordered A Company forward, perhaps without fully realizing they were engineers, as they were still wearing their boots from a road maintenance job. General Davis told them to go in and drive the enemy out of the town of Vossenack. They took off immediately. It was a mile from the edge of the woods to the church in town.[1]

As they took off, Captain Sam H. Ball, company commander, instructed the 1st Platoon leader, 1st Lieutenant William J. Kehaley, to take the right side of the street and the 2nd Platoon leader, 1st Lieutenant Kenneth J. Shively, to take the left. The 3rd Platoon, with 1st Lieutenant William Anderson, was in support.

There was heavy German artillery being fired at the men. They moved along fairly well and, when they got to the edge of the town, about 500 yards from the church, they moved the best they could under the incessant artillery fire. When a round would land close, they would hit the dirt; when the firing would let up, they would move again. This was repeated several times along the way. The men caught the first artillery at the turn of the road at (030326), and this artillery continued until they encountered the enemy. Friendly tanks were also moving into the town so fast some of the men had to jump into a ditch.

Major Baker and Captain Ball were at the head of the column as they moved along towards the infantry command post. After that, the company was to continue down the street towards the east while Baker and Ball remained in the command post. The engineers were just behind the command post when they encountered the enemy. They received harassing sniper fire, some mortar fire, and continuous artillery fire. Most of the sniper fire came from a couple of houses about 150 yards north of the town. The company weapons sergeant set up a .50 caliber machine gun and eliminated the snipers.

The company reached the road leading to the river, when they were stopped by fire coming from their front. On the way Private Doyle W. McDaniel climbed on top of a shed roof on the left side of the street to see where some of the sniper fire was coming from. When he jumped off, he landed on a German soldier, whom he then shot.[2]

When they reached the crossroad in the center of town, McDanial climbed atop another building across from the church, trying to see where the new frontal fire was coming from, a move which cost him his life.

While this was going on, the 1st Platoon had advanced down the right side of the street and taken the church, by what the men called run-and-duck tactics. They shot and ran, ducking and taking cover as they went forward singly and in pairs in short rushes. They went right in the front door of the church. There was a short battle inside the church, leaving eight men injured and eight to ten Germans captured. The building next to the church must have been a German command post, as the engineers found a lot of equipment inside.

By then it was getting close to 5:00 PM and was growing dark. Captain Ball got in touch with his platoon leaders to find out their situations and sent a message back to the battalion headquarters with their position.

By this point, they had fought forward and were holding all positions up to and west of the church on both sides of the street. The 2nd Platoon was holding the buildings and flank on the left all along to the back of the town. The 1st Platoon was holding the church and three buildings on the west side of the road to the river as well as buildings in the rear on the right side of the street. The 3rd Platoon was set up on the right side of the 1st Platoon. The company had harassing fire all night from German artillery.[3]

That night A Company received orders that they were to move out to the west. They started at 11:30 PM in total blackness. They moved to where the infantry command post was located, then moved south about 400 yards, before swinging to the east, with occasional artillery falling near them. It was all open ground, except for a small trail which paralleled the main road to the east. They went as far as (043327). There were a few barbed-wire fences they had to negotiate when crossing between fields. They discovered that the infantry guides did not know where their old positions were. They were lost.[4]

Captain Ball halted the company and sent Lieutenant Kehaley with one of the guides to try to find the positions. He came back in about fifteen minutes. They had not been able to find them. The leaders held a hasty conference and figured they might be too far east, so they swung back west about 20 yards from where some houses came out to a little point along the edge of the east-west road at (042327).

Captain Ball sent Kehaley and the guide out again to make another search. The engineers had tried to be very quiet and had not attracted any enemy attention.

When Kehaley and the guide were about 40 yards from the company, Captain Ball noticed a figure squatting. The figure stood up, pulled up his pants, dressed, reached down, picked up his pistol and put it in its holster. Captain Ball asked the soldier next to him to call to the figure to come to them. When he did, the figure said something in German and took off running. Captain Ball fired at him and he fell, moaning. Captain Ball's runner fired three more shots at the German. The German hollered and screamed. Alongside the nearest house was a hedge and Captain Ball noticed another German moving alongside it.[5]

The company then withdrew about 200 yards to the southeast, down a slight slope. They fell back in small groups. The shooting had apparently startled the Germans, for they started shooting at the engineers. At first, the firing was high and came from about four burp guns. The men hastily withdrew down the slope and the slight cover it afforded.

They were just about in their new positions under sporadic fire, when the Germans started to fire flares. The first one came down from the cluster of buildings, then another two swiftly followed. Three more came from the valley below the men, near the Kall River, along with some machine gun fire. Flares were coming from all directions. The engineers decided that since they could not find the infantry positions, they would go back to town.[6]

In pulling back, they dropped lower into the valley, in order to get as much cover as possible from the high ground at Vossenack. As they went along, they came out just below the road junction at (043323). After encountering some Germans, the group came to a small orchard. Captain Ball set off faster than the rest of the troops to contact the tank outposts, which he knew had been stationed there, and to let them know they were not a German patrol. The engineers made as much noise as possible, so as not to surprise the tank crews. They called out occasionally that they were an American company returning.

When they were stopped by one of the tank sentries, the tank commander, whom Captain Ball had met before, recognized his voice and cleared them to enter the perimeter. The night had grown miserable. Sleet and rain started to come down very hard and the temperature was falling.[7]

Captain Ball was briefed on a plan for a new attack that would begin in the morning with two tanks in support of the engineers. C Company would lead, while A Company would re-take the church and cover the left flank as the attack progressed.

They jumped off at 8:15 AM in the midst of the heaviest enemy artillery barrage seen to date. The barrage centered on the church. Two squads got their men across the street by infiltrating them one and two at a time, until eventually capturing the church. The German artillery continued to come in heavily and was gradually knocking down the buildings the engineers were in. The church was full of rubble. The roof had been knocked off. There were shell holes in the walls and it was raining. A large number of Germans were killed and ten prisoners were taken.[8]

It took all day to get through most of the town. When the fighting stopped, the engineers received orders to set up a perimeter defense of the town, with C Company on the extreme east and A Company taking the area beginning at the church and extending their men as far as possible to tie in with C Company. The men were ordered to hold there for the night at all costs.

Relief came that night from elements of the 2nd Battalion, 109th Infantry. The infantry commander and one of his lieutenants came to the engineers with guides and looked over their positions before moving in. The 109th men took over, building by building, from west to east, relieving the engineers as they moved in. The engineers remained in an assembly area until they had moved out of town completely in the darkness of the following morning.[9]

The engineers warmed up and rested a bit, but had to go back the next two nights, November 9 and 10, to put in about 1,000 yards of minefields as a defense at the eastern end of town. They went in at about midnight the first night, partially completed the job before light, and then went back the following night to finish. The mines were laid on top of the ground in a semicircle north and south across the road and covering the approaches from that end. In those two nights, C and A companies placed 1,462 mines.[10]

13

Reflections from Veterans' Memoirs

28th Division Veterans

Robert T. Bradicich, Company E, 2nd Battalion, 110th Infantry

We pulled back a few miles and got replacements, and the next morning we got onto trucks which drove us north to the Hürtgen Forest. Here we got off the trucks and started our march to the front. The weather was miserable, very cold, muddy roads, and snow managed to seep through the heavy trees of the forest. The thick covering of pine needles managed to keep the mud underneath from freezing. Walking through the forest your feet got wet and, with the zero freezing temperature, it went right through to your bones. Just walking to the front, I was ready to leave. If this was not enough, we had to contend with Germans and the 88s which always exploded high in the trees. These were called "tree-burst." The tops of the trees were broken off and came falling down, you hoped not on you. Along with the branches and the tops of the trees, the exploding shells rained shrapnel down on top of you. To sum it up, I was fighting the cold, the wet under foot, the snow, the tops of the trees, the 88s, the shrapnel and let us not forget the Germans.

These were the worst conditions I ever had to fight under. We didn't have any artillery support because they couldn't hit the bunkers, and the shells would explode in the trees, which was where we were. Something to do with the angle the shell comes in at, and you can't fire mortars in a forest. This was the hellhole of all hellholes. I don't think hell could be this bad.

We didn't have long to wait when the order came to move out at the German positions. But first we had to make sure our rifles were in working order and not frozen. The bolt on my rifle was hard to pull back but I managed to get it working. The guy next to me couldn't get his to move, so

I told him to put the rifle butt on the ground and I took my rifle butt and banged down on the bolt to free it. It worked. Now we started our advance and, as soon as the Germans saw us, they started to throw those 88s at us. I heard someone yelling and, as I looked up, I saw the top of a pine tree that was blown apart by an 88 shell. I tried to get out of its way but it caught me, hitting my helmet and my back, knocking me sprawling down in the mud. Two guys came over and lifted the branch off of me and I scrambled out. I'm lucky that I was hit by the end of the branch, and I had my helmet and my overcoat on, which blunted the blow somewhat. I was covered with mud and my rifle took a mud bath. As I got up, I checked my arms and legs to see if everything was ok and not broken. My guardian angel came through again; I seemed to be fine, but with this cold weather you may not feel any bruises. I wish my gun fared as well. The gun was covered with mud and I didn't know if it would fire or not.

It seems that things happen for a reason. As we started to get up to where the rest of the platoon was, we could hear a tremendous amount of small arms fire coming from up ahead. In a few minutes we were up there and found out that our platoon assaulted the bunker but was beaten back with heavy casualties. I started to clean my gun but was having trouble; my gloves were muddy also. Next to me was a dead GI and his gloves were cleaner than mine, so I took his gloves off of him and I managed to clean my rifle. His gloves were drier than mine, so I put them on. I aimed my rifle at the German bunker, put my head down and fired. If it blew, I didn't want to get it in the face. Well, it fired ok. I could have picked up another rifle, but a rifle is like your best girl, you always want her by your side.

We had two tanks coming up with flamethrowers on them, but I heard that they were bogged down in the mud and couldn't make the slight incline. As we waited we set up a defensive position and waited for orders, it looked like we were going to stay there that night. We set out personnel mines and booby traps in front to catch any German patrols that tried to come through. Usually there were no patrols sent out at night because you could not see your hand in front of your face. While it was still light, we put gauze from tree to tree which led back to the command post. I dug a foxhole but it was wet and muddy so I gathered up some pine branches and put them in the bottom. Here I settled in for the night. We were not going to attack and neither were the Germans. It was too dark to attack or go on patrol at night. If you had to relieve yourself, you went no more than 2ft. from your foxhole. If you lost your way, you could walk into the enemy or walk into a mine (booby trap). So if you got lost, you stayed right where you were until morning.

During the night something woke me up. I heard someone that seemed to be crawling towards me, but it was black and I couldn't see him. I told him to halt and he did. I gave him the password and waited for the counter word. It came, but I was still not sure whether it was a GI or an English-speaking German. I readied my rifle and asked him for his name and serial number. He told me he was a GI and got lost. He asked me if he could stay here till morning. Well, I asked him one more question, who was Babe Ruth. He answered satisfactory and I told him to come in to the foxhole. I had to see him so I did something that is crazy. I put the GI blanket that I had over both of us and then I put my hand over my flashlight and turned it on. It was a young, scared kid. I told him he could have gotten himself killed; he should have stayed where he was until morning, but he was too scared. The foxhole got a little crowded but it was warmer with two under the blanket. I told him to get some sleep but he said he couldn't. I said then be still and let me get some shuteye.

In the morning as it started to get light, I saw that he was a young kid. He told me his name was James from F company and he was from New Jersey. I didn't want to know too much about him because I lost too many buddies already. He got out of the foxhole and I told him the direction of F Company. He said "thanks" and started out in the direction of F Company.

We were told to get ready to attack but make sure our rifles were in working order. With the cold and the dampness, the bolt on the rifle could be frozen. I had mine under the blanket next to me, so mine was in good working order. As we started out through the forest, we had to be alert because, as we got nearer to the enemy positions, we didn't know which tree a German could be hiding behind. The Germans must have been watching us because, just as the trees got a little thinner, they opened up with their rifles and machine guns. I dropped down on my stomach and started to return the fire but I saw a few of our guys get it. We stayed there and fired at their positions but it seemed hopeless. They were too well dug in and we could not advance any further. However, the order was to keep going. I fired and then got up behind a tree and then ran to a tree about 4–5ft. up ahead. The trees were getting skinny and we were losing more men. Why I was still on my feet I do not know. The order finally came to pull back, but this was no easy task, for the Germans were still firing at us. As we pulled back, we gathered up the wounded and got them back as best we could.

When we got back, the Captain asked for a volunteer to go up and bring back the forward observers. If someone didn't get them out, they would be cut off and be captured or killed. We were a sorry sight, guys sitting on the ground with their shoes off, massaging their feet to get them warm, and then they might not be able to get their shoes back on. One of the guys cut off the bottom of his coat and had that wrapped around his feet. I guess I fared a little better than the rest; at least I had my shoes on, so I volunteered to go up and get the guys and bring them back. Volunteering is something you never do in the army but those guys were dead if no one went.

The Captain showed me the map as to where the men were, right up on a hill, which overlooked the enemy positions, and the enemy was expected to make a push through that part of the forest. It was about 300–500yds. up front.

I had two bandoliers of M1 clips and two hand grenades. I got two more grenades from one of the guys and now I set out on my mission. If I came across the enemy, I was not to engage them in a firefight; that suited me fine. I started out going up the muddy road but staying just along the tree line. As I got up the road about 100yds., I heard the noise of a tank up ahead. I went into the woods a few yards and inched my way up to where the noise was coming from. When I saw the tanks, I gave a sigh of relief, as there were two of our Sherman tanks at the crossroads. I came out of the woods, and, as I did, the crew of the tanks all pointed their carbines and the tank's machine gun at me. When they saw that I was a GI, they all relaxed a bit. I went up to them and told them what I was there for. They told me I couldn't go any further because the Germans were going to make a push, and they expected them to come down the road. I contemplated what the tank commander said, but I told him if I don't go, then those guys would be captured or killed.

They wished me luck when I left and I started up the road. I had to try to get up that road and get those guys back down before the Germans started the push. I thought that, if I went through the woods, it would take much longer than if I stayed on the road. But if I stayed on the road and the Germans were coming, I would be spotted immediately. Well, I had to get there quickly, so I stayed on the side of the road and ran up the road hoping they were not coming. I made it to almost the top of the hill but I didn't see any GIs. As I was looking around for them, I heard some noise coming from behind me. My heart must have stopped as I whirled around with my rifle ready, but to my surprise it was the GIs I came to bring back. There were four of them, and I told them that communications were knocked out and the Germans were going to make a push through here any minute. I came up to get them back. I said, "Come on. We'll follow the road back down. We don't have much time." Luckily, they had the radio gear all packed so we took off down the road. As we started to leave, we heard the most horrible sound to an infantryman, the sound of tanks coming towards you.

We knew they were German tanks and we had to get out of there fast. We started to run down the road but too late; they spotted us, and they started firing at us. We all immediately ran into the woods for a little protection but the German tank fired their 88. (This is the 88mm gun mounted on the Tiger tank.) It exploded near us and we all instinctively hit the ground. One of the guys got hit in the upper part of his leg. Two guys formed a seat with their rifle (two guys held the rifle on either end), and the wounded soldier sat on the rifle between both of them. As they were doing this, the corporal and I returned the enemy fire. We were in the woods far enough so we managed to get away. The Germans were probably trying to determine whether we were a few stray GIs or the main body. This gave us a little more time to go down the road.

We got down a little further and looked back, but could not see any Germans, so we got back on the road carrying the wounded GI. As we got around the slight turn in the road, we saw the two Sherman tanks that I saw before. They asked me what happened up there and I told them about the German Tiger tanks. They got on the radio to tell the main body that the Germans started the push. The message they got was to pull back. The commander told us we were in luck, they were pulling back, and we could get on the tank and ride back with them. We got the wounded GI on the back of the lead tank, and the rest of us climbed aboard. We got on the road and rode back on the tank without incident.

We found our captain and the guys told him what happened. The captain had some guy by the name of Superio write me up and I received a Bronze Star. I wasn't concerned about the Bronze Star at that time, but it did help to get me discharged faster after the war.

I no sooner got back, when we were told to get ready again for the German assault, but this time we were told that we would get artillery support. As we waited, we heard the artillery shells come over but they exploded in the treetops and were ineffective. The colonel from battalion came up to see what the situation was like. What he saw was men with their shoes off massaging their feet to get them warm. Some of the guys had their toes and feet turning black (frostbite). Other guys couldn't get their shoes on. My hands were numb and I was also concerned about my feet. I took my shoes off and I put them near the fire, which they let us start, but my toes were starting to get blue. You had to be careful because when your feet were cold and numb and you put them too close to the fire, they would burn without you knowing it.

I understand that the colonel called back to headquarters and told them that we could not attack with the condition of the soldiers. He was given the order to attack but refused. I found out that he was relieved of his command. That afternoon some officers from regiment came up to see for themselves. When they saw the condition of the men, they pulled us off the line and sent up the 3rd Battalion, which was in reserve. There was no way we could go up against the German tanks and infantry with the condition of the men. Guys could not get their shoes back on, our hands were so cold that we could not put a clip of ammunition in our rifles. It would be like just walking toward the enemy (if we could walk) and have the enemy shoot us.

Ernest Hemingway with captured artillery in Schweiler, Germany, 1944. (*John F. Kennedy Presidential Library and Museum*)

Heading out on patrol, 1944. (*US National Archives and Records Administration*)

The Schwammenauel Dam, 1944. (*US Army Center of Military History*)

Temporary shelter, 1944. (*US Army*)

116th Panzer men prepare for patrol, 1944. (*Bundesarchiv*)

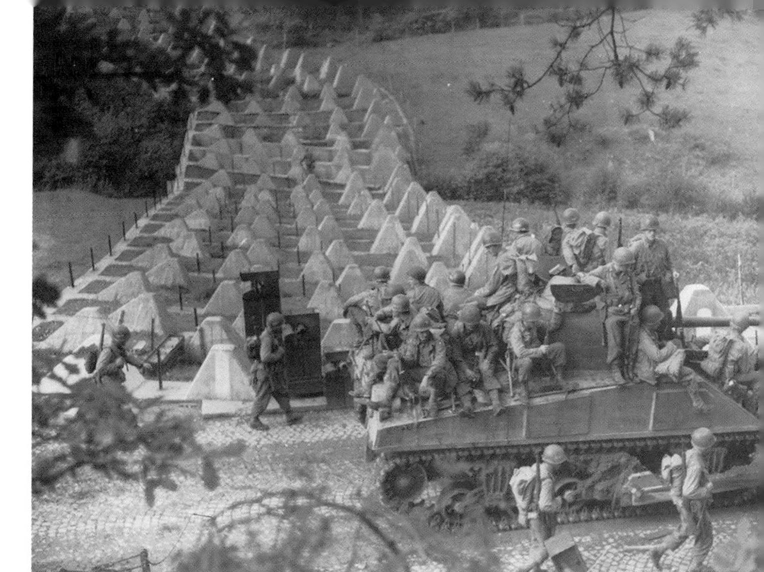

9th Infantry crossing the Siegfried Line, 1944. (*US Army Center of Military History*)

893rd tank destroyer heading into Hürtgen Forest, 1944. (*28th Division Archives*)

November rains, 1944. (*US Army*)

Protection from tree-bursts, 1944. (*28th Division Archives*)

Brief rest, 1944. (*28th Division Archives*)

9th Infantry medics, 1944. (*US Army Photo*)

Moving through the Hürtgen Forest, 1944. (*28th Division Archives*)

Tank destroyer, 1944. (*US Army*)

Below Left: Lieutenant Fleig, 1944. (*28th Division Archives*)

Below Right: Colonel Ripple, 1944. (*28th Division Archives*)

Clearing the forest, 1944. (*28th Division Archives*)

M29 Weasel, 1944. (*US Army*)

Artillery support, 1944. (*US Army*)

German pillboxes, 1944. (*US Army*)

Kall Trail, 1944. (*28th Division Archives*)

Looking at the Kall River gorge, 1944. (*28th Division Archives*)

Machine gun position, 1944. (*28th Division Archives*)

Moving through the forest, 1944. (*US Army*)

General Eisenhower and M. G. Cota (right), 1944. (*28th Division Archives*)

Due to the condition of the men (most of them had to be taken back by jeep or ambulance, trucks could not get through), each man had to be checked out by the medics for frostbite and exposure. Almost half the men went to the field hospital for frostbite. My feet were just on the borderline so I was not sent back. However, the nails under my two big toes remained black for years after I got home. I think this all came about because we could not have fires to keep us warm until it was too late. Word came down that the 112th was taking a beating trying to take Schmidt. They took it and were pushed back only to charge again and retake the town.

The Germans fought hard and lost a lot of men to keep us from breaking out of the Hürtgen Forest and now, in looking back, I can only make this assumption. If we broke out we would have exposed the large buildup of the German army which was getting ready for the big push called "The Battle of the Bulge." Little did we know that we, the 28th, would be taken out of the forest and put on line right where the German army was going to make the big push.

We got replacements but most of them went to the 112th, which took a beating around the town of Schmidt. Then the greatest thing happened to me; I got transferred to battalion headquarters. That's right I was off the front lines. They needed someone to code messages that went between battalion headquarters and regiment. Corporal Deener, who I knew in England, saw me back in Bastogne, and requested to the officer-in-charge to have me transferred. To my surprise it went through. I was promoted to a corporal technician 5th grade. Well, when I got the news, I got all choked up. I made it! I made it! I survived the war! Little did I know what was still to come.

To a rifleman, the front line infantrymen did most of the dying. The rest were cooks, bakers, truck drivers, doctors, planners, artillerymen, and generals. To the rifleman in the foxhole, they were as remote and safe and comfy as their own living room back home.

I was back in headquarters and set up shop with my coder/decoder. We got shelled from time to time, but hell, I didn't mind that at all. However, being a veteran infantryman, I got all the shitty details, like guard duty and taking replacements up to the front. I didn't mind this at all; this way I got a chance to visit my buddies at the front.

Yes, while I was in battalion HQ, I still didn't sleep inside. In fact there was no inside in this Godforsaken forest. I still had my foxhole that I dug and slept in, but this was paradise. No more watching the German soldiers coming towards you or you advancing on their positions not knowing if some German has you in his rifle sight or not, and no more killing.

I guess by now you know how I felt, so let me get on with what happened to me for the rest of the war. However, let me take a moment and tell you that the American soldier was not a gung-ho John Wayne type. He was an ordinary person who knew that Hitler had to be stopped or we would all be enslaved. When up on the front line, you have to kill or be killed. Yes, when we met the enemy, we were scared, but we did what we had to. The longer you survived on the front line, the killing becomes easier. Not like the first few times, in the beginning you sometimes hesitated, hoping that they would surrender (this hesitating could kill you). As a veteran, you do not hesitate; in fact it becomes second nature to you.

I am older now (76) and I look back at what I did and I'm glad we won the war, but I don't feel proud of what I had to do to help achieve this victory. It will be with me till the day I die.

Being in battalion headquarters, we were in a German pillbox at this time and I got the knack of coding and de-coding messages. We still had C-rations but now we could heat them over a small fire. The next day we were to move up to another pillbox, but the Germans mounted a counterattack and pushed us back to almost where we started. The next day a lieutenant colonel came up from regiment and wanted to know why we were not making any headway (I'd like to take him and put him on the front lines for two days, then he'd know).

When he arrived, the first thing he wanted to know was what all these enlisted men were doing in the pillbox. So we were ordered outside to dig foxholes for the protection of the pillbox. That went over well. The non-coms had a couple of shelter halves which they put together and made like a tent, and they slept inside the tent. I dug my foxhole about 5ft. from there, lined it with small pine branches, and was ready to get some shut-eye. I got into the foxhole with my overcoat and my rifle (it never leaves my side), and I put a blanket over us and got some sleep. At about 5:30 AM (dawn) an artillery shell came over and exploded inside the tent. The explosion sent shrapnel all over and a piece of shrapnel got me in the right hip. As I lay there, I could see that the blankets inside were burning, and some of the guys inside came out and were covered with blood. This got the officers inside up and they came running out. They went inside the tent and grabbed Maxwell, who must have been killed instantly because I remember he always slept with his hands behind his head, and this is the same position that they dragged him out. The medics came and patched us up and sent us back to the field hospital.

I was on the front lines for over five months, then back in headquarters about a week to ten days when I got wounded. When I got back to the field hospital, what I saw was sickening. The 112th was still taking a beating around Schmidt and there were guys on stretchers full of blood. The doctors were taking care of them and the medics were then moving them to cots. The nurses were doing a fantastic job trying to make all the guys comfortable, even when they knew they were dying. The doctor came over and took the piece of shrapnel out, patched it up, handed me a Purple Heart, and said you'll be ok. The nurse then bandaged me up, asked me how old I was. Because I looked young, she asked me if I wanted to go back to the hospital (for an extra day). I said "no" that I would go back to my outfit. I knew that if I went back to the hospital I would wind up in the "repel depel." This would mean that I would be a replacement to be sent up to any outfit that needed replacements. I don't know where I would have been sent. From the field hospital I knew I would be sent back to my own outfit. That is why I chose not to go back to the hospital.

We remained there, in the Hürtgen Forest, until about the third week of November 1944. I continued to send coded messages and took replacements up to the front. One thing sticks in my mind about a guy who came over with the outfit and got wounded eight times. I brought him up to the front the eighth time, and we kidded him about what lousy marksmen the Germans were. We all knew the unwritten rule that, if you are wounded nine times, you are sent back. We told him to stick his foot up over the foxhole for the Germans to see.

Well, he never made it. I found out that an 88mm from a German tank caught him and a piece of shrapnel ripped through his head. Yes, war is ugly and so unfair.

As our division was preparing to pull out, the replacing outfit started to come into the forest. We were being replaced by an Australian outfit. The soldiers I saw were all clean-shaven, and I said to myself, "Wait till they get up there in all that wet mud, snow and cold." They'll bat their heads against the wall the same as we did.

We had to walk out to get to the trucks because of the mud. The mud was about 6–10in. deep and we were walking through it. The trucks were really having a rough time. I was wondering where we were going, so I asked around and heard that we were going for some "R & R" (Rest and Relaxation).

This R&R was on the front lines but this was a quiet front. The 28th Division was stretched out about 30 miles in front. Instead of putting two regiments on line and one Regiment in reserve, all three regiments were put on line. But this was a quiet part of the front lines. The line companies had to put one squad in each town or hamlet and constantly patrol between the towns. Here we were expected to get replacements and get up to division strength. Trucks and jeeps had to be washed and repaired along with the tanks. We also had to get washed and receive new clothes because what we had on was full of mud.[1]

Albert W. Burghart, Company K, 110th Infantry

The Hürtgen Forest, on first observation, looked like heaven. The dense forest, with its towering pine trees, looked like a place where the German artillery observers would not be able to locate us. In the hedgerows, it was a fight for each hedgerow, and the casualties were severe. The Siegfried Line, with its pillboxes, was another world. The pillboxes, for the most part, were in large, open areas. They were camouflaged and had excellent fields of fire, and German artillery observers could watch our movement. It always seemed that the Germans had the high grounds. On second observation, when we got into it, the Hürtgen Forest looked ominous. It was dark, and as we went to our positions, we could see some of the problems that the 9th Division faced. The pine forest, which composed 99 percent of the forest, was littered with branches, and it was difficult to go in a straight line because of all the debris. We noticed the trees were scarred from shrapnel, and many trees were down from direct artillery hits. In general, the forest floor was a mess. This was caused by what we learned to fear—the tree-burst, which happens when an artillery shell hits high up in a tree, explodes and sends shrapnel raining down on you. The 9th Division and German dead were all over the area.

We relieved the 9th Division around the end of October. The guide from the 9th Division mortar section took our three squads to their mortar position. They were forced to construct underground shelter against the tree-bursts. These consisted of a dugout about 4ft. deep. The length and width I no longer remember, but I do know that you were always on your hands and knees. They were covered with layers of pine logs and dirt.

It had one entrance. There were a number of these covered dug-outs for all members of the three mortar squads. This mortar position, made by the 9th Division mortar section, was completely surrounded by tall pine trees. The clearing did not have to be large, because of the trajectory of the 60mm mortars. This helped us from being observed by the enemy. We had telephone lines going to the three rifle platoons on the line and one forward listening post to the left side of our defenses. We never found out who was on our left, but I think the mortar section was in a gap between one of our other companies, but I have no proof of this. The sergeants took turns at the forward listening posts, a very lonely and scary job. Every time we changed sergeants on this post, you wondered if you would make it to the post. Because of all the debris from the trees, it made an ideal position for an ambush or a sniper. Secondly, you wondered if you were hit in this tangled mess, if anyone would ever find you. At this period of time, we had more mortar ammo than I have ever seen. There were cloverleaf canisters which held 6—60mm mortar shells piled up about feet high for about 50ft., and there were no restrictions on the use of them.

If one of the rifle platoons asked for help, we checked on our firing charts and sent as many rounds into the German positions as was necessary. If a German was chopping wood for whatever purpose, we would send mortar shells into the area until the chopping stopped. We fired at night, so they couldn't sleep, the same as they did to our positions. During the firing mission, using two gunners to put the shells into the mortar tubes, one gunner put a shell down the tube before the first one went out. But nothing happened, because the brass plug was not blown out on the side of the shell—a built-in safety factor.

Because our position was so exposed, and we were never told who was on our left or ahead of us, we decided to rig an alarm system, which consisted of empty K-ration cans containing small rocks, attached to a line running around our complete area, so that if anyone hit the line, we could hear the rattle of the rocks and be alerted. We did this because, even though we always had sentries posted, your vision was limited at night in the forest. One night, between 11:00 PM and 2:00 AM, the cans began to rattle, and the battle started. We started throwing grenades out of our covered dugouts, and, since we were scattered in the clearing, no one knew whether the explosions were friend or foe, and this continued for quite some time. In the morning, when we inspected the area, it was a mess. The ground was torn up, and more debris from the pine trees was present, most of it being redistributed by the explosion of the grenades. The fellows on the line must have thought they were being outflanked with all the noise and flashes from the explosions. We never found any bodies, so possibly some animal must have hit the wire, but it sure gave us a scare and probably others as well.

One time, when it was my turn to be forward observer, I started out to my listening post. The shelling had brought down the tops and branches of the pine trees, and the forest floor was a tangle of branches. The only way you could find the listening post was by tracing the telephone wires through the downed tree branches. Each time you went up to this post, you didn't know if you would be shot by a sniper or captured, because there were no GIs in front of our listening post. I never heard anyone to my right or left, so the post must have been in a gap in the lines. One of the times that I went up to this post, the Germans must have heard me coming. It was almost impossible to move quietly, because of all of the debris from the tree-bursts. A mortar shell came down right in front of me.

I did not hear it coming (you never hear a mortar shell coming in because of the trajectory). It hit about 12–15ft. feet in front of me. The branches of fallen pine trees on both sides of me filled the air. Wind from the explosion gave me a wind burn, and the concussion forced me to the ground. I was covered with tree litter, and smoke covered the immediate area. I was sure that I was hit. I felt all over my body for the feeling of blood, but there was none. I was not knocked out from the closeness of the round, but I was dazed. I thought at this time that there was no way that I was going to survive, after all the close calls that I had, and most of my old friends were gone. I made up my mind that as long as I wasn't going to make it, I wouldn't quit either.

After coming back from one of these sessions at our listening post, we received a fire mission on a position in front of one of our rifle platoons. Since we had mortar ammo in ample supply, we decided to really do a job on the German position. We got all set up, and two gunners and ammo carriers passing mortar rounds, put up between twenty-five and thirty shells in the air before the first round hit the ground. We were aiming at their bunkers. It must have been devastating. It really sounded great.

In this time frame, an attack was planned. Our weapon platoon sergeant and the NCO of the mortar section went over the attack sequence. I was given a map of the area of what is now referred to as the Battle for Schmidt. We were never told what our mission was. In the attack, K Company's three rifle platoons were to secure an area 1,000yds. from our original position, dig in and hold. Using the map, I was to follow with the mortar section. There was a time given for the attack, but I no longer remember what it was. The artillery opened up, and soon after, the attack began. Our rifle platoon took off, but they were stopped before they had gone 100yds., and they took heavy casualties. The mortar section never left its position. I heard that a request to the air force to bomb the German fortifications in front of our position was denied because our positions were too close to the German lines.

After this attack failed, we were told we would be pulling out. Under cover of darkness, with what was left of K Company, we pulled back, and along with the remainder of our 3rd Battalion, became part of Task Force Ripple. After the war, when I was a civilian, I read about being part of Task Force Ripple and going to the aid of our trapped sister regiment, the 112th. Also, by reading from my collection of World War II books, I learned that our objective was the town of Schmidt and the Rur Dams, in particular the Schwammenauel Dam.

On the way to join the 112th Regiment, we went through Vossenack, a village in flames. It was late at night or early in the AM. It was just like you see in a war movie, smoke and fire all over. The smell of the burning buildings, gun powder, gasoline, and oil from burning tanks, and the ever present smell of death were very evident. The eerie light from the fires showed damaged buildings everywhere, and when a shell exploded, you could see a church steeple in the distance.

It was during one of these flashes of light that I saw what was left of a GI who had been run over lengthwise by a tank. I could tell it was a GI because of his clothing—webbing, steel helmet, etc., a sad sight to see. There were many bodies in the village, both German and American, which you could see by the light from the fires as we passed through. Part way through Vossenack, we left the main road and turned right to pick up the Kall Trail.

We went down into the Kall Valley and across a stone bridge wide enough for one vehicle. This part of the march to aid the 112th Regiment had less shelling, because the Germans did not know where we were at the time. A light but steady cold rain was falling. After we crossed the bridge, we started up the Kall Trail. The trail was very narrow in spots. There were no vehicles with us, and we had to carry our 60mm mortar and ammo, which was very difficult because of the steep terrain. The Germans finally found us, and the shelling picked up. In combat you see many things that your eyes were never meant to see.

The order of march for a rifle company usually is 1st platoon, 2nd platoon, 3rd platoon and the 4th platoon, which is called the weapons platoon. In combat we rotated the platoons. It was raining and starting to get light enough to see. A shell hit somewhere ahead, very close. When I got to the area, a shell apparently had hit the top of a tree (tree-burst). There were five men hit. Four of them were dead. They looked like rag dolls that were carelessly thrown around. Their arms and legs were not in normal positions, and the medics had not arrived on the scene. As I came up to one of the men, he was in a sitting position, looking sort of in a stupor. I don't know if he was watching the water from the rain, along with his blood which had turned the little stream red. As I passed him, I looked at his face, but I'm thankful that I didn't recognize him. It had to be one of the fellows I knew, because of the line of march and the time element. I was able to look down inside of him, because of the large wound in his shoulder. I am quite sure that by the time I passed him, he was dead due to the depth of the wound. This all took place in a matter of seconds, but at the time, it seemed like hours.

My last days with the 3rd Battalion, 110th Infantry were on the reverse slopes outside of Kommerscheidt, a short distance from Schmidt, Germany. With what was left of the 3rd Battalion, we dug in and waited for the word to renew the attack on Schmidt, but because of the problems that the Kall Trail presented, the attack was delayed. No tanks or supplies were getting through. The Germans could not shell our position with their regular artillery because of the reverse slope, but they were able to use mortar, due to the higher trajectory. We hadn't eaten in three days, except for a roll of life savers, which I shared with a friend, and there wasn't any part of me that wasn't cold, wet or damp. The damp part was having the hell scared out of me. While in this position outside of Kommerscheidt, the wounded increased at an alarming rate, and they could not get proper treatment. Our medics negotiated a temporary truce. I was told by our medics that the Germans checked each stretcher to make sure that only the most seriously wounded were being evacuated.

Sometime on the 8th of November 1944, word was radioed that we were trapped and that our troops would not be able to break through to us. We were to abandon our position, and all our mortars and machine guns were to be destroyed. We were to break up into small groups and get back to our original company areas. Since I was in charge of the 60mm mortars, I destroyed the mortar sights with the butt of my rifle, and buried the base plates, bipods, and the mortar tubes in different spots and camouflaged the area.

When the group I was with took off late that night, we went down the Kall Trail and across the stone bridge over the Kall River. It was guarded by troops. We came upon it very quickly, and it was very dark and raining. My platoon sergeant and I, when discussing this years later, are sure that the troops were Germans, but since our group was larger than theirs, and this happened so fast, no action resulted. After crossing the bridge, we went cross country out of the Kall Valley, up some very steep slopes, suitable only for mountain goats. Everyone was very quiet, and we received no incoming fire. The Germans apparently had no idea that we had left our position. It was during this time that someone lost their helmet. It went crashing down the rocky slope to the bottom of the valley, making a tremendous amount of noise. After getting away without being detected, we thought we had had it, but nothing happened.

When we arrived at the top of this valley, we came to a flat area where we were challenged in English by a sentry. Whoever was leading us, satisfied the outpost that we were GIs, and we passed through to our company area. We were too tired to dig in. We just laid down and went to sleep. At first light, when I awoke, I was covered with the first snow of the season. The medics arrived and were checking everyone. When they came to me, they asked me how I was, and I said that other than being cold, wet and hungry, I was okay. They asked me how my feet were. I said, okay, and proceeded to take my M1 and hit my left foot with the butt of my rifle and felt nothing. They had me take my boots off and examined my feet. They were as white as the new snow. The medics wrote out a casualty tag, and put it on me. They brought up a stretcher and told me to get on it, which I thought was great. It was great until the circulation started to try to get back in my legs and feet.

When they took my M1, I saw for the first time that 6in. of the barrel were missing, probably removed by shrapnel. I have no idea when this happened, because my rifle was always within my reach. This started me on my way to the States, through numerous hospitals in France and England, and on a hospital ship, the S.S. Exchequer.[2]

John J Farrell Jr., Company I, 3rd Battalion, 112th Infantry

The night of November 3–4, 1944, found the men of the 3rd Battalion, 112th Infantry Regiment in a buoyant mood. They had successfully crossed the Kall River; using the Kall Trail as their main axis of advance, they had entered Schmidt after passing through Kommerscheidt, having received only desultory fire from some snipers in the un-cleared parts of the town. The men settled down as best they could among the shattered buildings of Schmidt.

Company L deployed its 3rd Platoon astride the Hasenfeld Road to the southeast of Schmidt, with the 2nd Platoon to the left and the 1st Platoon on the left of the 2nd at the Harscheidt Road to the northeast. Contact patrols operated between these fanned-out rifle platoons to ensure the ground was secure. Company I, consisting of two rifle platoons and a Light MG Section dug in along the North of Schmidt. The 3rd Battalion was now deployed in all-round defense of Schmidt.

In one of the many foxholes dug alongside the track leading from Schmidt out to Kommerscheidt were huddled two sergeants. At 22-years-of-age, Staff Sergeant John Farrell Jr. did not look like a veteran, but having been in the Army for nearly two years, survived France and now in Germany, he must have felt like one! He shared his hole with another sergeant, Edward T. Jones of Vermont, USA. He was five years older than Farrell and had enlisted in March 1941, perhaps having seen that America was bound to come into the war in Europe in the near future. He wasn't a college boy like Farrell but had three years at high school behind him and now in full-time employment. The war had brought them together.

As the inky darkness fell and the temperature also, both men no doubt whispered words of encouragement to their fellow riflemen.

The sun came up at 7:32 AM on the morning of November 4, but the men of the 112th were already awake and alert. German artillery fire had startled those who had managed to sleep. Shells began to fall all over the town, from the northeast, east and southeast. Those that survived recall the shelling appeared to come from all points of the compass at once.

Soon thereafter the enemy infantry came on. At first, apparently in an uncoordinated assault, but then in greater numbers. Soon Schmidt was being assaulted from almost every direction, save from the North. Now German tanks entered the fray, at least ten coming towards Jones, Farrell, and their comrades. The tanks were merciless, firing into individual foxholes, the concussion killing those whom the rain of jagged steel failed to claim.

The survivors of this vision of hell broke to the southeast, away from Schmidt, a town they had occupied almost without a shot being fired shortly before now being left hurriedly as it erupted in fire and steel.[3]

GEORGE W. GRIZZLE, COMPANY E, 2ND BATTALION, 112TH INFANTRY

I don't think I have too much to add... We took the place of the 9th Division a couple of days before. The weather didn't clear enough for air support, so it was decided to go ahead without it on [November 2]. After clearing a few mines, we really didn't encounter much resistance. The trouble came when we were deployed on the edge of the ridge (in the town of Vossenack) and subjected to constant bombardment for five days. We were way under strength, and the mental casualties began to be a big factor. The higher levels of command couldn't understand why the division was so under strength.

There had been blunders—failure to follow orders and plans, communication failures—way back to Normandy. One time then we were supposed to take a hill at 2:30 PM.

We got there at 2:00 PM and were able to take it without any real trouble. However, artillery support had been ordered for 2:30 PM. The captain said it wasn't necessary now, so we would call it off. The message didn't reach its intended recipients, because the barrage rained downed on us at 2:30 PM. I remember the captain yelling at the radio man to get them on the radio and stop it. But they must have laid the radio down for the entire time, because it continued for the planned time on target. I believe we lost fourteen men.

Another time that comes to mind was in the planning of the Siegfried Line offensive when we were sent in unfortified jeeps to an area 6 miles or so inside the line. I was in the second jeep. The first one got by, but then they discovered us, and our jeep was hit. The three men riding in it with me were all casualties. They could have used an array of more heavily armored vehicles, which were certainly available.

I was captured on November 7 along with many others and put on railroad cars for about ten days or so and taken to Stalag IIA at Neubrandenburg. They took 160 6–180 of us to another camp in an isolated storage area in a wooded place at Dannenwalde where there were concrete storage buildings camouflaged and brush growing on top of them. We mainly spent our time here making roads with picks and shovels, working ten hours a day, seven days a week. In about six weeks (shortly before Christmas), we started receiving Red Cross rations and about every two weeks thereafter. Prior to receiving these rations we had boiled vegetables such as rutabagas, potatoes and cabbage.

Sometime after that we were moved out of Dannenwalde back to the town of Neubrandenburg—about February 1. They had us building a concrete wall on the south side of the town to defend it from the Russians. The last we saw, it was about 200yds. Long—never finished. They had not taken the forms off when we left there (thank goodness as we had intentionally not put any cement in the concrete mixture and it would have just crumbled).

One evening after this we were taken out and marched toward the Western Front. This was the last we saw of Neubrandenburg. It took four days or so to get to the Western Front. We arrived there a couple of days after Hitler had killed himself. The war continued and a couple of days later the Russians came in and took Berlin. The road to the Western Front had been filled with everything and everybody, on foot, as there was no gasoline for motor vehicles—baby buggies, carts, etc. We had left Neubrandenburg in the evening as the Russians were getting very close, traveling the 100 miles or so on foot, resting at night whenever possible, and eating what Red Cross food we had left. Eventually I was separated from anyone I knew.

One night towards the end of this trek, I slept in a haystack (along with several others unknown to me there, until all emerged the next morning). I had only travelled a half mile or so when I met up with an American staff sergeant who was having all the Germans disarm and pile their weapons along the side of the road, a pile approximately 3ft. high by 20–30yds. long. We continued on up a hill and had breakfast at a camp kitchen and were then taken on a truck to a collection point for POWs at Schwerin Air Corps Camp. There was a long row of brick, two-story barracks there where we were housed until a large number of us were collected and then a convoy of trucks came and took us across the Elbe River (actually the front line).[4]

Richard F. Leach, Company D, 109th Infantry

After many battles in the Siegfried line, just inside the German border, we became stymied for approximately two weeks. We were pulled out of the line and sent northward to the Hürtgen Forest to relieve the 9th Division, who had been held up in the vicinity of Vossenack, Germeter and Schmidt. These little towns seemed to string out along the highway which the Germans were using to shift troops back and forth.

After several days of fighting and crawling in and out of the basements of houses in Vossenack and Germeter, our regiment was ordered to launch an attack to the northeast to the town of Hürtgen. The attack was through heavy forest all the way, so we massed all of our machine guns, both .30 caliber and .50 caliber, to throw interdictory fire on the roads near the town of Hürtgen.

We even took the .50 caliber guns from the kitchen trucks and had them operated by headquarters and kitchen personnel to increase firepower. We also laid out a ladder-like barrage for the 81mm mortars, which could be dropped ahead of our troops as they advanced through the forest. I went along with Colonel Strickler and his headquarters group. which was following C Company, then commanded by Captain John Ritter, so that I could call the mortar barrages down ahead of the battalion as it advanced. I had a radio operator and several runners along with me.

The attack went quite well for a while and we made good progress until the German counterattack started hammering shells through trees that had not been blown down. About 1 mile after we had jumped off to go into the forest, we came across Captain Ritter, who had just been shot through the mouth. He was on his feet and gargling with cognac and spitting blood and broken teeth, but still leading his men and directing the company. Strickler ordered him to immediately turn over the command of the company to someone else and go to the rear. I found out later he did not do so and kept on fighting. We advanced probably another mile within sight of the town of Hürtgen. The remaining Germans that we had not killed were flushed out of the forest and across the fields. As they ran back across the open fields our riflemen picked them off.

We held up at the edge of the forest to regroup and reorganize. Many of the men were completely lost and separated from their units as they made their way through the fallen trees. About that time, we were hit with a German heavy artillery barrage. I hit the ground, as did everyone else, until it was over. When the barrage lifted, I started to get up and found my left elbow wouldn't work. I looked down and saw the hole in my jacket where a piece of shrapnel had pierced through. Lieutenant Myron Buyers was nearby and he fashioned a sling for my arm; he was also wounded in the hand and a number of other men around us were very badly wounded. We used our belts to make tourniquets for a man who had lost his leg. Since very few of the soldiers knew where they were and I had the advantage of previously studying the maps, I led a party of approximately fifteen walking wounded about 2 miles back to where we had launched the attack that morning. I had only one good arm so I threw away my rifle but kept my little 8mm movie camera.

When we returned to the company command post, my bedroll had been riddled with a mortar burst right where I had slept the night before. I turned over all the maps, and the command of the company to Lieutenant Allen. My driver then drove me to the aid station.[5]

Gilbert Mass, Company K, (Heavy Weapons), 110th Infantry

In the Hürtgen Forest, that gloomy expanse below Aachen where the trees, terrain and weather, even without entrenched Germans, make formidable opposition, and mud-sluiced roads and clinging snow penetrate like a plague in the bones, American troops have fought a great but unsung battle. They were soldiers of the 28th Division, Pennsylvania's own, men who are destined to be overlooked as a greater campaign resumes, but whose fourteen-day sacrifice, as they butted their heads against steep hills and the blazing muzzles of Tiger tanks, may one day be appreciated by military historians who know what they attempted to achieve.

In a broad sense, the division, known to the Nazis as the "Blutig Eimer" (Bloody Bucket) after its crimson keystone patch and the ferocity of its onslaught near Mortain, attained its objectives. It has about killed, captured or wounded 4,000 enemy troops. It took and held Vossenack and Germeter and a considerable amount of the woodland surrounding them. It crossed, without benefit of roads, the ridges protecting Kommerscheidt and Schmidt, seizing those two villages, and holding both for a time. It destroyed thirty-six enemy tanks and self-propelled guns and three Messerschmittaircraft and wrecked a whole series of pillboxes and blockhouses. Its very mission, to distract and occupy as many German troops as possible, indicated the nature of the assignment.

Survivors sat silently staring straight ahead, and if there were heroics to recount, someone else had to talk for them. The men of the 28th would not. Too many of their companions remained behind, too many were missing or wounded. If they never saw the Hürtgen Forest again, it would suit them. If they never traveled its fragrant ravines or pitched another tent or new-hewn hut to ward off fragments and falling treetops, if they never saw a timbered slit trench or smelled the tangy odor of burning cones and felt springy bed needles that carpeted the forest, they would not care. They hated Hürtgen Forest, where the stately Douglas firs, with their epaulets of snow, ranged like frosted grenadiers, close-ordered on the hillsides, immutable, impenetrable, and cold.

It was November 2, 1944, when the 28th Division churned over the plateau from Luxembourg to try to negotiate the thick barrier that lies between the Siegfried defenses and the plain of Cologne. The mission was not easy and the staff knew it. Enemy artillery zeroed upon every narrow road, enemy mortars dropped on all exposed turns and openings. The enemy knew each captured pillbox and could shell with card-index certitude, while the Germans also realized that the loss of Schmidt had definitely isolated whole sections of the lower Siegfried line. The Hun would fight for Schmidt with all he had—and did. From the Nazi standpoint, the whole idea of the Rhineland stand has been to contain the Americans in this western fringe of homeland. If they can keep our troops from reaching the Rhine, if they can force winter upon the allies and bolster their slave-built defenses, if they can muster secret weapons for spring, as each soldier has been promised, they may yet escape punishment. Schmidt and Hürtgen Forest are strong links in this chain of reasoning.

When the 28th attacked on November 2, there were strong enemy infantry forces before them, plus light- and medium-artillery batteries and 88mm guns, only a few 105mms, and no tanks. When the 28th completed its fortnight's battle, the Germans had thrown in many new troops, heavy artillery, and tanks, of which some were Mark VIs. There was a complete flak regiment engineer battalion which immediately attacked and lost 480 men, and the German guns were firing eight to ten rounds a minute for periods of twenty minutes on a twenty-four-hour-a-day basis to keep our troops from advancing. Hitler's best troops had retaken Schmidt under orders to restore the line at all costs.

On November 3, a regiment commanded by Lieutenant Colonel Carl Peterson, of Bradford, Pennsylvania, struck toward Vossenack, overran Germeter and took both places before nightfall. Things looked good. One of these prisoners taken at Vossenack couldn't understand why the yanks were coming through the forest. Why take Vossenack? "The road leads nowhere," he said. But the Germans fought like fiends to retake it, and it's worth your life to show your head there today.

Lieutenant Colonel Richard Sieg's engineers built a road around the shoulder of a steep hill so tanks could cross, but when he finished and three vehicles traversed it, the rock gave way and the remainder couldn't pass. By then the attack of Colonel Peterson's regiment had turned on Schmidt, and the engineers had to reopen the road. They hauled away the disabled vehicles and blasted away the debris to clear the route. Meanwhile, Schmidt had fallen and been retaken by the Germans and that in itself was a story.

Colonel Ripple was assigned to lead a task force to take back Schmidt in a spearheading operation pending arrival of a regiment to relieve it. It was composed of one battalion commanded by Lieutenant Colonel Bill Tait, of Indiana, Pennsylvania, a composite company of tank destroyers and two companies of a tank battalion. The task force left its bivouac at 2:00 AM on November 4. It was frosty in the woods at that hour.

On the way, Colonel Ripple's elements reached Kommerscheidt, where five big enemy tanks were overrunning the village. The commander left the regimental dugout just ten minutes before a Mark VI rumbled forward through light arms fire, straddled the command post and stayed there, shooting our men as they tried to run out. Survivors say they still can envision that tank squatting on the dugout like a prehistoric monster, spitting slugs through our men.

Everyone was exhausted by now, for it was twenty-four-hours-a-day fighting, as the enemy increased his strength steadily and hurled more tanks into action. Tanks were sneaked up at night and when daylight came; they fired their cannon at 200yds. point blank into GI foxholes, or sprayed them with their machine guns. Three officers were in one slit trench when it took a direct hit. One was killed and the second had his arm blown off. He said, "They winged me, but haven't got me!" He demanded a tourniquet, walked to the first-aid station unassisted. The third officer was blown right out of the trench and suffered not a scratch. It was the first combat for Ripple, who has a wife and children in Bethesda, Maryland. He directed the fight against the tanks.

Captain Bruce Hostrup, commanding the tank company, ran through heavy artillery and small arms fire while trying to dislodge the tank from the command post. He's from Port Clinton, OH, and showed extreme courage but the enemy tank refused to budge. Eventually the remainder of our men in the dugout had to surrender.

Lieutenant Ray Fleig, platoon leader, kept the battle going. They called him General Fleig because he directed three tanks as if he had an army behind him. Fleig was walking ahead of the tanks with Sergeant Tony Spooner of Alton, Illinois, a section leader. All three vehicles were under heavy mortar and artillery fire. The first tank hit a mine, was disabled and blocked the road, but Sergeant Spooner, with a cable, used the lead tank for an anchor and hauled the others through. Lieutenant Fleig jumped in, rode through intense artillery fire to Schmidt, where the infantry men were so happy to see him that several almost cried. "There are Heinies with lots of tanks over that hill," they told him, to which Lieutenant Fleig said, "I'll do what I can, boys."

They then proceeded to knock out three German tanks at 75yds. and another at 400yds., until Sergeant Spooner and the two other tanks joined him. The three tanks then beat off the German infantry-and-tank onslaught and secured a ridge at Kommerscheidt. When the Nazis came with twelve tanks, Lieutenant Fleig radioed his commander, "We can hold them," and he did. Every time the Germans showed face, our fellows beat them back, getting one probable, until by November 4 they joined with the infantry setting up defenses, until Lieutenant Dick Payne came with five more tanks and defended the left flank.

On the next day they repelled four counterattacks and not until the enemy sent an overwhelming number of tanks at them did they retire and relinquish Kommerscheidt. And that was only one of the 28th's feats in Hürtgen Forest![6]

John F. Marshall, Company B, 707th Tank Destroyer Battalion

I'll go on to where we moved into the Hürtgen Forest. Here we were to house-clean the tanks and fine-tune them to be combat-ready. Nothing was to be in the tank that wasn't issued. Mike told us that this meant all the food we had accumulated! That order hurt; you might just as well have stabbed me with a knife. We pleaded and reasoned with him but to no avail. That's the orders he got from the platoon leader and that is the end of the discussion. I thought of all the times I was hungry and didn't break into this food, saving it. Now after carrying it from England and across Europe we have to bury it. What a rotten break. As I prepared to throw the cans of butter, cheese, jellies and bread, etc. in the hole, Mac said, "Wait a minute" and climbed up on the tank to the racks we had welded on the turret to carry our bed rolls. Among them, deflated and folded was a Mae West jacket issued to us when we boarded ship to cross the channel. Mac saved his (or maybe it was his air mattress); he cut it with his trusty knife so that it resembled a sheet of canvas with rubber backing; for no particular reason we packed and wrapped all our precious food in this and buried it. I feel it stemmed from our upbringing during the depression and the teaching that it was a sin to waste food. After all our conniving, wheeling and dealing to acquire this food it came to this. We even took branches to use as brooms to cover the digging and tank tracks so no one would know we've been here. I was beginning to hate Hitler and all Germans.

We moved out that day, deeper into the Hürtgen. When we reached our position it was late afternoon; through the trees we could see the hilly countryside and buildings. We dug our trench. As we were going to back our tank over it, Mike was summoned to a meeting of all tank commanders and officers; feeling it may be orders to move again, we waited for Mike to return. Meantime two infantry men from the 110th Regiment asked us if they could have our freshly dug trench; it would save them a lot of digging, as they were very tired; we told them they were welcome to it (within an hour or so, it was to be their deathbed). The Germans began a concentrated artillery fire to this area. A heavy shell landed directly in their trench, leaving nothing but a few body parts and a shredded overcoat.

When Mike returned he seemed upset and told us, "We move out tomorrow." We asked him, "Out to where? What are we to expect? How far away are the Krauts? (Unknown to us the Krauts were already among us.) Will we be fighting with others? If so, who are they?" Mike was embarrassed and frustrated because he could not tell us more and said, "That's all they (the officers) told me." We thought what a senseless way to lay our lives on the line not being informed. Mac said he was going to fix something to eat and pulled out a Bunsen burner to light it and heat some food for all of us. The sly fox did not bury all the bread, jelly, soup and cheese that we were ordered to bury yesterday. He had "squirreled" some of it from sight in a 75mm shell cavity. Mike reminded us that it was against regulations to light one of those up inside a tank especially one carrying 125gal. of gasoline.

Mac looked at Mike and smiled as he would when making a final point and said, "If I'm going to get killed tomorrow at least for tonight I'm not going to be cold and hungry. Mike said, "Why not." Mac lit the burner. As though we were all thinking the same thing, John, Jim and I climbed out of the tank and unfolded a huge canvas tarpaulin and tied the four comers to trees just over the tank, as it would act as a roof to keep the rain out and allow us to keep the hatch open for ventilation and keep the Krauts from seeing any light coming from inside the tank. We had just climbed back in the tank when the Germans started shelling the area; we quickly closed the hatch as aerial bursts set to explode at tree-top height, so that the shrapnel would go down into tank hatches and fox holes.

After a tremendous explosion rocked the tank, we ate in silence knowing that those two 110th infantry men were killed with that blast. It was about 1:00 AM, Mike did not eat; at this point in time, he had but five more hours to live. We were being shelled all night long; none of us slept. At 5:45 AM word came for us to move out. It wasn't quite daylight yet, foggy and dreary. We had only travelled several hundred feet, when Mike leaned out of the turret to ask two 110th Infantry men what is the situation and in what direction are the Germans. With my hatch closed, I watched the men's expressions through my periscope, they were less than 24in. away. They were dirty, unshaven, tired and excited. I did not realize they were here days before we arrived and we were rested, clean and fed. It wasn't too many minutes after 6:00 AM, when, at this moment, there was a tremendous explosion as a heavy mortar hit our tank between the two front hatches.

I was crushed by a strange numbness from the concussion; although I had blood in my mouth, my nose was bleeding and I was temporarily deaf, I was not wounded. I was alive. I looked over at Alyea; he was dazed, staring straight ahead as in a trance, I concluded he was not hurt either. I removed my shattered periscope and replaced it with a spare and looked at a scene I can still see to this day. All that remained of the two soldiers was a leg with the shoe still on; a head bared to the skull and some pieces of clothing. I tried to believe this was just a bad dream, until I heard Mac calling me as though he was miles away in a cave, "Mike got hit and needs help." I crawled back to the turret, and as I tried to make Mike comfortable, I could see his chest was torn from his body. I dumped all the powder we had on his wound (I believe it was sulfa). His last words were, "Don't kid me, how bad am I?" I answered, "You'll be okay but you won't be able to write for a while." I know he died before I finished the sentence. The shelling continued exploding so close that mud showered into the tank, but none were direct hits. We decided Mac should be tank commander and I would be gunner; Jim would stay as loader and John would stay as our driver.

He turned the tank around and raced back to find an aid station. It was a pitiful scene: two men carrying a dead man; a couple of severely wounded men helping each other, they say, "Men don't cry," but they do, whether it's from frustration, hopelessness or pain—men do cry. Mac jumped out of the tank and stopped a medic running to help someone and asked him to come to the tank, hoping beyond hope that maybe something could be done for Mike. The medic refused, as he was swamped with work and we were several hundred feet away from the aid station, and because of all the vehicles and ambulances we couldn't get closer. Mac pointed his gun at the medic, and he came to the tank; not that he feared Mac's gun but he was a tolerant and understanding man. He climbed up on the tank and looked in the turret and in a way of appeasement said, "Bring him in." We turned Mike over to the medics. They examined him and placed him with others that were killed. I recall seeing bodies stacked three or four high in rows 40–50ft. long; there were probably more, but I saw two such stacks, likened to a cord woodpile only made of humans.

We then went back to Vossenack to take our place in the platoon. Lieutenant Anderson, noticing our presence but not aware Mike had been killed and that now we were only a four-man crew (as we could only receive transmissions on our radio, we could not transmit), ordered us to get on the road and proceed towards the only church in Vossenack. We did this for about 200yds. under very heavy shelling. Mac said, "John listen to me." He gave orders to drive off the road, as we were completely exposed and drove parallel to it, staying in the field, as it turned out, just in the nick of time. We moved ahead only a few hundred feet or so, when we received a direct hit in the left rear of the tank. It went forward for about 15–20ft. down a swale and into a tremendous burst of exploding mortars. The tank dropped into this "instant-made" tank foxhole, rendering it immobile. We now discovered that the turret would not traverse. The shell that killed Mike had jammed the gears; the 75mm gun was useless. We were alive and for the moment safe because the tank was a little lower than the road and a grassy mound on our left gave us some protection.

The Germans could see our turret, and they knew we were in the tank; they kept shooting at us many times with their 88mm guns. The bullets would slam into the mound and tear through the earth like a giant ground mole, only to glance upward with a sickening whirring sound, raining dirt, rocks and grass into our tank.

It seemed like forever but the shelling directed at us temporarily stopped because the Krauts found other targets for the time being. The tank was a mess, with the blood and flesh mixed with mud and debris. With the gun not working, we decided to abandon the tank. I was all for jumping out while it was still daylight, but John, Mac and Jim thought it would be unwise; we should wait until dark. John then suggested we should set up a machine gun outside the tank and take turns on guard; we had guns but not the stand (legs), so we decided against that move. John often wished he had an M1 rifle of his own. The field to our right was littered with dead American soldiers lying near M1 rifles.

Just to hear myself talk, I said to John, "There's your chance to pick up a rifle for yourself." John thought for a moment and then opened his hatch unseen by the Krauts as his section was lower than the turret. Nothing happened until he ventured a short distance from the tank to pick up the rifle and was now in view of the Krauts and then all hell broke loose again prompting John to throw the rifle down and race back to the safety of the tank. So we waited, mostly in silence; there was a little daylight left when we decided on our evacuation procedure.

One man at a time was to exit the tank, run 40–50yds., dive into a shell hole and then get up and run again when the next man exited. We would continue this procedure, so that we would all be heading towards the command post 40–50yds. apart. As soon as Jim, the first man, was out of the tank, the shelling started again, but we stuck to our plan, except for me. When I got about 300ft. from the tank I realized we had no blankets, actually nothing but the clothes on our backs (Mac had taken the firing pin out of the 75mm), so I turned around and went back to our tank for my bedroll, which was placed with the others in the rack I mentioned earlier. From the explosions on and near the tank all day, these rods were twisted and knotted around the bedrolls like ordinary rope. I pulled and tugged but couldn't dislodge my bedroll. It was now dark and I was angry with myself for not sticking to our escape plan.

I really started to worry when I heard someone sloughing their way towards the tank, for I had no gun. I slid off the tank and crouched against the tank in the shell hole; I waited then I heard someone ask, "Marshall?" It was John Alyea. Although he had almost reached the company area, he had come back to see what had happened to me! Together we each pulled a bedroll free and in the fog and darkness made our way back, our imminent danger being shot by our own outposts. We found Jim and Mac lying under a tank on blankets. Mac knew there would be bedrolls lying all over the forest floor just for the taking. Their owners didn't care as they were lying in the fields—dead. I learned that Staff Sergeant Jack Goldman of B Company, 707th Tank Battalion would risk being killed by the Germans or our own guards and enter this forbidden forest under the cover of darkness to gather up these idle bedrolls and would distribute them to men that lost all their possessions as we did. It's men like Jack Goldman that help win wars, as he did this voluntarily. Jack did not surrender in the Bulge and returned to the company to fight across Germany to the end of the war.

We all squashed under the tank to rest; we were together again. Then a thought struck me, should the tank commander get orders to move out in a hurry we very well could be crushed, so I crawled out, rapped on the turret hatch to let the TC (tank commander) Sergeant Clough know that we were sleeping under his tank. About 11:30 PM Mac alerted us, as he heard someone calling our names. It was our company jeep driver looking to take us back to company headquarters, about a half mile at the most (which is like a 1,000 miles when you are that close to the enemy), and for a hot meal (C-rations), which is like a gourmet dinner when you haven't eaten in twenty-four hours.

After we ate, one of the cooks, Booger Bates, offered John and me his tent to sleep in for the night. Mac and Jim used another cook's tent alongside of ours. I laid in silence thinking of all the things we had gone through on this first day in battle, far more I thought than I ever dreamed I could endure, never dreaming this was just the beginning of our nightmare in the Hürtgen Forest; many more days were waiting to be endured. We were exhausted. All of us had Mike's blood on our hands, face and clothing; washing up was the furthest thing from our mind. This one part of combat we never learned about in training.

We had lost our tank commander, the first man in the platoon to be killed, and all our possessions; our tank combat loaded with bullets and grenades and we didn't fire a shot. During the night, Howard Thomsen and his crew undertook a daring task. They were to go into Vossenack and retrieve our tank, knowing the Germans had infiltrated back in the town and taken positions in it as well as around our tank. Somehow in the darkness, they were able to "steal" the tank from under their noses and bring it back to our company area!

We were up before daylight cleaning the inside of the tank—the ammo, guns, and instruments were covered with mud, flesh, and blood. The maintenance crew worked on the tracks, turret, gas, and oil. Except for the inability of the turret to be able to turn 360 degrees, the new 'Bea Wain' was ready to roll again. However, when we climbed out of the tank in daylight and faced one another—the first time actually, in twenty-four hours, our facial features had changed so much to cause Mac to remark, "Lord, do you guys look different!" I said wait till you get a chance to look at yourself, for he had changed also. Several days later, when Mac took his tanker helmet off, all the hair from his head was in it—he was bald!

It had been raining and all tanks leaked. Hoping to dry myself quickly and to be able to stand erect for a while during a "lull," I climbed out and stood behind the tank so that the exhaust dried my back. About a hundred feet away, Veryle was doing the same thing behind his tank, when he saw me and he came over to talk. Within a few minutes the shelling started again, one shell that struck a tree about 60ft. up did not explode but glanced down and was tumbling end over end towards us. We watched, dumbfounded. There were two fallen trees between us and the oncoming projectile which we thought would stop its progress like a loose football; the shell took an odd bounce and went over the trees! Luckily, once on our side, it stopped about 50ft. from us. It was a German 88 HE shell. It could have had a delayed fuse or it might not have hit the tree detonator first; anyway, it didn't go off. 1 said to Veryle, "I'm getting in the tank. If that 75mm goes off, we'll be blown to bits." Veryle corrected me and said, "That's an 88. Look, I'll show you." I didn't attempt to stop him, he picked up one of our empty 75mm casings lying by his feet and walked over to the 88, stood it up and tried to sleeve our smaller casing over it. He said to me, "Look dummy, it won't fit!"

The shell that killed the two men in the foxhole on our first night tore our tarpaulin to shreds, leaving only the four ropes tied around the trees. A few days later our tanks were in another location; Veryle again chanced a quick visit with me. While "chatting," we were peeling scales of dirt off that build up between your knuckles and fingers from not washing for long periods of time. It was quiet because the Americans had made a deal with a couple of Germans to stop all firing until all the dead and wounded were picked up from the woods and fields, as the bodies were getting covered with snow. Tankers stayed with their tanks as observers. The efficient Germans included mobile crematoriums in their combat hardware. Infantry men put aside their guns to be litter bearers, as a truce was in effect. This led to a feeling that, if it is that easy for Americans and Germans to get together and call a truce, this probably is the start of the end of the war. However, all German artillery men did not get the message, as we were to find out. Nearby was a Hitler Youth Camp made up of fragile wooden buildings, except for the kitchen, which was constructed of concrete. Here German youths would live and train to become soldiers. Veryle suggested we take advantage of the "lull" and check out these buildings.

We ran between the first two buildings. To our left was the kitchen and wooden buildings; on our right were the classrooms and the sleeping quarters.

I glanced in the first building, which was a classroom. I noticed that the area we were in Vossenack, Schmidt, Germeter, etc. was detailed on a sand table, topographically and distance-wise correct, with cardboard cutouts of American tanks and vehicles with a remarkable likeness. There was also a compass left on the table; they used it to simulate the distance of targets and I put it in my pocket. I still have it to this day. I saved it not as a souvenir but because it was so much better than the one issued to me. I stepped out to tell Veryle to come and look at the classroom; I noticed a tarpaulin lying a few feet away blown off a tank that had been hit before. I asked Veryle to help me fold it before it gets covered with snow and later help me carry it back to my tank. Veryle said, "Later, after we look at this place. Let's start with the kitchen." I started to argue with him; he simply reached over and grabbed my arm and yanked me into the kitchen. At that moment there was a tremendous explosion skidding me across the floor on my stomach. Veryle was roiled up like a wet sack of potatoes on the other side of the room. When we got our composure back, I said to Veryle, "You saved my life." He answered, "I saved my own." That was the extent of our conversation in regard to this, I didn't even tell the crew what happened because I knew what they'd say, "Now maybe you'll stay in your own tank."

The school room was reduced to splinters and the tarp to shreds. We realized while we talking about the tarp the shell was on its way to get us; it failed. In the kitchen were huge iron pots or caldrons suspended from a tripod; they still had cooked potatoes in them. Except for a few scrapes and bruises, we were okay and decided there was nothing in the remaining buildings we wanted to see. Actually we ran like hell back to our tanks. For the rest of the war I had no desire to pick up discarded tarpaulins, as I felt they really weren't necessary to operate a tank.

In training our communications officer Johnson was a stickler for radio procedure, use of codes, proper handling of inter-platoon messages, and fine details. That is until we got into combat in the Hürtgen and made a complete turnaround. He saw German tanks and so did we. They were far out of the range of our guns, but we were not out of range of their superior 88s. When his tank slid off the road into a ditch and a few German shells exploded near his tank, he started screaming for aerial support. "Tell them to bomb where my smoke shells hit. I'm 75yds. away from the only church in town," he kept broadcasting this message. There were disabled tanks all over the area abandoned by their crews; now some probably were occupied by Germans listening to every transmission.

When the planes (P47s or P51s?) arrived about two hours later, we were enveloped in smoke. The Krauts were smoking us, and our own planes were bombing our tanks and killing infantry men. We finally waved them off by exposing ourselves to cover our tanks with identification panels. The officer Lieutenant Johnson abandoned his tank and men, ran back to an aid station, where a medic classified him as suffering from battle trauma, hung a tag on his neck and shipped him back to a rest area. He never did come back to the company, but he probably got the Purple Heart and Bronze Star for heroism.

With all our setbacks, we persevered, as John Alyea would say, "Thanks to Mac, our invisible shield." I for one believe it existed. I should tell you this: Mac was annoyed with using an empty ammo box for a toilet inside the tank (we all did), so he climbed outside in spite of the exploding shells near us, then quickly and noisily climbed back in the tank, for he had gotten hit by a burst of shrapnel. We removed his torn clothes to find five or six puffy red welts on his chest. The force of the burst had expended itself when it reached his flesh and pieces of shrapnel had stuck between his skin and underwear! After that using an ammo box was just fine with him! Around the middle of November, we were relieved and were to go to a rest area. We would leave Germany and travel through Belgium and into Luxembourg.[7]

Howard Rallard, Company B, 110th Infantry

I was in the 110th Regiment of the 28th Division, and it was a cold but clear day on November 10, 1944, when our company commander ordered everyone to prepare to move out. The woods were covered with snow. In fact, it was the coldest winter that the Germans had ever recorded in history. It had been a fairly quiet night. The usual shots were heard during the night, but no patrols had been encountered. Our orders were to infiltrate the enemy lines, attack and destroy the effectiveness of two pillboxes, which are gun emplacements made of thick concrete walls dug into the mountainside.

These pillboxes were directly in front of our position and provided an opening in the Siegfried Line, that strong defensive line on the German border. We were in the Hürtgen Forest near Schmidt and Vossenack. The 28th Division, of which I was a part, had broken through that absolutely impenetrable Siegfried Line, which protected Germany from all its invaders from the West.

Our mission then was to obtain control of these pillboxes to make it possible for the American Army to continue its invasion into Germany properly. Our B Company, the 110th Regiment of the 28th Division, moved toward our assigned goal in the early afternoon. The sun was covered by clouds and the temperature was dropping. My squad, we moved toward our assigned positions. The plan was to move quietly through the German lines, reorganize, and attack the concrete bastion from the rear. The movement through the German line was quiet and uneventful.

In fact, only a few rifle shots were heard throughout the afternoon and every squad was soon in their designated positions. Because the snow was about a foot deep, it was a simple matter to dig in and wait for further orders. The unit with the fire shooting bazooka made the first attack and immediately silenced all activities in pillbox number one. However, the German soldiers in pillbox number two called for artillery and mortar fire and things got noisy and rough. We too had mortar support, which protected our flanks, but the mortar shells only bounced off the solid concrete walls of the pillbox. Our troops began to suffer heavy casualties while we were pinned down by the enemy.

Then the bazooka failed. Several attempts were made to send a runner back for new batteries, but each of these attempts failed. So it was decided to stay down, dig in, and wait for darkness. Several large logs and an abandoned American tank offered some protection for the diminished number of survivors of the heavy shell fire. There was no screaming or other sounds to indicate when a shell took a victim, but the still bodies told the tale. As darkness arrived and there was no moon, it was black dark.

We began to call and whisper to others to see who were still alive. Out of over 200 that started the attack that early afternoon, seven of us began our trek home. The soldier in charge was a sergeant and I was the next ranking soldier, a private first class. The sergeant took the lead carrying a Browning automatic rifle and I brought up the rear with the same kind of weapon. The going was rough and our hearts were in our throats as we tried to move back to our lines without a sound. We all shared the wonder of why God had spared us, but in single file we knew it would be a difficult night and every step would be fatal.

As we began to cross the road, which we knew we had to cross to move back to our lines, we heard German footsteps. They wore heavy, noisy boots. The first five of our group got across the road before the Germans got too close. The last two of us decided we better not try to cross the road before the enemy passed, so we waited in silence. The two German soldiers stopped right above us as though they had heard a sound.

We waited a long time, we smoked a cigarette, but finally tromped down the road. We waited until we could no longer hear their footsteps. Then the two of us made our way across the road to try to catch up with our buddies. It was so dark we dared not call out, so we decided to go on our own.

Almost crawling through the woods, we moved slowly but carefully in the direction of our friendly forces. No stars guided us, no landmarks to steer by, just dead reckoning in the grace of God. We never heard from our five fellow soldiers again. They were not taken prisoner to my knowledge and were never reported as returned to duty. My companion was Pedro, a Mexican fellow about my age who spoke only broken English. Together we wormed our way back up the hill. It was icy and suddenly Pedro slipped and began sliding down the icy hill. This brought shouts of halt from the enemy unfriendly forces nearby. The air was immediately full of German conversation as they searched for their enemy.

What to do? Where to hide? The thoughts whirled through my mind as I lay still as possible. The area was then teeming with German soldiers excitedly conversing, when suddenly Pedro was located. Screams of joy echoed through the night while the searchers continued for whoever else might be around. Little did I know there were only two of us. Should I try to shoot my way out? Where could I go? Could I get away? Will they start shooting before I can? Should I give up? The questions whizzed by as I tried to think. No one was speaking English and I spoke no German.

But that indecision came suddenly to an end as I felt a German boot in my back. I too had been discovered. More cries of glee, fast German conversation, and orders that indicate I should stand up and give up my weapon. At that moment I experienced the feeling of complete helplessness, knowing that for the immediate future I must relinquish the freedom I had so much cherished and had been willing to give my life for and learn to submit every moment to my captor's whim and to be willing to leave my future in the hands of God. I've learned to accept what is said in Philippines 4:11 [Not that I am speaking of being in need, for I have learned in whatever situation I am to be content]. I've learned to be content with whatever the circumstances.

I did think a lot during those moments about my parents. This was November 10. On November 4, 1944, my parents had celebrated their twenty-fifth wedding anniversary. Our dad had written that he was giving mother a new wristwatch from us boys. And there we were. My oldest brother aboard a troop ship bound for the China-Burma theater. My twin brother on the front line just a few miles from me later wounded in the Battle of the Bulge and me now listed as missing in action. What an exciting twenty-fifty anniversary for our parents.

Our B Company was composed of 250 men. Twelve of those on November 10 were assigned to guard duty at regimental headquarters and other soldiers were on company detail, cooks, clerks, and so forth. So they did not take part in our skirmish. At the end of that fruitful day, except those who did not participate, Pedro and I were all that was left of B Company, 110th Regiment of the 28th Infantry Division.[8]

William F. Train, 112th Infantry

My story of the Battle of the Bulge starts on November 2, 1944, in the Hürtgen Forest, southeast of Aachen, Germany, when the 28th Division replaced the 9th Division, which had made a salient into the German Siegfried Line. From these positions the 28th Division launched its main attack towards Schmidt, which overlooked the dams on the Roer River. The dams had to be captured to prevent their being destroyed by the Germans, thus flooding the lower reaches of the river, where the main attack would occur at a later date.

When the 28th Division attacked, it was the only unit in the First Army sector on the move. Hence, the Germans operating on interior lines were able to concentrate their forces for counterattacks against the early gains of the division. The 109th Infantry Regiment, commanded by Lieutenant Colonel Dan Strickler, attacked to the north toward the town of Hürtgen to secure the left flank of Division's sector. The 110th Infantry Regiment on the right, commanded by Colonel Ted Seeley, was confronted by enemy pill boxes as it attacked eastward. The main attack was made by the 112th infantry Regiment, commanded by Lieutenant Colonel Peterson. The 112th Infantry Regiment from positions in Germeter attacked along the Vossenack Ridge, crossed the Kall River, captured Kommerscheidt and pushed on to Schmidt. Unfortunately, the roads-end trails through the Kall River gorge were very steep and precarious, which severely limited the number and size of support weapons which reached Schmidt.

After occupying Schmidt for only a few days, the Germans counterattacked, decimated the units of the 112th infantry Regiment, and drove them back to Kommerscheidt, where they were practically surrounded. Lieutenant Colonel Peterson was wounded and evacuated. The regimental executive officer, Lieutenant Colonel James Lockett, en route to Kommerscheidt, was captured. A relief column, a Battalion of the 109th infantry Regiment, under control of the assistant division commander, Brigadier General George Davis, was misled into the sector of the 110th infantry and never reached the LD. Colonel G. M. Nelson was transferred from the 5th Armored Division and assigned command of the 112th Infantry Regiment to replace Lieutenant Colonel Peterson.

Accompanying a combat patrol, Colonel Nelson was able to reach the remnants or the 112th Infantry Regiment at Kommerscheidt and took command. After a brief reorganization, Colonel Nelson executed a rear-guard action and successfully withdrew the survivors of the 112th Infantry Regiment to bivouac areas west of Germeter, passing through the 2nd Ranger Battalion, commanded by Lieutenant Colonel James Rudder, which had been attached to the 28th Division. The regiment was directed to reorganize and prepare for recommitment in the division's sector. The 112th Infantry Regiment required 1,600 replacements after returning to our lines.

During the battle in the Hürtgen Forest, I was the executive officer, 109th Infantry Regiment. This regiment had been successful in securing positions along the road towards Hürtgen, although many enemy soldiers held a salient within our lines. After several days, during which most casualties seem to result from minefields and tree-bursts of German artillery fire, the 12th infantry Regiment, 4th Division, commanded by Colonel James Luckett (Lieutenant Colonel Joe Golden was the executive officer), arrived and was assigned to take over the positions of the 109th Infantry, which was displaced eastward on the north side of Vossenack Ridge and in the town of Vossenack.

About November 14, Colonel Strickler called me to his forward command post in a pillbox and assigned me the mission of inspecting the front lines along Vossenack ridge and ensuring that the troops were in position east of the town. He told me to remain in the command post until complete darkness and prepare my plan for this mission. While I was waiting for the time of my departure, Colonel Jesse Gibney arrived at the command post and told Colonel Strickler to call the division commander. From the conversation, it was apparent that Lieutenant Colonel Strickler was being relieved of command. Colonel Gibney, who had just recently joined the division, was assigned to command the 109th Infantry, and Lieutenant Colonel Strickler became the executive officer. I was then reassigned to command the 1st Battalion, 109th Infantry, which was deployed along the Vossenack Ridge and its eastern end beyond the town.

Upon assuming command of the 1st Battalion, I moved to the command post and got a briefing of the deployment of the Battalion. The area was receiving artillery fire, and I decided to visit all my units the next morning, although the previous battalion commander had been killed the day before along the ridge. Early the next morning, while on Vossenack Ridge, en route to inspecting the front line companies, I received a message which relieved me of command and transferred me immediately to the 112th Infantry Regiment as executive officer. I turned over command to the battalion executive officer and left to find the location of the 112th Infantry regimental command post, where I met Colonel Nelson.

The weather during our operations in Hürtgen Forest was miserably cold, with heavy rains, snow and wind. The mud, together with fallen tree limbs from artillery tree-bursts, made the forest trails practically impassable and the bivouac areas of the 112th Infantry Regiment were a quagmire.

Because the Regiment was supposed to be recommitted soon, Colonel Nelson and I were busy receiving replacements or men and equipment and providing inspiration to the badly demoralized units which had only about 25 percent effective strength on withdrawing from Schmidt. Many of the newly assigned officer replacements had been serving in anti-aircraft or anti-tank units which had become surplus due to air superiority, etc. Although they had received refresher training in infantry tactics, some officers were less than enthusiastic about joining the front-line infantry. A morale problem confronted us from the beginning of the reorganization.

The 112th Infantry Regiment was in the process of preparing itself for recommitment, when, on November 18, orders were received to move the 28th Division to the Luxembourg border in a piecemeal transfer with units of the 8th Infantry Division. The 112th Infantry Regiment initiated the transfer and we moved out of our bivouacs at night. The roads were icy and the weather cold. While there was some straying and delays, the 112th infantry Regiment relieved 8th Division units along a 6.5-mile front in the vicinity of Ouren, Germany the next day.[9]

German Army Veterans

NB: After translating from German, some minor edits were made to enhance readability.

Hubert Gees, Fusilier Battalion, 275th Infantry Division

About fifty-five years ago, in the early morning of October 7, 1944, we moved here on the winding path down into the valley of the Weiße Wehe [9.0-mile loop trail near Hürtgenwald] for a counterattack against the Americans, 39th Regiment, 9th US Infantry Division. Our 2nd Company attacked behind the bridge at point 312 on the western side of the valley in a southerly direction. We did not get to point 365, where we were to take the bunkers again, but after about 1,000m in front of a small tributary of the Weiße Wehe, we came to rest in the defensive fire of the American infantry supported by grenade launchers and artillery. The sad balance of the first day: more than a third of our combat strength of 100 soldiers, thirty-five losses due to wounding and death. Among the wounded was also my commanding officer, Lieutenant Tatze, among the dead my platoon leader [*Kompanietruppführer*], Unteroffizier Zeppenfeld. Together with him, I had shared our resting quarters with the farmer Schmitz, on the Albert Leo Schlageter Highway 92 in Gürzenich, on the days before. He rests today here at the Hürtgen military cemetery in grave number 584. After two to three days, Lieutenant Lengfeld took over our 2nd company.

On the afternoon of October 7, we had retreated to a swath and dug in there. On October 8, two armored vehicles, coming over a slight hilltop, pushed us in the back. A courageous soldier eliminated both with the bazooka. On October 9 our company withdrew once more. About 300m south of the bridge, at point 312, a contiguous front was hastily built from the Uferstraße in a northwesterly direction. We had to get into the ground quickly, because we suffered the greatest losses due to tree screens. All available entrenchment equipment such as saws, axes, pickaxes and shovels were in the front line.

We of the company troop had to laboriously work our way into the slate rock into the depths with our small flat spades.

Up to the main road to Germeter, all hell broke loose for days. Uninterrupted infantry, artillery, and tank fire. The valley resounded in reverberation. In the area of the bridge at point 312, we were regularly hit by artillery fire. Where the Weiße Wehe comes very close to the Uferstraße, I wrote to my relatives on October 17: "I've been really lucky that I've gotten away with my skin intact so far. Just pray that this happiness will continue to be with me—How nice it could be if one could go about one's work at home in peace and quiet."

On October 18–19 we moved to the east side of the Wehe-Bach. The two other companies of the battalion joined the Germets stream up to the Wittscheidt sawmill. Again we had to hurriedly drive new holes in the slate rock with our primitive children's spade. At noon, the first artillery salvo hit us at the Pferdesiefen Bach. Bullet frenzy and deafening explosions in the treetops above us were one. Instinctively, we lay in our still shallow holes in the ground. Strong-smelling powder steam lay over us. A paramedic had been hit in the back by a fist-sized shrapnel. He did not survive. Was that, sarcastically asked, the most beautiful death in the field? So we boys had been taught to sing in patriotic songs. But not everyone hit was lucky enough to end so short and painless.

At the beginning of darkness, an artillery volley hit us again, a splinter penetrated the foot of our stretcher. Late in the evening, a shrapnel tore off a lower leg bone of the comrade from the company command group [*Kompanietrupp*], who was lying next to me in the hole in the ground. He died of an embolism in the morning of the next day, as a paramedic from the first aid station on Arnsberger Weg told me. An Unteroffizier did not return from the scouting party—shot in the stomach. Hardly a day without losses.

But the front area in the direction of Deadman's Moor was constantly circling an American reconnaissance aircraft, called "crow" by us. The garrison directed the artillery fire at everything that could be seen on the paths and aisles. Our horse-drawn supply vehicle was hit hard in those days up on the Ahrensberger Weg. With leaflets and loudspeakers, the Americans urged us to defect. Overflow? No, had we not sworn allegiance to the fatherland? However, the holes in the ground of about twenty replacement soldiers, who had been assigned to our company shortly before, we found empty the next morning. They were soldiers of the so-called "People's List 3," more Polish than German.

At the end of October, there was another change of position: from the right wing in the valley to the left wing of the Fusilier Battalion, up here adjacent to the main road, at the edge of the forest in front of the Wittscheidt sawmill, which the Americans had firmly in their hands with the main road via Germeter-Richelskaul-Raffelsbrand-Peterberg after fierce fighting since mid-October.

On the morning of November 2 (All Souls' Day), a huge barrage (12,000 shells according to US literature) broke out on our positions. Earth and air shook for an hour. The 109th Regiment of the 28th US Infantry Division collapsed to the north. We lost our third move—All telephone and radio connections had failed. So our artillery observers and I were ordered to report the burglary and situation to the battalion as quickly as possible.

We hurried along the often tattered telephone cable and stood barely 500 meters from here, stepping onto the aisle leading from here to the top of the forest, suddenly, barely twenty paces in front, a group of Americans advancing with rifles ready to fire. In the moment of shock, even before the GIs had raised their rifles, the two of us had jumped back into the forest. We ran for our lives. The Unteroffizier screamed staggering. He had been hit by the furiously sent fire. Up and on, only when we approached our positions again, did we take a closer look at his shot elbow joint. We noticed a heavily bleeding Unteroffizier at that moment.

In the early afternoon of November 2, the 1st Battalion, 109th Infantry Regiment occupied the edge of the forest in front of Hürtgen, with the forester's lodge there, and on November 3, across the main road there, a small box-shaped forest. In the afternoon of November 2, we immediately angled our position to the Wilde Sau minefield, which had already been laid behind us on the western side of the road. In front of the mine-free alley, which led here to today's cemetery grounds, a machine gun secured to the rear. We held this position until November 20.

On November 3, our troop command threw the 116th Panzer Division (greyhounds) into the torn front between Schmidt and Hürtgen. On November 4, fiercely led counterattacks began. In the area of Vossenack-Schmidt, fierce fighting raged, accompanied by heavy artillery fire and tank fire. The US air force constantly intervened in the ground fighting. Thank God the bad weather (fog) also hindered the aircraft mission on various days.

At Hürtgen counterattacks against the front arc of the 109th Infantry Regiment began as early as November 3. This front sector of the 109th Infantry Regiment was taken over by the 12th Regiment of the 4th US Infantry Division. From November 7–8, with Lieutenant Lengfeld, a reconnaissance party went to an outpost position, which, thank God, had not yet been reoccupied. At noon on the 10th of November, our artillery opened with half an hour heavy barrage on the Americans. Southwest of Hürtgen a new attempt to throw back the enemy by all available means was made. After days of heavy fighting, this forest peak fell back into our hands on November 13–14, after the forester's lodge had changed hands there several times. In this regard, I quote from war diaries of some units of the 116th Panzer Division:

"November 10 morning—The Artillery Regiment 275, 1020 and the Panzer Artillery Regiment 146 put the strongest drum fire on the room to be cleared in a twenty-five-minute preparatory fire."

"November 10 evening—Southern shock group penetrated up to half in the forest area. Meets hard resistance, stays put. The northern shock group has reached a forest lodge near Hürtgen and then turned north. In the section there are three fresh battalions. Parts of it are cut off in the forest area and in fierce fighting with their own infantry. Weather—driving snow, rain."

"November 11—Heavy fighting in the area southwest of Hürtgen. Small group of enemies included, but I'm too weak to destroy them. The exhaustion of the troops is very great, as are the absences. Very bad weather; the men have been lying outside in the wet for days."

During the night of November 12, the Americans broke through the newly formed Heerestruppen Kampfgruppe at the bend of the road and reinforced its broken parts by two more companies. The forester's lodge near Hürtgen was lost once again. At around 9:00 AM, the situation was restored in a counterattack with the help of the assault guns of the Panzenjägerabteilung 228.

The battles swayed back and forth in uninterrupted severity. It rains, wet wisps of fog or snow clouds sweep over the puddle-ridden, soggy land. Wading in the mud and water, lying and fighting, the German soldiers are close to complete physical exhaustion. The reported combat strengths are dropping alarmingly. The artillery battle rolls uninterruptedly. In the forest itself, it looks great. The trees lie through the constant fire cross and across each other, and the paths are completely soaked. Everywhere the water is feet high. No rest for over a week and no dry thread on my body; because it rains all the time. Fog is also constantly present. It is a bush war, man against man with tremendous efforts for the individual men. The infantry of the division is completely finished. There are only very few German soldiers. Even men who can no longer be brought forward with a pistol are also there.

On November 13, the attack against the encircled Americans was resumed. The mass of Americans escaped to their own lines. Only twenty-seven prisoners were brought in. The front line now ran from the western edge of Jagen 181 unit on the west bank of the Weiße Wehe stream to the northwest corner of the Wilde Sau minefield. On the evening of November 13, General Field Marshall Model visited the staff of the 116th Panzer Division in the bunker near Grosshau. Replacements for the division were finally ordered. It is also high time, as was very battered and exhausted.

On November 10–11, we left our positions south of the Wilde Sau minefield to reconnaissance in a westerly direction. After crossing the first aisle, we suddenly came across an American scouting party in the low undergrowth. The command-like "Hold" of a GI made me instinctively duck. I didn't see anything of the enemy, "You or I": here our leader decided the question for himself—and thus also for the three of us behind him—by perhaps only a fraction of a second—Hard, these memories, you can't get rid of them in life.

Two of our machine gunners from the machine gun securing the mine-free alley in the rear were shot in the head by American snipers who had infiltrated us on the east side of the road. But we had even more enemies: the vermin—lice! For weeks now, without being able to wash ourselves and change our underwear, we had been living in the damp puddles of earth. When I discovered a white band of nits/lice eggs on the inner hem of my Wehrmacht sweater, I threw away the sweater without further ado, although I would have urgently needed a second one because of the wet and cold weather. In my last letter from the front, on November 11, I wrote of a severe cold and "we still have heavy fighting here, but it seems that the matter will soon be resolved." On November 12, after the soldiers of the 12th US Infantry Regiment had retaken the forester/hunting lodge Hürtgen at night and lost it again in the morning, our company was hit by a heavy blow.

In the early morning, an apparently seriously wounded American called for help. It was located in the middle of the Wilde Sau minefield on the edge of the embankment of the eastbound side of the road in no man's land. My commanding officer, Lieutenant Lengfeld, sent me to the rear with the instruction, if paramedics would come to rescue the seriously wounded man, not to use a weapon. Since the heartbreaking cries for help continued after hours, Lieutenant Lengfeld ordered our paramedics to form a rescue team.

It may have been around 10:30 AM that Lieutenant Lengfeld was walking at the head of the rescue team on our side of the road in the direction of the minefield Wilde Sau. The road itself was secured with anti-tank mines, the location of which was relatively easy to see. Just as Lieutenant Lengfeld was about to cross the road at the level of the severely wounded American, a detonating anti-personnel mine pulled him to the ground. In a hurry, he was carried back to our company command post to provide first aid. Two bullet-sized holes in the back suggested serious internal injuries.

He groaned in severe pain. Under the leadership of a slightly injured noncommissioned officer, he was immediately carried back to the first-aid station Lukas Mühle. In the evening he succumbed to his fatal injuries on the main first aid station in Froitzheim. He has his final resting place today in grave no. 38 in Düren-Fölsdorf.

With Lieutenant Lengfeld, I had lost my best superior. He had meant a lot to me in the difficult weeks behind us and had given me inner strength. He was an exemplary company commander who never demanded more from us than he himself was prepared to give. Walking with him at the head, I was in a scouting party up to the American outpost positions. The American explosive ammunition of the infantry with a bright-whipping bang on the trees gave us the impression that the enemy had broken in.

On November 14, we established the connection to the neighbor to the north here on the site of today's Hürtgen military cemetery. The 12th US Regiment had retreated from the roadside about 300m to the northwest corner of the Wilde Sau minefield. The retreat had been hasty. Weapons, machine guns, bazookas and also dead people had to be left behind. Our interest was primarily in the food left behind in cans and packages, C- and K-rations, which had usually been inserted at the inner edge of the hole cover.

Lieutenant Heer took over our company, which was still just under forty men strong. On November 16, the day of the major attack of the Americans on a broad front from Gelsenkirchen to Vossenack, where Düren was reduced to rubble and ashes by bombers in clear skies, I was once again in the deserted positions to fetch supplies of C- and K-rations.

At noon on November 17, we carried back a dead man through the mine-free alley. My comrade Alfons Bösl took a few steps ahead. He showed us the safest way through the thicket of crisscross tree remains. Suddenly, we were startled by the nearby detonation of an anti-personnel mine. Comrade Bösl lay bent over a tattered treetop. No more moans and no more breath—finally dead. He is buried today in grave no. 36 in Vossenack.

Even before we had reached our destination, the forester's lodge Hürtgen, in the early afternoon, we were attacked by heavy artillery fire from the Americans on the grounds of today's military cemetery. Late bloomers only crashed after a dull earth impact and whirled up earth, which pattered down on us like rain. Seeking shelter, the four of us jumped into a close, large shell crater and crouched tightly on the ground in front of the bursting shells.

After a few seconds, I saw an American man right next to me. Soldiers, stretched out on the embankment of the earth crater, dead, as his deathly pale face made me recognize. He stared with wide open eyes at the sky above Hürtgen. I was not indifferent to this dead man. What thoughts must have moved him at the hour of his death? Relatives?—Home?—Where in the vast America will a mother mourn him? I thought. How would my mother weep for me if the same fate befell me? Thoughts and questions that moved me at such a moment.

I became quite aware of the senselessness of killing each other. Why, why did we fight each other here? This soldier had braced himself against death until his last breath. This was told to me by his expressive face, with stern features that still seemed alive. His open mouth seemed to have exclaimed something else. Alone in foreign soil, he had ultimately lost the fight against death. But wasn't there also hope in his face? This dead man from the 12th Regiment has always remained very close to me. I have never forgotten his face in death. Remembrance teaches me to pray for the fallen of the Hürtgenwald. My Christian faith gives me the hope that one day in eternity I will be able to reach out to him for reconciliation.

The war soon caught up with us again. Arriving in the cellar of the forester's house, we were again attacked by heavy artillery fire. Bright reddish clouds of phosphorus grenades darkened the cellars. From the front line, about 300m away, fan fire began. After a short time, five to six prisoners were hurriedly brought to the forester's lodge. A GI wounded in the back received medical care; then the group was brought back to Hürtgen in a hurry.

North of the Wilde Sau minefield, the attack had been repelled. On the other hand, a unit of the 12th US Regiment had broken through to the main road south of the minefield. The remnants of our company (only eighteen soldiers left) had formed a small bridgehead in front of the mine-free alley.

At nightfall, the neighboring company fired from the east side in front into our positions at the edge of the forest. That was the agreed signal for us to advance. Proceeding with extreme concentration, I reached a shelter with my comrade Brand, which belonged to a machine gun position. Entrance curtain torn in advance and illuminated with the pocket lance—were one, executed in a flash. But we didn't have to shout, "Hands up." The dugout was empty. The Americans, a shocked troop, had retreated to their own lines, taking their prisoners with them. At our machine gun position alone, which I now took over with comrade Brand, there were three dead; among them was our leader who had been ordered to the front ten days earlier as an officer candidate.

We set up the position, improved the camouflage. Engineers placed mines in the evening in the darkness about 50m in front of our positions in the forest, but I waited in vain for their detonation the next morning at around 9:00 AM. At 8:00 AM I had relieved my comrade in the machine gun stand. Peeking under a tree top, I suddenly saw two GIs on the meandering path towards our machine gun position. Was it my trust in the laid out anti-personnel mines?—Did the meeting of the day before with the dead GI in the shell crater still have an effect on me that I instinctively reached for my smallest weapon, an egg hand grenade? When the two, a machine gun crew, were only about 30m away from me, I opened fire with the egg hand grenade. Comrade Brand jumped from the side dugout to me in the position and all the machine guns rattled off. The artillery also intervened to provide support.

Heavy shells hit not only close to our positions, but also into our positions. A dead man from the previous day, lying in front of the side shelter, was hit again. Later we found only his lower body. This shell, which burst only 3–4m from our position, after the shortest bullet frenzy with a deafening bang, left only a bare stump from the tree next to our hole in the ground. Brand and I had instinctively thrown ourselves to the bottom at lightning speed. My eardrum had been damaged, and it was not until late in the evening that I gradually regained my hearing.

The captured American, a machine gunner testified that the troops had wanted to advance further across the main road reached the day before. About two to three days later, one of our men hurried back from the corridor to the neighboring company on the eastward side of the street: "Americans are standing there in front of the command post!" How could that be? We had not heard any noise of battle. Were they perhaps, as I read a few years ago, GIs from the 1st Battalion of the 109th Infantry Regiment, who had infiltrated north of Vossenack behind the German front lines and which could never really be brought under control from our side?

Our situation on the western side of the road had now become even more difficult. The mine-free alley of the Wild Sau was only left as the last rear connection. Our company troop leader and I received orders to make contact with the battalion on the east side via Hürtgen. When the two of us were still at a medical station in Hürtgen, the remnants of our company were already following suit. It was said that the unit north of the minefield would take over our section to the main road.

With about twelve men left, we reached the battalion command post not far from the Bosselbach around noon. We must have been seen,for there we were greeted by a fierce grenade launcher overfall [attack]. After a sharp command, we squeezed into the dugouts there. A comrade's skull had been torn wide open. His brain evaporated in the damp cold November air. We were integrated into the unit at the eastern edge of the forest of the valley pasture on the Bosselbach. The situation there was confusing on both sides. On the left wing, a good 500m from the lower village of Vossenack, we had no connection to a neighboring unit. There, too, we still had losses due to grenade launchers. A slightly wounded sergeant said goodbye to us old comrades with the words: "If we were still a company, I would come back from the first-aid station, but as it is... Farewell!"

In the night of November 27, our unit moved to the village of Hürtgen. As soon as we arrived, via a side path at the church, heavy artillery fire let us take full cover at dawn. With four men from the old 2nd Company, all born in 1926, we ended up in the cellar of the Hürtgen forestry office, where we were taken prisoner in the morning of the next day.

Hürtgen was and remained in American hands when the noise of fighting at the last houses in the direction of Kleinhau died down in the afternoon. The final phase had concluded a week earlier, following the start of the 8th U.S. Infantry Division's insertion. Supported by strong tank forces, they advanced here on the main road from the direction of Wittscheidt. Fighter-bombers (Thunderbolts), as we could see well from Bosselbach, 1.5km away, repeatedly intervened in the ground fighting; their on-board guns hammered on the last defenders of the Waldspitze here. It was our great luck not to be in position there anymore. Fate and God's providence led us here down into the valley into captivity: seven men—the rest of the 2nd company, Füsilier Battalion 275.[10]

August Güvert, 116th Panzer Division

On November 3, 1944, we were loaded in Wegberg and arrived on November 4, 1944—I think it was a Saturday—via Nideggen to Schmidt at 9:00 AM. In the forest in front of Schmidt we were on standby. The tanks were serviced again. There was food and additional tank food. "Don't eat old things right away," our tank commander Sergeant Dolezal said to us. The others followed his advice. But I ate it all. "What good is the best food if I'm dead and can't eat it anymore!" were my thoughts. We heard the noise of battle in Schmidt, which reached our ears ominously. Everyone was near the vehicle. Again and again, the possibilities of surviving if the tank was to be hit were thought through in their minds.

I withdrew a little from the others, took my rosary, which I always carried with me, and prayed. Today I don't remember what laws I prayed. In any case, this prayer did me good, and I felt in God's hands. At 2:00 PM the order came: "Driver march! Attack on Schmidt!" Sergeant Dolezal's tank had to drive at the front; I drove with my tank past Schmidt on the right towards Kommerscheidt.

After a short time we reached the first houses. [August Güvert does not remember exactly where this was. It was probably the Haas house opposite the pond in Kommerscheidt, perhaps another one in this part of Kommerscheidt.] Then, suddenly, the order came: "Stop! Reset!" We had probably already driven too far ahead. The commander then ordered: "Bubi, [as August Güvert was called by Sergeant Dolezal] back immediately! Tower at six o'clock!" Tower at six o'clock means: The cannon points backwards. This was like a death sentence for me. When the tower is at six o'clock, the driver can no longer get out because the "backpack" on the tower protrudes over the driver's hatch, blocking his way out.

We had just started to reset when a tremor ran through my tank. The shell of an American tank had hit my vehicle in the turret. The hit was so unfortunate that Commander Dolezal and also the gunner were killed instantly. The loader and the radio operator were wounded. Without my knowing this, both left the tank. [Lieutenant Fleig, commanding the US tank, was surprised that the crew immediately abandoned the vehicle after it was hit by an HE shell. It was his first shot of the day, following the strenuous drive from Vossenack along the Kall Trail, and it resulted in an immediate direct hit.] I didn't notice any of this down in the tank. I only heard in the headphones: "The sergeant is dead!" However, there was a noncommissioned officer in the tank; the commander was Sergeant Dolezal. I tried to turn the tank, but I got a hit from the front. He penetrated the radio operator, who fortunately had already gotten out. The radios next to me kept the splinters from the grenade; I only got a small splinter in the right eyebrow. I was lucky there. When I hit it, my hatch flew away. I didn't think twice and climbed after it.

At first, I took cover behind the tank. Then I noticed a garden gate to my left. I crawled towards it and wanted to go through it to get away from my vehicle. But as soon as I was out, behind the tank, the bullets whistled around me. The Americans took me under fire. Immediately I took cover behind the tank again. But now I noticed that it was burning. Since there was still enough ammunition in the tank, it could explode at any moment. I now looked to the right and saw the entrance to a chicken coop. Next to the tank lay my cap, which I picked up, then I jumped into the chicken run and then into the house. The house was already completely destroyed.

After a short time I saw Sergeant Pichler, who was also on his way back with his tank. He waved to me to jump on his tank. This I did, and here I met my loader and my radio operator again. Both were wounded, just like me, but we were still able to cling to the armor of comrade Pichler. I don't remember how far and how long I was on the tank. But it was pure hell. Only now did I realize what a fire spell is performed on a tank. With rifles, machine guns, rifle grenades and PAK—with everything the Americans had at their disposal—our tank was shot at. I could literally see the shells whizzing through the air. We heard their eerie and deadly whistling and rushing, and we pressed ourselves against the cold steel as if it could save our lives. We saw the fountains of dirt shoot up when the shells exploded, the splinters howled over us. Fortunately, we were not hit.

After some time I noticed a bunker; I jumped off the tank and ran towards the bunker, opened the door and went in: "Come in my boy and shut the door!" So I was welcomed by Americans who had occupied the bunker and had waited for and survived the attack of the Germans. They offered me space, dressed my wound on my right forehead, gave me a cigarette, which I smoked with them. Sometime later, in the bunker, we heard the sound of a tank, the hum of the engine and the rattle of the chains. I said goodbye to the Americans, who let me outside without further ado.

With this tank I then drove back to Schmidt. There I met the tanks of Lieutenant Adams; I think there were three tanks. Now we first provided makeshift care for the wounded and then took them away. At the church I saw an assault gun standing on a meadow next to the road. Only one man of the crew was left. The driver was dead. Next to the assault gun lay five wounded comrades. It was very difficult to get these people onto the assault gun, but with mutual help we finally succeeded. Then I drove off with the wounded in the direction of Harscheidt. There was a military hospital in the forest. Here I brought the wounded woman. On the way, however, one had bled to death, as there was no paramedic to be found far and wide, and we could not help.[11]

Erwin Kreßmann, Tank Destroyer Division 519

I was captain and head of the 1st company of Panzenjägerabteilung 519. We were corps troops. In October 1944 we were subordinated to the 116 Panzer Division and transferred to the Western Front, after we had been reorganized at the MILAU military training area and equipped with tank destroyers [*Jagdpanther*]. My company had fourteen tank destroyers at that time.

The 2nd and 3rd companies were equipped with Sturmgeschütz III assault gun (7.5cm combat vehicle gun). Our previous commander, Knight's Cross-bearer Lieutenant Colonel Hoppe, had been transferred to the 33rd Tank Regiment at the beginning of October. Until the arrival of the new commander, Major Rosenthal, the department was led by me as the longest-serving company commander. The new department commander was transferred to us at the end of October. It was the announced Major Rosenthal. I don't know much about him. He defected to the Americans shortly before the Battle of the Bulge.

We had been in the training area since October 26, as a reserve of the Seventh Army. Until then, we had been deployed in the Aachen combat area in the area of Stolberg and Würselen (as corps troops we were always divided). We were only deployed twice during the entire war (the first time was with Schmidt and the second time during the Battle of the Bulge). We moved by chain from training to Nideggen, where we arrived on the afternoon of November 3 (on that day Schmidt had been taken by the Americans). The whole detachment moved into the small town, and our vehicles, which were of considerable size, were parked and camouflaged between the houses. Our stay was not supposed to last long anyway. I immediately started exploring for a counterattack, as I wanted to take advantage of the brightness for that.

We rolled early on November 4 from Nideggen towards Harscheidt, where we were to establish contact with the 1st Battalion of Grenadier Regiment 1055 of the 89th Infantry Division until 6:30 AM. This unit had already been lying at the edge of the forest about 1,000m northeast of Harscheidt since the evening of November 3 and sealed off there. It was to be feared that the Americans would continue their attack in the direction of the nearby Rur Dam after reinforcements had arrived. This intention was to be thwarted by a counterattack by our 89th Infantry Division. The commander of this division was General Bruns.

The attack began at 8:00 AM. We attacked on the left side of the road to Schmidt and unfolded as soon as we came into somewhat more open terrain. The attack progressed well.

I had ordered my crews to immediately and ruthlessly use the weapon and fire as much as the barrels would allow. When attacking a town held by enemy infantry, there may be an anti-tank gun around every corner or enemy close-range squads lurking. Besides, we didn't know if the Americans had tanks. So I wanted to intimidate the enemy infantry and have them fight without regard to ammunition, as our heavy and cumbersome Jagdpanther were very vulnerable to them. A big advantage we had over the Americans was the long range of our 8.8cm guns, and we wanted to take full advantage of that. Of course, we would also shoot at individual foxholes if we had recognized American soldiers in them.

At about 11:00 AM, their own forces had succeeded in taking Schmidt to the church. One of my commanders, a noncommissioned officer who wore the German Cross in gold, but whose name I have forgotten, hopped an enemy command post in the course of this attack; I believe it was a battalion command post. I still remember this noncommissioned officer very well. He was not to be disturbed by anything or anyone. Even in battle, he was calm personified, and his crew liked him and trusted him very much. The way he had taken the command post was typical of him. He had calmly driven slowly towards the house in which the command post was set up, had put the muzzle of his cannon against the door and thus knocked. The Americans then showed a white flag and surrendered. The Americans had occupied the town with a complete battalion, and their resistance was getting stronger and stronger. When we reached a hill at the north exit of Schmidt around noon, we couldn't go any further at first.

About one hour later we received the order to continue the attack towards Kommerscheidt at 2:00 PM. I thought I could not believe my ears because we were to attack in broad daylight with strong enemy artillery superiority and good visibility, which could make the use of enemy fighter-bombers possible at any time. In addition, we were supposed to drive over a front slope from Schmidt in the direction of Kommerscheidt. But it stayed that way. We fired from the hill on which we were standing into Kommerscheidt and used the same tactics as in the morning.

Past us, our own tanks attacked into the village without infantry support. We received reports that the first American tanks had been seen in Kommerscheidt and that a tank battle was developing in the village. We were then deployed to support our own tanks and rolled down the slope under mutual protection. Four of my tank destroyers stuck to the ground and two were shot down. On the evening of November 4, Kommerscheidt had not been taken and the attack was stopped. The attacking German forces had high losses of tanks.

As I was sitting on a meadow on the back slope of the hill north of Schmidt on my tent track in the evening sun, the commander appeared. As far as the attack in the afternoon had gone pretty much exactly as I had feared, I reported to him, somewhat resignedly, that my company was no longer ready for action due to the failures. The commander, however, did not accept my report, shooed me up, kicked me in the buttocks, and ordered me to get my vehicle afloat again—personally. After dark, I managed to recover all six tank destroyers by dawn by using the Bergepanther [recovery vehicle based on the chassis of the Panther tank] and the 18-ton tractors.

On November 5 we confined ourselves to shelling the Americans in Kommerscheidt and Vossenack with our long-range guns. On November 6, all tank forces were combined into a combat group and the further attack on Kommerscheidt was ordered for November 7. My company was also planned in the main focus, since, on the one hand, we were corps troops, i.e. "fire brigade," and on the other hand this company had the heaviest vehicles at its disposal.

I planned the positions of my trains and vehicles and recorded this on a sketch that I made on a sheet of white DIN A4. I assigned a position to each individual vehicle, which I assigned numbers to, divided according to platoons, and gave corresponding alternating positions the designation of left or right.

The first vehicle of the 1st platoon, for example, had the position 1.1 and the alternating positions 1.1-left or -right. This had proven itself many times in Russia and I could know at any time where my fighters were. I put the sketch on the sheet of paper in a cellophane sleeve so that it wouldn't soften in the rain and put it on a shelf in front of my commander's seat.

The attack began on November 7 in the morning while it was still dark. My company attacked with twelve tank destroyers. We were to smash the Americans once and for all in cooperation with our infantry and retake Kommerscheidt. As we approached the village, we received artillery fire from the opposite slope, from Vossenack. After a few hundred meters, I came across an open mine barrier with my tank destroyers, which had to be bypassed. The barrier ran across a meadow in front of us and also crossed a path. Since I did not know whether mines were still buried in the meadow, and we could not lose any time because of the shelling, I decided to disembark and pull the mines away with my hands on the way in order to let my tanks pass through this alley. This he did. In the course of the attack, my company managed to destroy eight enemy battle tanks or tank destroyers, two of which I shot down myself. After the shooting down of the two Sherman-type tanks, I saw another disappear behind a house wall. He was only half visible, as he was reversing and obviously wanted to retreat. I [identified the target aloud to the crew] and, after the loader had given the ready signal, gave the order to fire. When the electric firing was activated, however, no shot was fired. Another attempt to fire the cannon also failed. I ordered the emergency firing to be activated, but even with this measure, we did not get the cannon to fire.

I looked for the fault and found out that the last time it was fired, the cellophane sleeve in which my mission sketch was located had slipped off the shelf because of the vibration when the cannon was fired and got into the return track. During the cannon's advance, it had been guided forward and melted due to the heat generated during firing. So we were defenseless at that moment. I immediately gave the order to swerve backwards and ordered the hunters standing near me by radio to cover our deviation and close the gap that had arisen. We retreated into a depression behind us and tried to repair the damage there under cover of the terrain. However, we did not succeed because the melted plastic shell had literally glued the cannon. I looked for a building where the gun of the tank destroyer could be placed against it and pushed back to open the gun cradle. I hoped that by the resistance of the wall the gun would be pushed back into the interior of the tank and thus the breech would be freed.

The first farmhouse near us had walls made only of clay. When we drove our tank with the muzzle of the cannon against the wall and slowly accelerated, the soft clay wall gave way and collapsed. The same happened to us at a second house, which was made of half-timbering, but whose clay filling also did not withstand the pressure of our Panther. So it was not possible to start with the houses here in the village.

Nearby, at a bend in the road into a hollow, there was a pond, around which stood some mighty willows. I chose the thickest of them, which could easily be embraced by two men. The strongest part of such a tree is where the trunk ends and the thin branches of the crown begin. There we put the muzzle of the cannon and drove slowly against the tree. However, due to the soft soil, the roots came loose from the earth and the tree toppled over. When it was completely on the ground, I noticed that the roots still held the willow very well. We tried our luck, continued to press the cannon against the tree and the hoped-for finally happened. Thanks to the high weight of the tree and the strength of the roots, the tree did not roll away. The counterpressure was enough to push the cannon back a bit and open the cradle a crack. I fished the plastic cover out of the breech raceway with fingertips and the mounting lever and then locked the gun again. The contact light for the electric firing was lit and our cannon was clear again. I ordered the grenade in the breech to be fired to see if the gun was working again.

Since it was necessary to catch up with the comrades, who had already attacked further, we were in a hurry. Our repair had cost us at least half an hour. Without looking backwards, I gave the driver the order to back up, so that we could drive out of the soggy trough. When the tank had moved back a bit, there was suddenly a huge jolt. I was thrown backwards in my commander's hatch and suddenly saw only cloudy skies. What had happened?

In our effort to hurry up and take part in the battle again, we had driven backwards into the cesspool of one of the farms. The tank had tipped over the stern and was now stuck in the pit at an acute angle with its bow pointing steeply into the sky. The engine was still running and it dived through the red-hot radiator ridges into the engine compartment. It stank to high heaven! There was a danger that our engine would drown and there would be a water hammer (or slurry) that would have inevitably destroyed our tank. But the shot was still stuck in the barrel and I still didn't know if our cannon was ready for battle again. We aimed the gun barrel at the highest elevation and fired a test shot. The gunner literally chased the grenade into the blue [meaning, it traveled so high and far that the gunner had to follow it visually into the sky].

The cannon worked again and now it was time to get the tank afloat again. Before I had embarked on an officer's career, I had been trained as a driving instructor on wheeled and tracked vehicles. The knowledge of the technical behavior of vehicles benefited me in this situation. I talked to my driver reassuringly and let him drive out of the pit very slowly but with a powerful gear ratio in second gear. If we had tried to drive out of the pit in first gear, the rapid movement of the tank tracks would have crushed the enclosure of the cesspool and we would not have been able to get out. We now hurried to catch up with our comrades, who were of course much further ahead. When we reached them deep in the village, the battle was already over. With great joy and relief I found that we had not suffered any losses in this battle. The two tanks shot down were returned to us after they had been repaired in the next few days.

For the deployment and success of my company in Schmidt and Kommerscheidt, a few days later I was nominated for the Knight's Cross, which was awarded to me on December 9, 1944, for the decisive act of the battle. However, I did not receive the award itself until January 1945.

On September 9, 2004, sixty years after the Battle of Kommerscheidt, I met a former member of the 89th Infantry Division Mr. Fritz Tillmanns at a veterans' meeting in Schmidt. He told me that he had been lying with his 1st Battalion Grenadier Regiment 1056 at Gerstenhof on November 7 and had observed the battle from a distance. He and his comrades watched in fascination as the American tanks were shot down by us one after the other and more and more columns of smoke formed at Kommerscheidt. They drew each other's attention to the new shots ("There, look, another one!") However, a Sherman escaped under artillery fire and disappeared behind the forest backdrop. He was then found a few days later by soldiers of his regiment standing at the edge of the forest. He would have thrown both chains in his quick escape.[12]

Harro Kunst, 1st Artillery Regiment 189, with the 89th Infantry Division

Nideggen and the Kall Valley, as well as the Eifel plateaus from there to the west to the Belgian border into the Eupen region, with their wild forests and gorges, have always been a landscape of austere and beautiful character and a popular local hiking area for the people of Aachen, Düren, and Cologne. Dense forestation of the often canyon-like slopes and the undulating plateaus, loneliness, and poor agriculture gave the area its unique character in peacetime.

In 1944, World War II came in this country and devastated it through a material battle of hitherto unknown artillery firepower and fire density in a week-long trench warfare. The destruction had not completely disappeared even ten years later, and traces of the infantry fighting were still found effortlessly forty years later. Today, the villages are heavily populated by emigrated city dwellers [people who had left urban areas to settle elsewhere, usually in rural areas or smaller towns] and ever-increasing tourism, camping, and water sports, and a never-ending motor traffic of cars and trucks from Aachen and the Rhenish industrial zones floods over the winding hillside roads, which does not care in the least about the many 70 km/hour signs that have been erected in the meantime.

In this country, I got caught up in the Battle of the Hürtgen Forest in 1944. I was celebrating my nineteenth birthday out there. A few days later I was pretty sure that it would be my last and that the anniversary of my death was very imminent. I was a corporal, a radio operator trained in 105mm artillery, and had survived the Normandy Battle at Caen and Falaise and on the Seine. On the retreat I had been caught in the airborne landing of Arnhem and witnessed the fight for this city. Now, I have been in the Eifel Battle for forty days. So far, fate had left me several kilometers behind the armor in action.

On this morning of November 16, I climbed the concave steep slope of the Kall valley at the southern exit of the paper-mill town of Zerkall to the hilltop village of Bergstein with a comrade. There I was supposed to report to the B-officer of my artillery department for combat deployment as a radio operator. We did not follow the curve of the road, but climbed steeply uphill from the house at the end of the village over its orchard. Even today, this steep slope is still there, but partly settled with weekend houses and provided with access roads. At that time we climbed through absolute wasteland, sheep pasture-like and interrupted by blackthorn bushes. This steep slope was the usual footpath from behind to front for the Bergstein plateau. And there were artillery shells who conquered this steep slope, a difference in altitude of a good 200m even with horse-drawn infantry carts, not only uphill, but also downwards, and sometimes also in artillery fire.

Once at the top, we were at the edge of the rear slope of the Bergstein plateau. The edge was covered with deciduous forest to the left; there was the castle hill of Bergstein. After going straight ahead, we ran directly towards a wide residential bunker that was embedded in the rear slope. Dead straight ahead of it is still the church of Bergstein. The bunker was, I believe, number 370, and it remained undestroyed and is still there today: the "new" (now very old-looking) forester's lodge of Bergstein rises on it today. Our bunker became the basement of the forester's house! At that time there was an artificially raised mound of earth on the bunker, in front of it an earth wall, in front of it a slight depression over to the church and to the village street of Bergstein. This area has been completely changed today, because after the war someone came up with the idea of filling up there (presumably with house rubble) and creating a village sports field.

In the multi-room bunker was the B-point (observation point) of our department, with a combat room, telephone exchange, and sleeping room with two bunk beds. To my delight, the B-officer was our former battery commander lieutenant. I reported to him and was told the armor was about 4km ahead of us in Vossenack; from that direction we received artillery fire. It was not possible to go in front of the bunker in the direction of the church and the village of Bergstein because the area there was already seen by the enemy. Since our laid telephone network was being shot down more and more often, radio operators were now needed for radio communication. However, this is dangerous because it is immediately targeted by the enemy and leads to immediate massive, accurate artillery attacks by the enemy. Therefore, the B-Stelle bunker cannot be a radio station. I am therefore assigned the neighboring bunker, into which I now have to go.

The neighboring bunker was also embedded in the rear slope, about 60m to the south, i.e. in the Hochwald directly on the highest elevation of the entire Bergstein plateau. It is exactly 400m above sea level and bears the name Burgberg. This bunker, one of the normal Westwall residential bunkers with two rooms, is still there today.

When I visited again in 1985, there was a café on it! Undestroyed bunkers are an excellent building foundation. Unfortunately, there is no one there today who knows what we went through in these bunkers. Cheerfully, as if nothing had happened, life goes on. Happy people move around there.

This bunker was now to be the radio bunker of the B-Stelle. What I never found out at that time, constantly moving under cover on the rear slope, was that the bunker was located on the highest elevation of the entire combat area still held. This elevation is basalt, dome-like, and can be seen not only from Vossenack, but also from the main road Vossenack-Hürtgen and from the plateau of Schmidt. Accordingly, the castle hill of Bergstein was to be under massive enemy fire in the following weeks.

When I arrived, I found only one man in the bunker as the only inhabitant, my battery mate Spielar. He was Viennese, tall, blond, 20-years-old, married in Breslau, one child. With every mail delivery he received longing letters from his young wife. He was a musician by profession, and he had carried a violin with him all over Normandy. He still had it with him, here in the bunker, and fiddled on it: "Do you hear my secret calling?"

In the bunker there was plenty of space for the two of us, a table, several chairs, two bunk beds (so-called "air-raid beds"), but no light, no electricity, no water. The latter had to be fetched in buckets from somewhere. That's why none of us washed or shaved. For drinking, we had Muckefuck brought in daily from behind in jugs or knapsack tanks. Every day we got small bread rations, tiny margarine cubes, and a slice of sausage from the neighboring bunker. There was no more hot food. I lived in this bunker for eight days. Due to the danger of bearing, we had a strict radio ban until further notice. [Because sending radio signals could give away their position, the unit was forbidden from using radios until it was safe.] Several times a day, usually early in the morning, the American artillery carried out grenade raids on our bunkers. Since she did not know their exact location, most of the projectiles exploded in front of us on the hill in the forest. But we also got unexpected hits directly in front of the bunker entrance and on our supply path around the rear hang. Moving around there was a matter of luck; often there was complete silence for hours, and even then you ran to receive food or orders only at a run, in a stooped position, with open ears and elastic knees, to lie down immediately. We took turns to get food.

When I went up there on this gloomy November Thursday, there was nothing to hear or feel of enemy artillery. Once again, the deepest peace lay over the front area on the day of my arrival, as I had experienced several times now. As soon as I arrived at the B-Stelle bunker on the rear slope of Bergstein, I was already assigned to the field service. A construction team from our telephone platoon was tasked with laying a new line from Bergstein to Obermaubach, routed to be better protected and less vulnerable to artillery fire.

In Obermaubach and the surrounding area were our firing positions for the 89th Infantry Division. Obermaubach, like Zerkall, lay down in the valley, down the rear slope. While we were still busy in deepest peace on the edge 1,500m north of Bergstein in the hillside forest, American bomber groups suddenly flew over us, coming from the west, about 4,000m high in such numbers as I had not seen since Arnhem. We suspected they were flying to Cologne.

The cloud cover had cleared, and the planes, flashing in the sun, were easy to see and count. They did not receive antiaircraft fire and, as usual, flew unchallenged. We were sure that we were not their target. However, her goal was closer than we suspected. As soon as they had flown over the Rur valley behind us, we heard the typical, full-toned noise of hundreds of explosive bombs dropped at the same time. Each time it sounded as if a huge steam pipe had burst. Where would the carpet bomb hit? After three seconds we could observe it in detail from our mountain height: The city of Düren, about 10km behind us down on the plain, was razed to the ground. Clouds of smoke and debris rose kilometers high, and the large city began to burn over a large area. Whoever was there now was lost. The city had not yet been cleared of its civilian population. It was not a Wehrmacht base. Entourage, depots, resting places of our troops were never located in large cities, but decentralized. The bombing of Düren was one of the typical American miscalculations and senselessness against innocent people. Schoolchildren and babies were murdered. The city of Düren was wiped out. The German defensive front, 12km in front of it, remained standing and held for many weeks.

On Friday, November 17, more and more new faces also appeared at our department B position in Bergstein: the troop was noticeably replenished with replacements. Most of them came from the home garrison of Verden an der Aller, but did not come from northwest Germany, as before, but from the entire Reich. Many had been recovering from wounds on the Eastern Front. They were most endangered in our mission because they were hardly used to enemy artillery and bombing from the Russian war and therefore moved too carelessly in the terrain and were often the first victims of sudden enemy fire attacks. It was a peculiarity of the Americans that they constantly observed our rear area with special measuring troops and, as soon as they saw something moving, within a few minutes they fired very deliberately with a cannonade of whole batteries of guns, even at individual soldiers. Such a fire attack could consist of non-stop volleys for fifteen minutes, so that our soldiers kept saying: If we could eat with ammunition like that, we would still win this war!

Among the new arrivals was our new battery leader of staff battery of Artillery Regiment 189. It was a young lieutenant, no more than 22-years-old and very caring and sympathetic, but a sporty, brisk guy who knew how to carry you away. He was from Lübeck and was called Knutzen. The day after my arrival, Lieutenant Knutzen came over from the B-Stelle to our residential and radio bunker, Westwallbunker 371, on the Burgberg, to visit comrade Spielar and me. He inspected our radio, which we had made ready for operation with a throwing antenna outwards into the trees, and he had also brought us something that I hadn't seen in years, let alone tasted: a small round tin of Schokakola dark chocolate (a combination of chocolate and kola nuts). "Special ration for the front," he said.

But he continued: "Unfortunately, this is my last can. I want to share it honestly with you and the others who have not yet received anything; so I can only give each of you a quarter slice of chocolate!" I fell over this portion with ravenous appetites, because I hadn't had enough to eat for weeks. Inwardly I was angry, not at Lieutenant Knutzen, but at this kind of supply of special rations. Where did the chocolate cans get stuck, or did the Reich really have no more for a fighting soldier than a quarter sector of a thin, circular slice of chocolate?

On Saturday, November 18 at noon, Lieutenant Knutzen had me called to the B-Stelle bunker: "You have to go troubleshooting! Our telephone line to the infantry has just been shot down. Unfortunately, our telephone soldiers are all deployed at the moment, so I have to fall back on you as a radio operator. And unfortunately you have to go alone, because I don't have a man off otherwise. But you are experienced and can do it! The pipeline runs from here over the bunker apron diagonally to the northwest towards Brandenberg. But be careful and make sure that you can always take cover immediately; it may be that the area is inspected and you get fire."

With a rifle slung over my shoulder, a repair kit in my bread bag, and a gas mask can, I set off at noon. The air was damp, but clear. The pipeline led over arable fields on an open, unwooded plateau. To my left, the village of Bergstein remained behind me. Several kilometers ahead to the left were huge round mountain ranges. Where the shot-up church tower towered up, Vossenack lay. From far away, the church tower of the village of Schmidt greeted us.

I was not instructed in this situation at the time, only warned against shelling. There was absolute silence. So I moved fearlessly across the fields, letting the cable slip through my left hand; it was, as usual, laid on the floor, with a generous tolerance of space against shelling. I made sure that I went as far as possible into furrows in the field or through small erosion channels, so that in a matter of seconds I could lie stretched out covered in case of fire.

After about 1,000m, in the middle of the height, my cable ended up being shot. Effortlessly, a few meters further on, I found the other end, connected both ends with a weaver's knot, scraped the wire bright and reconnected it, and wrapped the patch with insulating tape. I did not have a field telephone with me, so I prepared to return without checking the connection. I had not yet gone 10m from the patch when it hissed very lightly for less than a tenth of a second, and the first American shell hit 20m away from me. Just in time before I came to rest in a small hollow. I felt no fear as a whole barrage of about twenty impacts came up to about 15m from me. I was still inexperienced in Eifel trench warfare and thought the whole thing was random scatter fire. I got up again, saw that the telephone line had remained intact, and calmly walked the 1,000m across the field to the bunker in a stooped position. It was not until a few days later that I was to experience what American artillery meant in the Eifel and realized the mortal danger I had been in.

From Sunday, November 19 Spielar and I were left alone in our bunker, 371, up in the castle hill near Bergstein. The two of us led a quiet bunker life because we were forbidden to radio. When we set up our receiver, we always heard numerous American voices, but never a German one. American radio, often roaring loud, always began with the word "Hello," followed by a code word, often a number. The whole radio message consisted mainly of code words and numbers, and it always ended with the word "Over!"

We hardly received any artillery hits at the beginning of this week, and we used the rest to clean and mend our stuff and to write letters. We also had discussions about this and that, especially about care, about women, and about home. We knew each other very well since Düsseldorf, where we had several guards together in the same collective quarters and Spielar was loved by a French foreign worker.

Darkness came earlier and earlier in the evening, and our only lighting in the bunker consisted of "Hindenburg lights," wax-filled tin cans that could hardly be lit by a newspaper. The Hindenburg lights were always good for cracking lice. It was done by holding the neckline of the undershirt or tunic close to the flame. Up in Bergstein, however, we were lice-free. I had gotten rid of the last lice eight days earlier at the regimental headquarters in Heimbach. Outside there were already cold November nights. Our bunker had no stove, so we lived and slept in warm clothing in the cold bunker all the time.

On Monday, November 20, around noon, comrade Spielar was ordered to the neighboring B-Stelle bunker. After some time he came back with fear on his face: "I have to go to VB!" (VB is the forward observer in front of the infantry position directly in front of the enemy.) He took his bread bag, gas mask, steel helmet and rifle, shook my hand and said, "I have a feeling that I won't come back." I tried to encourage him: "It's not that bad!". Then he left. From now on, bunker 371 belonged to me all alone, for four days. No one on the B-Stelle seemed to care about me lonely radio operator.

Since the day was completely without the noise of battle, I decided to go on an excursion at noon and take a look at the area in front of my bunker. So far, I only knew my bunker space at the covered rear and only entrance. I walked up next to the bunker and found myself in dense autumnal deciduous forest that covered the entire top of the mountain. The undergrowth was made of raspberry bushes. I walked from depression to depression in a stooped position, always ready to take cover in case of a sudden fire. But it remained calm. To my surprise, after about 60m up in the deep forest, I found an almost intact single house, picturesquely situated and abandoned by its inhabitants. It was the forester's lodge of Bergstein (which has since disappeared without a trace).

The doors were open, the windows shattered, the furniture complete and intact! However, some comrades had already visited, looking for something useful, and had left objects scattered on the ground. I climbed into the basement, actually only because it was the most protected, and to my surprise found a clean room with shelves full of filled preserving jars. I decided on a large jar of pear compote, which I took upstairs. There was no one far and wide. Since there was still no artillery fire, I visited the comfortably furnished living room. Between hunting and forestry literature, I found a local history book of the North Eifel in a bookcase. I took this with me to the bunker to read. In it I learned for the first time about the Rur dams, about the history of Mariawald, about the Heimbach excursion site, and about the climbing rock in the evenings. I learned that I was in a region full of romance, which was just about to be destroyed, as was the beautiful Normandy from which I had come here. Starved, I devoured the sweet pear compote. In the light of Hindenburg candles in the autumnal cold bunker.

Since it was still quiet and dry weather on Tuesday, November 21, I went on another excursion, but this time to the hinterland of the bunker. Directly behind the bunker exit, the terrain does not immediately drop steeply into the Kall Valley, but there was dense high forest there at that time, which led to a steep-walled mountain spur with shrub terrain. There I lay down in the autumn sun. It was warmer than in the bunker. Next to and in front of me the terrain fell steeply into the valley, and over there, as if within reach, lay the town of Nideggen, in its castle fortifications. For me, this was a fairytale view, because as a North German I had never seen a fortified old mountain town.

Nideggen was still intact on November 21, and from down in the valley, the road that led up to the city gate greeted you next to the railway line. When I had just gotten up again, there was suddenly a quiet hiss above me. The hissing came straight to me in a flash. Before I could throw myself down, I saw the flashing of four impacts in the mountain face opposite below Nideggen! The shells must have flown only centimeters above my head over my mountain spur, then over the whole valley to the rock face over in front of Nideggen! I had heard the deadly hissing closer to my ears than ever before; I almost thought I had felt the draught. Uncertain, I retreated to my bunker. To this day, I am tormented by the question: Had I been spotted by the enemy, or was it merely a coincidence? Between me and the HKL (main battle line) lay the castle hill of Bergstein. The shells barely cleared my mountain spur before detonating on it. A little later, I would experience the same in the Kall Valley before Nideggen, where individual men were struck by artillery as if specifically targeted. It was unimaginable—how could they have seen us? The entire area was supposedly sheltered by the rear slope of Bergstein.

From November 22 onwards, everything changed in Bergstein. Immediately after breakfast there were shells in the hilltop forest in front of my bunker. I had considered sneaking back to the front of the forester's lodge and getting something to eat from its cellar supplies. But out of the dream of my castle-hill romance, the American artillery shot at our high altitude terrain, which was visible from afar. Between 10:00 AM and 11:00 AM, the impacts came closer to my bunker. I was in it reading a book. Suddenly there was a terrible boom with an air-pressure wave. The bunker seemed to be rocking, and since I had experience in being buried from Normandy, I lay on the concrete floor in fear and listened. The air pressure had blown out my four Hindenburg candles, and it was now pitch dark around me. I felt my way to the bunker entrance and looked out cautiously; nothing had changed. However, my antenna had been thrown down from the branches above the bunker and lay on the ground in front of the bunker entrance. Apparently, the bunker roof had been hit, but had held. After all, the concrete roof had been lightly covered with earth and vegetation. I understood something about impacts and estimated: This impact came from at least a 15cm shell.

Soon after the impact, there was dead silence around the bunker again. So I climbed up the side of it to see if there had been any damage. What I found was only this: Up on the bunker roof, at the level of the entrance, the turf and earth cover had been swept away all around. And in the concrete ceiling there was a flat, elongated funnel about 60cm in diameter and about 30cm deep.

The bunker roof had actually taken a direct hit! Nevertheless, the structural integrity of the bunker remained intact. (When I revisited Bergstein for the first time in 1955, my bunker, 371, was still standing intact in the forest thicket on the back slope of the castle hill. We climbed up—and saw, unchanged, the deep concrete notch of the direct hit of November 22, 1944! Strangely enough, it was still not overgrown. Did toxic chemicals keep the vegetation away from the impact crater?)

When I came to the B-Stelle bunker at noon on November 22 to get food, I was greeted with the message: "Spielar is gone." When I asked, I was told: "Missing". Poor comrade Spielar ! But if he had been lucky, he was now in American captivity. I never heard from him again. From that moment on, I felt miserably alone on the Eifel front. On the way back from the neighboring B-Stelle bunker to my bunker, 371, uphill through the high forest, I had to throw myself into a leaf hollow with my filled cookware at lightning speed: fire attack directly on my path. Artillery shells shredded the treetops in front of my bunker entrance for the first time. Branches and twigs fell on my head. And I thought to myself: now the dangerous tree-crackers are starting again![13]

Günther Schmidt, 272nd Volksgrenadier Division

At Cologne-Mühlheim there was an air-raid warning. The train stopped between houses, no one was allowed to get out of the train. It was a strange feeling when the FLAK started to shoot and some bombs fell in the distance. In the early morning, the train stopped before it entered Düren station. From time to time heavy enemy artillery fired at the railroad tracks. Every few minutes an enemy "greeting" came rushing in, but it didn't cause that much damage. It took about an hour before we finally got on to Vettweiss.

There our train was unloaded under the protection of light FLAK. Shortly thereafter, enemy planes appeared and they threatened the whole area. Our companies were marching in a long, stretched column in the direction of Nideggen, using every cover that we could find. In the distance we could hear the rumbling of the front very clearly. After marching for a while, we recognized the explosion of every single shell. No one knew what was going to come the next day, and the men were in a depressed and quiet mood. Once in a while, we meet civilians with all their belongings, some with horse-drawn carts, handcarts, and even with baby carriages or bags and backpacks for their most important things only. Their faces expressed what they had to live through, having to leave their home and belongings.

The front-thunder was coming closer; we could hear the bursting menace of the exploding shells. Our tension grew when the front came closer. I marched with our commander, Hauptmann Schneider, at the lead of the battalion. At the crossroads in Brück, I stopped a truck to ask for the road to Harscheidt. When the truck drove on, I saw what it had loaded. The legs and boots of about twenty dead soldiers could be seen under the canvas. Some officers' boots were among them also. We shivered thinking about the reality.

After we walked the road uphill, we finally reached Hill 366 at the wood line of Harscheidt. The lead of the column waved for the rest of the men. Rest! The impact of the enemy artillery was very close; they were coming from the direction of Bergstein, where the truck had come from. Hauptmann Schneider ordered me to the regimental command post, which was on the edge of the village of Schmidt, at the road to Heimbach to return with further orders and a runner. It was already dark. We barely reached the first houses of the village and were standing between some horse carts, when the first shells came in and exploded very close. We quickly jumped into the ditch for cover.

There was a lot of confusion in the street: horses backed up; we heard screams from the men that were hit. Before we could think about what to do, the next round was falling into the moving column. I decided to go around the village on the left side through the fields, which wasn't difficult because of the clear night. Soon we reached the hunting lodge while Schmidt was still under heavy artillery fire. We quickly got back to where we came from with the orders for the retreat, while shells were coming in only a few hundred yards away at the village of Schmidt. Our battalion moved through Schmidt and into the defenses around Rollesbroich. I talked with the commander and suggested that only vehicles and carts should go through Schmidt because of the artillery that was coming in on the village; the men shouldn't go through.

We started marching in a long, stretched column and went around the village. After crossing two valleys we safely reached the road in Gerstenhof. We rested for a short while and marched along in the direction of Strauch. At the wood line on the right side, we were to meet some runners at a pillbox who would lead us to their line of defense, but we couldn't find these men. Finally our Hauptmann ordered us into a firebreak to the right and we kept walking downhill. I had a bad feeling about this. I thought something stinks. That's why I suggested we walk back to the main road. If we had followed this firebreak, we would have walked right into Simonskall.

The next day the Americans started their attack from the Kall Valley to Kommerscheidt and Schmidt. After another search along the road to Strauch, we finally found the spot where we were to meet the runners. In the meantime our vehicles had crossed the village of Schmidt. They had some wounded. Pillbox 139/40, which was located a few hundred meters inside the forest, was our battalion command post, and the other half of it was a first-aid post.

We were glad that we finally found it. A sergeant of the unit that we were to replace called my name.

In September we put up an alarm company together at Venlo in Holland. This was just a small experience but it helped to make me familiar with the new circumstances. The burning logs in the small stove gave a comfortable heat. Our predecessors informed us about our new tasks. They showed us on the maps where several companies, the heavy weapons, and the communications were. Telephone wire was partly dug in, and the rest was lying on the open ground. The other half of our double pillbox was used as a first-aid post. Inside was the assistant doctor, Dr. Egel. It was still night when our companies were brought into their new defenses.

The old troops were released and were gone by daylight. Our communications unit was not far away from us at pillbox 142. It was coming and going at our command post. The telephone kept ringing and the runners were coming in from all directions, while others were going again. At daybreak we could see the steeple of the Lammersdorf church. The Americans had an observer positioned there and every imprudent movement at our wood line resulted in a few incoming rounds.

Today is November 2, the weather wet and foggy, temperature around 32 degrees. It was pretty miserable outside. Part of Grenadier Regiment 983 (275th Infantry Division) on our right side were involved in a heavy fight to defend the Raffelsbrand Forest with the pillboxes 372, 372a, JG2, JG3, and 22. We could easily hear the fighting in that area. During the next days there was a hard and tangled fight for Vossenack. The Americans pushed through the Kall Valley to Kommerscheidt and Schmidt. At first we didn't know what was going on. On the morning of November 2, we sent four runners with bicycles by way of Schmidt to our supply unit at Heimbach to lead the carts with supplies and provisions to our new defensive positions. We waited in vain until the next morning for the return of our runners and our supplies.

During the next day, we were informed by the unit on our left side that the Americans had taken Schmidt and about the hard fighting behind our backs. The supplies still hadn't come on the second night. After a few days we were officially informed by the regiment about what happened behind our backs at Kommerscheidt and Schmidt. They found the bicycles of our runners east of Gerstenhof, but the men couldn't be found. When I look back, I must say that it was unjustifiable of the regiment not to inform us about the happenings at Kommerscheidt and Schmidt. We should have protected the backside of the road to Gerstenhof at once. If the Americans were a bit faster, they could have pushed through the front to Simmerath without meeting any resistance.

The Kall Valley south of Raffelsbrand was under heavy mortar fire day after day. The unit on our right side told us that there were tremendous losses.

In the meantime our companies became familiar with the half-finished defense positions. Our heavy infantry weapons, mortars, infantry guns, as well as our artillery had ranged in their guns in certain areas. When enemy attack took place, our battalion gave messages to the fire command and a little later our shells were on their way to the Americans. We didn't have much rest at night either. Engineers were working at the defenses. Barbed wire and mines were brought at night. A whole battalion of Russian volunteers was digging trenches every night.

During daylight, the Americans at the Lammersdorf church steeple could see every little move that we made. Our area looked as follows: 5th Company at the Schmidt-Simmerath road, west edge of Rollesbroich; 6th and 7th Company at the southern height of the Kall Valley Dam to the Wasserscheide bei Kallbrück road. The 8th company, with heavy machine guns and mortars, were west of the Tiefenbach Creek. The enemy quickly recognized we were working on our defenses. The nightly artillery fire at our lines was getting stronger and stronger.

One day the Russians mutinied and didn't go out front to dig trenches because of the high losses of dead and wounded. These dead were buried in a small cemetery at the wood line south of the Schmidt-Strauch road. Within a few days the enemy attacked at the east bank of the Kall Valley Dam. North of Rollesbroich and at the dam itself, the Americans succeeded in taking the east bank of the Kall Valley Dam. By late afternoon the enemy forces were pushed back again by our counterattack. We didn't have too many losses. The Americans probably didn't expect a counterattack and they fled back.

The next day our battalion commander, Hauptmann Schneider, and I visited the defenses of the 8th Company at the Tiefen Creek Valley, pillbox 510, our front-line at Rollesbroich, and the retaken east bank of the Kall Valley Dam. Everywhere we found a lot of equipment that the Americans had left—weatherproof sleeping bags, little tents, cans with rations, little cookers, coffee, tea, and cigarettes. They were probably digging in and preparing for the night when our counterattack took place. Our own losses in the first two weeks were about 15 percent, mostly by artillery fire. Our first-aid post in the pillbox beside us was a great help during those days. From there the wounded were transported by ambulance by way of Schmidt and Heimbach to the field hospital at Mariawald.

On November 15 our battalion was shifted to the right. The 7th Company stayed in their old defense at the east bank of the Kall Valley Dam and in the area of the dam itself. The 5th Company was to defend the warehouse at Kallbrück (the Pub), pillboxes 111, 112, 113, and 115, and 6th Company was given pillboxes P2, 22, JG3, 372, and 372a. From this area there was no connection to other units until the clearing of pillbox 372 at the end of January 1945. Unit

8910, which was to be released, had had tremendous fighting in this area since November 2 and was seriously weakened because of heavy losses.

We were just getting used to our new defenses, when, on November 16, the enemy attacked pillbox 111 and held it for a short period. Oberleutnant von Ruden, who cleared the enemy at the Kall Valley Dam was very fast on the spot and was able to retake pillbox 111 without too many losses after a counterattack. Only a few Americans escaped. The rest were taken prisoner. Although we had some snipers in the area, imprudent Americans kept crossing the firebreak in front of pillbox 22 day after day.

During clear nights, Hauptmann Schneider and myself often checked the defenses from pillbox 124, via pillbox 111 to 372a. This wasn't possible during daytime because of enemy observation. The pillboxes were connected with trenches. In front of the trenches there were mines and barbed wire. Between all this lay the rest of the completely destroyed fir tree forest.

Inside the pillboxes the men could rest after their duty in the trenches outside, but most of all they were safe from the constant incoming shells. It really wasn't an easy task for an attacking force. Our heavy infantry guns, mortars and artillery had zeroed in very well at areas directly in front of our defenses. Most of the pillboxes were connected by telephone with wires buried deeply in the ground. Wires in the open field were only laid in short lengths between the concrete wire connecting pits behind our front. Besides that, we had several field radios with the forward observers.

In the next days the Americans attacked pillboxes P2, 22, and JG3. Most of the attacks ended in front of the barbed wire because many of their men were lost in the minefield and because of our soldiers' defense, aided by our heavy weapons. The supply of the 5th and 6th companies gave tremendous problems. The horse-drawn carts with supplies were coming from Heimbach by way of Schmidt to pillbox 124 alongside the road to Kallbrück. From there, we had to carry all the supplies by hand to the front and back again inside the old command post, Pillbox 125. The operation was completed without any problems. Until January 10, it was really quiet at our sector. Only now and then the Americans fired into our positions. We could almost believe that the war had ended. The Ardennes Offensive had disrupted the enemy, which gave us a bit of relief. On a clear night I walked with Hauptmann Schneider and two runners to the defensive positions in front of pillboxes 111 to 372. We wished all the men a Happy New Year and everyone received a small present of cigarettes, chocolate, or alcohol. That night there was hardly any firing. The look of the snow-covered forested landscape could almost make you dream. It took us 'til early morning before we were back at our command-post pillbox, 125, by way of the firebreak at pillbox P3. The quietness seemed to last too long and we started to worry about it. We could see that the enemy was organizing large-scale firing exercises behind their front at Rötgen. Every day we could see an increasing number of vehicles taking the road from Lammersdorf to Germeter. There were hundreds of them.

Our own artillery fire didn't trouble the enemy that much. During those quiet days we prepared our defenses some more. We checked a second defense line on the right side of the Kall River at Buhlert, and with the support of an engineer and alarm company, we started to work. Besides that we were working on a plan to get the two foremost companies at Ochsenkopf over the Kall River in case of a flood caused by a possible blowing of the Kall Valley Dam. Engineers stretched a cable from pillbox 122 to pillbox 121, and we placed two rubber boats at this spot. The snow stays till the end of January. On January 10 it happens. The enemy attacks the whole sector of our 5th and 6th companies, but the attack is stopped in the minefields after the concentrated fire of all.

After about an hour, the enemy concentrates the attack at pillbox 22. Our men keep fighting from inside the pillbox for half an hour. Till the very last moment we have the men inside the pillbox on the phone. Suddenly there is a crack in the line and it's over. From there, the enemy moves to pillbox JG3 and starts pressing on it from all sides. In about an hour, this pillbox has the same fate as pillbox 22. The enemy stopped its unsuccessful attack under heavy losses around noon at the sector of the 5th Company. During the night our reserve company arrived to try to retake the old positions in the early daylight in an attack from pillbox P2 and 119. Twice these attacks were repelled under severe losses for our troops. In the meantime they pushed in another reserve unit, who attacked a third time without the support of heavy weapons. As it was meant as an unexpected attack, it was a costly failure as well.

The next day the Americans attacked again and managed to take pillbox P2 pretty quickly. Pillboxes 372 and 372a kept on fighting. On January 12 another battalion arrived with about a hundred men. Their winter clothing was not sufficient. We placed our battalion command post inside pillbox 119, where I stayed with our commander. At 9 AM our heavy weapons started firing. After a successful beginning, our attack broke down in the heavy enemy fire. In some places the enemy pushed us back to our line of departure. We had severe losses. Our men were lying in the snow in the open. Without foxholes to hide, they were exposed to the strong enemy mortar fire. Our losses are tremendous. After a short while our command pillbox 119 changed into a first-aid post. Severely wounded were carried inside—the wailing and groaning—medics tried to dress the wounds.

Severely wounded soldiers were dying. They were carried outside and new ones were brought in. At noon there were about fifteen dead piled up at the hollow road in front of the entrance. Other wounded were trying to help each other while they were going downhill into the Kall Valley. It was late afternoon before the severely wounded could be transported down into the valley. The badly mauled and beaten stayed in their defensive positions. I stayed with a few men inside pillbox 119 until morning. The work on our defensive positions went on night after night. Engineers brought up our weapons.

A few days later the enemy unexpectedly started its attack at pillbox 115. They succeeded to blow the pillbox with a special charge, but they didn't destroy it completely. A reserve force is sent up front to retake the pillbox, which is now manned by Americans. The attack is a failure, despite the support of our heavy weapons. We lost a lot of men. We received another order from our regiment at noon. Pillbox 115 is to be attacked again the next day and to be retaken.

Our Hauptmann Schneider tells the commander of the regiment, Oberstleutnant Rösener that another attack on pillbox 115 wouldn't make any sense and is unjustifiable. Our men were lying in their foxholes in the snow between pillboxes 119 and 372 at Ochsenkopf. Our last men were lost at pillbox 115. The rising, open ground offered no opportunity for a successful follow-up attack. Hauptmann Schneider asked the regiment commander to come over to have a look himself at this area. Finally the divisional commander, General König, came on the line and said that it was an order from the Führer headquarters to retake pillbox 115 and that this order must be obeyed, even if it seemed impossible. Hauptmann Schneider said that he couldn't take the responsibility to waste his men for a useless attack, that we were already too weak for the defense. It was suggested not to start the attack. They would tell the Führer headquarters that the new attack had failed.

Our regiment commander said that he would come up front to see that the attack started as ordered. And that's how it went. He watched how not a single one of ten men came back and how they all got killed. This had a big impact on our Hauptmann Schneider. The enemy tried to take pillbox 510 in front of Rollesbroich for several days. These attacks resulted in great losses for the enemy. Once the Americans asked for a ceasefire to get their wounded out and that's indeed what took place. Finally the Americans fired for several days with a big gun directly at pillbox 510. Some men inside were wounded from pieces of concrete that were falling off. Another infantry attack was repelled again.

Since January 10, 1945, we have had very little sleep. There was always something going on. We slept in turns. Mostly I slept between 6:00 AM and 9:00 AM. Enemy observation planes could easily make out the paths that we made through the snow between pillboxes and the defensive positions. The result was the enemy mortars fired at the entrances of the pillboxes continuously. Since January the Americans have also been shooting with white phosphorus, but with no great effect because of the snow. Enemy artillery increased from day to day along the whole front. On February 2 we received orders that on February 3 we were to clear several of our defensive positions. Our engineers were to blow or to mine the pillboxes.

We could get out without any problem or difficulty. The new sector went from the Schmidt-Strauch road, near pillbox 190, along the line of pillboxes to pillbox 128/129, and from there on the right bank of the Tiefenbach to Kall Valley. The men dug in as good as possible. Some rested in the snow lying around. The fighting at Raffelsbrand weakened the companies severely during the last few weeks. After heavy losses the strength of our battalion is about 20–25 percent. The enemy artillery kept firing day and night along the whole front and only increased. Our new battalion command post is now inside pillbox 136.

On the night of February 5 at 3:00 AM, we received orders to increase the battalion sector by 800m to the left. This order widened the line even more and severely weakened our front. Some company runners were called immediately. A written order had to be made for every company. It was pretty late to accomplish such a difficult change of front lines. It took till the early morning before all companies reached their new sectors. The consequence was that we did not even have enough men in our sector to man all the pillboxes. We repositioned our battalion command post in the early morning to pillbox 220/21, south of the Schmidt-Strauch road. The first-aid post stayed inside pillbox 139/40 and in the main line of defense.

We had hardly arrived at our new pillbox when we received the first shocking message. This first message was made by telephone and came from the old RAD camp where our mortars and infantry guns were positioned. The enemy suddenly appeared there by the hundreds from the direction of Simonskall. There was some short fighting. It didn't take long. No more messages from the RAD camp. A bit later a message from our first-aid post told us that the Americans had broken through the defense almost without any sound. We must give up! Now the enemy came from the RAD camp and attacked along the road to Strauch without much resistance. Finally, our communication pillbox 717a near the road was involved in the fight. It didn't take long until the Americans took this pillbox. We could talk to them on the telephone!

The enemy took the pillboxes along and north of the Zäunchen road at noon. In the afternoon, the enemy pressed against the pillbox armed with a 75mm PAK to the north of us. They pushed through the forest to the south, until they could open fire on the backside of the pillbox. This pillbox was manned only by an officer and three men. They ordered me, with three men, to go and reinforce that pillbox. The firing compartment was pointing in the direction of the dragon's teeth and Steckenborn. With binoculars we can see that a fight was going on in the village, but we couldn't discern friend or foe. The dragon's teeth to the road at Zäunchen were still free of the enemy. The enemy fired at the backside of the pillbox from a distance of about 120m inside the forest. From a foxhole at the emergency exit, the defenders fired back into the forest. Finally, the gunner was killed by a shot in the head. In the meantime they were firing also at the big steel door on the backside.

Our way back over the open fields to our command post was cut off. We were trapped. We destroyed the breech of our gun—we couldn't blow the gun because we didn't have any explosives. The hammering of the bullets on the steel back door became unbearable. We crawled out of the firing compartment into the open and became prisoners. Two of our men were wounded by a shot in the arm when this occurred. The rest of our battalion staff gave up their pillboxes at dawn and gathered in front of Gerstenhof. The enemy attacked the next morning with tanks and infantry alongside the road. After a short fight these men surrendered to the enemy.

So the next day in a cellar of a house in Rötgen, I met our commander, Hauptmann Schneider, Adjutant Lieutenant Peters, as well as Unteroffizier Möbius and Unteroffizier Matzkewitz from pillbox P3 again. Our losses in the last few days were so tremendous that our battalion didn't exist anymore. After this the regiment gathered all men that were left in a small group. The last of this group was destroyed later in the area around Leipzig. That's how the costly fighting of our battalion came to a tragic end.[14]

14

112th Infantry Medical Evacuation Report

The following report was submitted to the surgeon for the 28th Infantry Division by Major Albert L. Berndt, regimental surgeon for the 112th Infantry. The attack of the 28th Infantry Division on the town of Schmidt in the Hürtgen Forest in early November 1944 occupies a special place in the history of the US Army's operations against Nazi Germany in World War II.

Fought in awful weather conditions over very difficult, heavily forested terrain along the Kall River on the German-Belgian border south of Aachen, Germany, the Battle of Schmidt was one of the bloodiest and most wasteful American operations of the war in Europe. The 109th, 110th, and 112th Infantry Regiments of the 28th Infantry Division and attached units were all engaged in these operations. However, the 112th Infantry Regiment bore the brunt of the fighting and casualties in the towns of Vossenack, Kommerscheidt, and Schmidt, and along the Kall Trail that connected Vossenack with Kommerscheidt and Schmidt to the east of the Kall River.

Within days, medical personnel of the 112th Infantry completed these reports, which provide a graphic picture of the challenges that regimental and battalion medical personnel faced in caring for and evacuating the wounded and sick soldiers under such appalling conditions. Captains John S. Howe and William J. Fox, 2d Information and Historical Service, European theater of operations, subsequently interviewed many members of the 28th Infantry Division who had participated in these operations. They did not, however, apparently interview any of the medical personnel. They did collect a number of reports that medical personnel had already submitted to the regimental surgeon for the 112th Infantry and the division surgeon.

These documents are part of the larger collection of 28th Infantry Division interviews and draft historical reports that were compiled by the 2d Information and Historical Service for use by the historian's office of the European theatre of operations. The information concerning medical evacuation in the 112th

Regimental Combat Team during the attacks on and the defense of the German villages of Vossenack, Kommerscheidt, and Schmidt is provided below in chronological order. In reading the report by Major Albert L. Berndt, regimental surgeon for the 112th Infantry, several pertinent facts should be borne in mind. Firstly, the majority of material given here was based on reports and information received at regimental headquarters medical detachment from a wide variety of sources. Secondly, since no station log was kept of those reports, they are being repeated from memory of the writer and of those people to whom access is available at present. Thirdly, accurate information of both past and impending operations was difficult for the writer to obtain subsequent to the removal of regimental advanced headquarters from the pillbox at (015331) to the village of Kommerscheidt. Fourthly, communications between the aid stations of the 1st and 3rd battalions, the collecting company and the regimental headquarters aid station were completely lacking after 3:00 AM on November 6, 1944, except for occasional messages carried by medical department personnel. Fifthly, and most importantly, the difficulty of the terrain over which military operations took place made the evacuation of the wounded possible only under conditions of the utmost physical hardship. Sixthly, the efforts of two reinforced regimental combat teams and at least two task forces flatly failed to secure the main supply route over which evacuation had to be made. No further allusion to these facts will be made herein.

(All map coordinates refer to Map 2. Topographic Map of the Hürtgen Area)

The chronological report follows:
November 2, 1944: 9:00 AM
2nd Battalion, 112th (White Battalion) attacked Vossenack, reaching objective at 1:45 PM. The 112th had crossed LOD at 1:00 PM. Evacuation was excellent.

November 3, 1944: 2:50 PM
3rd Battalion, 112th (Blue Battalion) reported Schmidt captured. The 1st Battalion, 112th (Red Battalion) followed in support of Blue Battalion, occupied Kommerscheidt. Positions of battalion aid station at 6:00 PM: Red Battalion in valley at (014307); White Battalion in barracks at (022329), where it remained until November 8.

November 8
Blue Battalion in rear at (018333) and forward in church at (038326). At this time the lines of evacuation were stretched, but evacuation was quite successful and the aid stations counted on moving forward at dawn the following morning.

Major Berndt's Report

November 2, 9:00 AM
112th White Battalion attacked Vossenack, reaching objective at 1:45 PM. 112th had crossed line of departure at 1:00 PM. Evacuation was excellent.

November 3, 2:50 PM
112th Blue Battalion reported Schmidt captured. 112th Battalion followed in support of Blue, occupied Kommerscheidt. Positions of Battalion Aid Station at 6:00 PM: Red in valley at (014307), White in Barracks at (022329), where it remained until November 8, Blue rear at (018333) and forward in church at (038326). At this time the lines of evacuation were stretched, but evacuation was quite successful and the Aid Stations counted on moving forward at dawn the following morning.

November 4, 1944, 9:05 AM
112th Blue Battalion Reported driven out of Schmidt, withdrew to Red positions in Kommerscheidt. 2:00 PM—regimental commander requested investigation of medical evacuation from Kommerscheidt. Assistant Regimental Surgeon visited Red Aid Station at (054308) to determine the tactical situation, the methods of evacuation and needs of the Aid Station, found casualties heavy, the Aid Station under direct fire of enemy artillery, but evacuation continuing successfully. 5:00 PM—Message received from Blue Surgeon requesting additional Medical Personnel immediately. Four Technicians, Carr, Marinclin, Lopes and Moss, were sent from the Regimental Aid Station to give help. Upon their arrival they found they were not needed, and upon the suggestion of the Blue Surgeon, continued forward to the Red Aid Station where they might be needed. Carr and Marinclin remained at the Red Aid Station overnight, returning the following afternoon to Regimental Aid Station. Lopes and Moss departed the Red Aid Station with seven casualties in a weasel. They brought a request from the Red Aid Station for food and Medical supplies, arriving at Regimental Aid Station at 1:00 AM next day. 6:00 PM—Location of Aid Stations: White unchanged. Red in house on edge at Kommerscheidt at (054308), Blue at dug-in log cabin at (046316). Ambulance loading point at (045317) at edge at woods on forward slope of hill. Casualties are being moved by weasels from Red and Blue Aid Stations to Ambulance Loading Point.[1]

November 5, 1944, 8:30 AM
Rations, Medical supplied and water were sent by weasel from Regimental Aid Station to Red Aid Station in house in Kommerscheidt. This was the first food received by the Red Aid Station in two days. Evacuation continued successfully.

Afternoon—Red Aid Station house received three direct hits by enemy artillery high explosive shells, killing one Medical private, destroying the supplies which had been received. Feeling that the house was no longer tenable, the Red surgeon waited until dark, then withdrew the Aid Station from Kommerscheidt and joined the Blue Aid Station in the log cabin at (046316). Both Aid Station groups continued to occupy this location, operating a joint Red-Blue Aid Station until the evening of November 9. Evening—Casualties were carried from front to Red-Blue Aid Station by weasel, from Aid Station to Ambulance Loading Point by litter carry because of blockage of road by stalled tank.

November 6, 1944: 2:00 AM
Lieutenant Johnson departed from Red-Blue Aid Station leaving Aid Station free of casualties. 3:00 AM—All communications between Advance and Rear Regimental Headquarters were cut off by enemy penetrations from northeast and southwest along valley to bridge at (047313). No further reliable information received from Advance Headquarters. 8:00 AM—Tech Sergeant 5 Benninger, from Red-Blue Aid Station, arrived at Regimental Aid Station saying that he had been cut off from the Red-Blue Aid Station by a German patrol about 10:00 PM last night, had taken shelter in an abandoned tank, had finally managed to escape from the pursuing patrol by following the defile of the woods from the area of the bridge to road junction 446 at (019324). Benninger, one of our most reliable men, reported that the Aid Station was cut off by the enemy both from the Red and Blue battalions in front and from White Battalion to the rear. He also reported that the route by which he had escaped was impossible for litter teams to cross with casualties.

During this day, and subsequent days, the Red-Blue Aid Station was in German-held territory. Several times each day German Medics and infantrymen visited the Aid station. They permitted walking wounded to cross through their position while returning to the Aid Station from Kommerscheidt; they made no attempt to interfere with the operation of the Aid Station. They offered to supply the Aid Station personnel with dressings and sulfanilamide; they stated that the Aid Station personnel and wounded would not be molested as long as no American infantrymen tried to bring their weapons into the area. The truth of these statements cannot be denied; they have been confirmed by all the Medical Officers and men in the Aid Station. However, the Germans did capture all the vehicles belonging to the combined Air Station. Subsequent evacuation from the Aid Station could be made only by litter carry uphill from the Aid Station to whatever point could be reached by ambulances or other evacuation vehicles.[2]

8:04 AM—White battalion was forced to withdraw to the center of Vossenack. Although the situation was temporarily restored by a counterattack by Engineers, the status of the control of the eastern half of the village was continually doubtful according to all information reaching the Regimental Aid Station. As a result, the main road from Vossenack to Kommerscheidt was denied to Medical Vehicles from Vossenack to the ambulance loading point. This necessitated forward moving vehicles to leave the main street of Vossenack at (033326), turn south to the border of the woods, then follow the defilade of the woods in a most circuitous route to the Ambulance Loading Point. Further difficulties were added by sharp sideways slope of the path, which at places almost caused the weasels and ambulances to fall over on their sides, and by a German battery in the vicinity of (065334), which fired on every vehicle seen to be moving in the field south of Vossenack.

Visibility from this battery, or from its observers, apparently permitted the vehicles to be seen but was not sufficient for the Red Crosses to be seen. Hence the battery fired on Medical vehicles as on others. During this day the further evacuation of wounded from the combined Aid Stations was impossible.

November 7, 1944: 1:00 AM

A Regimental Supply Train of weasels departed for Kommerscheidt, successfully passed through the German-held territory in the valley by the Red-Blue Aid Station, returned with twenty-two casualties from the Kommerscheidt area. These were the last casualties to be evacuated from Kommerscheidt area other than several walking wounded who made their own way through the enemy lines. This last train stopped at the combined Aid Station and an officer knocked on the door. Either the occupants were asleep, or more likely feared a German ruse, and did not answer the knock. Since the waiting Train was under fire, the knocking was not repeated and the Train continued without having picked up any casualties from the Aid Station. The twenty-two casualties were delivered to the Regimental Aid Station at 7:30 AM.

5:00 AM—Rain rendered the defilade route previously used by evacuating weasels too slippery for further use. 8:00 AM—Second Lieutenant Morrison from Red Aid Station, together with three or four walking wounded arrived at Regimental Aid Station, having followed the valley used by Benninger previously. He requested that wounded be evacuated from Aid Station, but said that the route he had followed could not be used by litter bearers because of the length of the haul and the steepness of the terrain. At noon 2nd Lieut. Morrison returned to the Red-Blue Aid Station afoot using the same route.

3:00 PM—First Lieutenant Page, of Collecting Company, left White Aid Station with three litter squads to evacuate wounded from Red-Blue Aid Station to Ambulance Loading Point. Arrived at Aid Station, evacuated seven walking wounded and three litter cases, during which two litter bearers were shot by the enemy. Lieutenant Page and the litter bearers remained at the Aid Station overnight.

3:30 PM—Lieutenant Johnson departed White Aid Station with a weasel, followed slippery mud track at edge of woods, arrived at (045316), where the wounded brought by Pagewere loaded on the weasel and a 0.25-ton trailer found nearby. He returned, leaving only seven casualties in the Aid Station, by the route along the woods, almost overturning on the slope at (041318), arriving at White Aid Station at 6:00 PM.

7:00 PM—In view of the impossibility of the evacuation of wounded from Kommerscheidt hill, I suggested to S-2 and S-4 of Regiment that a truce be arranged with the enemy for a period of several hours in order to sweep the Kommerscheidt area and evacuate our dead and wounded. The suggestion was declined. Instead, a second attempt to run a Supply Train through under cover of darkness was ordered. I suggested that supplies be dropped to Red and Blue battalions and to the Aid Station by air. This, too, was declined.[3]

November 8, 1944: 1:00 AM
The Regimental Supply Train, including two Medical Technicians from Regimental Headquarters Aid Station, attempted to penetrate the enemy lines, was fired upon somewhere south of Vossenack and was ordered to return by the commanding officer. Regimental S-4 spent most of night exploring, unsuccessfully, for an alternate route of approach to Kommerscheidt. No supplies got through, no casualties were evacuated either from Kommerscheidt or from the Aid Station. Morning—Lieutenant Johnson reported five attempts by himself to get a weasel down to the ambulance loading point. Fired upon each time by the enemy battery at (065334), he was forced to withdraw and abandon the attempt.

1:00 PM—I recommended to the Division Surgeon that a truce be arranged to permit removal of casualties from inaccessible Kommerscheidt and the Aid Station area. Together we went to make the suggestion to Brigadier General Davis at the Regimental Rear Command Post. General Davis was not there. The Division Surgeon departed for Division Headquarters with the statement that he would make the suggestion to Commanding General.

3:00 PM—All other methods of evacuation having failed, Lieutenant Johnson reported that he was taking five ambulances and eight litter teams to establish a new Ambulance Loading Point at (029313) from which he proposed to travel to (033314), (037316), and across the nose of the hill to the Red-Blue Aid Station. This route, a last resort, would have required an airline litter carry of 1 mile with extremely difficult descent and ascent of two high hills.

5:00 PM—Lieutenant Johnson reported that attempt had failed. Having reached (037316), he was informed that L Company had been forced back to that point and that further progress down the valley would lead into enemy lines. Johnson continued despite this warning, encountered heavy mortar fire at (039318), was forced to withdraw.

6:00 PM—All remaining troops of Red and Blue battalions withdrew from Kommerscheidt Hill by breaking up into small groups and making individual escapes through enemy lines. Red-Blue Aid Station remained at same location.

9:00 PM—Lieutenant Johnson and Page returned to Collecting Company for the night.

11:00 PM—Division Surgeon called via telephone, said that Division G-4 had ordered thirteen weasels with armed guard to proceed immediately to Red-Blue Aid Station to evacuate fifty casualties known to be there. Regimental S-4 was contacted, agreed with me that arming of convoy was dangerous. S-4 wanted Lieutenant Johnson to accompany the convoy and had sent a message to him. I sent another by courier, in case the S-4 message was lost. I arranged for ambulances to meet the returning convoy at the White Aid Station, now taken over by 109th White. Lieutenant Johnson received message too late to catch convoy.

November 9, 1944: 2:45 AM
M29 Weasel convoy reached original Ambulance Loading Point vicinity but overshot road in darkness, could not find Air Station. At (045321) the convoy was fired upon and Private First Class Shumacher, of the Medical Detachment, who had volunteered to accompany the convoy as a guide, was killed. One weasel was disabled. The remaining vehicles withdrew, having failed to reach the Aid Station or to evacuate any wounded.[4]

8:00 AM—I phoned Division G-4, volunteered to go under a flag of truce to the German lines to arrange a truce to enable us to evacuate wounded from Kommerscheidt Hill, now free of American combat troops. I requested authority be given me by Division Commanding General to make definite arrangements with the enemy for the truce. My request was denied. G-4 suggested that I merely determine the attitude of the enemy toward a truce, leaving the details and official confirmation to be made later.

9:50 AM—With Tech Sergeant 4 Wheeler W. Wolters acting as flag-bearer and interpreter, I departed from Vossenack on foot across brow of hill toward Aid Station. Arrived at Aid Station without being fired upon, found Aid Station personnel loading forty-four casualties into two 2.5-ton trucks and one weasel which had been abandoned along road at Aid Station area by Services Company. Ten litter cases remained in the Aid Station. All Medical personnel there, including two MOs (medical officer), two MACs (mission assurance coordinator), two Chaplains and six enlisted men, together with thirty infantrymen, tankers and engineers, enlisted men who were acting as emergency litter bearers, were in good shape. Wolters and I continued past the Aid Station down the hill to the bridge at (046313), which we found blown out. After a short delay a German Lieutenant with five men came out to join us on the road. They were most courteous, made no attempt to search or harm us. I stated my intentions. The German Lieutenant said that all American wounded had been evacuated from the Kommerscheidt Hill by the German army Medical Department and that the German Medical Officer and enlisted men had completed the evacuation and had withdrawn only twenty minutes before my arrival. Since there appeared to be no further need of arranging a truce for evacuation from Kommerscheidt, I stated that we were going to remove three truckloads of wounded from our Aid Station and that two of the trucks would return for the remaining wounded and medical personnel.

The German Lieutenant offered to evacuate our wounded, but I declined in order to give him no opportunity or excuse to capture our Medical Department personnel. He agreed to permit the vehicles to pass out without interference by his men, but added that he had no communications with his superior officer to inform him of my request. He said that he expected a telephone line to be completed shortly and that he would inform both his superior officer and the German artillery to permit the vehicles to get out unmolested. He said and repeated that the German army scrupulously observed the Red Cross and would not fire upon anyone or any vehicle which clearly displayed the Red Cross. Following an exchange of salutes, I returned to the Red-Blue Aid Station. There I found that the loaded trucks had tried to get up the hill toward Vossenack but were completely blocked by two medium tanks. I returned to Holland White Aid Station, reported to Division G-4, outlined the situation to Lieutenant Johnson, who took numerous litter bearers and ambulances to the Ambulance Landing Point at the stalled tanks and evacuated all the wounded, all medical personnel, some of the assistant litter bearers, the MAC officers, and all members of his own party. German soldiers who helped with the ambulance loading restrained the Medical Officers and Chaplains from leaving. Lack of further information from these officers indicates that they were captured and held.

Summary

Evacuation of casualties during the Kommerscheidt-Schmidt operation was impeded by the most difficult type of terrain, by a wretched road network which was worsened by daily rain, by a shortage of vehicles at the beginning, and by the early loss by capture of the Red and Blue battalions' Medical vehicles, by frequent blockage of the single road by knocked-out tanks, by lack of communications, and by being in the position of operating a two-battalion [Aid Station] for three days behind German lines. Despite these handicaps, evacuation was continued intermittently until the American infantry failed to regain the valley in which the Aid Station was located. Then it stopped. Negotiations carried out under a flag of truce enabled every casualty at the Aid Station and most medical personnel to be removed safely.[5]

To the credit of the Medical Department, let it be well noted that the Red-Blue Aid Station personnel remained in their Air Station behind the German lines, taking care of their wounded and making every humanly possible effort to evacuate the wounded themselves, for a period of more than twenty hours after every other member of the 112th Regimental Combat Team had withdrawn to positions in the rear of the original Line of Departure of the Vossenack attack.

Let it also be made a matter of record that only one method of total evacuation proved feasible: under the flag of truce; that this method was suggested to the Regimental Staff and later to the Division General Staff in plenty of time to permit the evacuation of all American wounded from the Schmidt-Kommerscheidt area; that these suggestions were declined until it was too late to reach this area and these wounded were left by the withdrawing Infantry to be picked up by the enemy; and that, had the suggestion of a truce been adopted when first made, evacuation would have been completed with no detriment to the eventual tactical outcome of the operation.[6]

15

German 89th Infantry Division Mirror

On November 2, heavy attacks were launched again in the area of Germeter-Vossenack, which brought Vossenack into the hands of the enemy. On the morning of November 3, the enemy launched a surprise attack from Vossenack towards the south. They succeeded in breaking through our right flank and penetrating into the rear areas of our division's positions. After the breakthrough to the west, it appears that the enemy now has a clear path through Vossenack and Schmidt towards the Rur River and Düren. At this point, General Krüger, who is currently in this area, sends Colonel Ulbricht with two assault companies to counter the enemy. These units form the first solid barrier against the enemy, preventing an unimpeded advance. Regiment 1055, which was marching towards Lammersdorf-Rollesbroich, was halted.

The thoughts of the men, who have repelled every enemy attack since the beginning of the forest battles and inflicted heavy losses on the enemy through patrols and raids, undergo a sudden change. Gone are the hopes of rest and replacement; the harsh necessity demands a new effort. For the enemy's victory here would mean the continuation of their advance over the ridges of the Rur and the capture of Kommerscheidt. Another enemy breakthrough must be prevented at all costs, or all the efforts, suffering, and sacrifices of the past weeks and months would have been in vain. Regiment 1055 is tasked with this mission. In swift, improvised movements, the enemy is confronted with a determined stand. Tank destroyer units move forward, and new reserves are brought up. However, the enemy's pressure also increases, and their artillery fire becomes more intense.

At 4:15 PM, the report arrives that Schmidt is in enemy hands. Shortly after, Battalion Wolf has set out. The barriers on the road are being prepared for demolition. *Puppchen* antitank guns are being positioned. Reconnaissance patrols set off into completely new terrain, but they return with important reports. Determined and resolute, Colonel Issel gives his orders for the construction of the new positions, preparing for the upcoming attack. Assault guns and tanks move in. The soldiers are eager for battle; they haven't seen "these heavy lads" in a while. Now they know that when things get really critical, the necessary weapons are also present. Our artillery adjusts to the new targets. Throughout the day, fighter-bombers fly over our positions, and loud noises can be heard from our right flank. Our own attack aircraft are reported, engaging the advancing enemy with bombs and machine guns.

On the morning of November 4, the enemy launched a stronger attack in the area of Simonskall. In the region of Germeter, Hauptmann Schütz led a heavy counterattack. We advanced from the west towards Harcheidt. The first successes began to show. Hauptmann Wolf, with a platoon and some signalmen, broke into Schmidt. Assault guns rolled through Schmidt and, along with Wolf's men, pushed the enemy out of Schmidt. Slowly, the enemy retreated north. Then the report arrived that the enemy had penetrated Simonskall. Our front was in motion. The battalions advanced step by step. Regiment 1056 also received orders to join the battle. Storm clouds gathered over the battlefield. Despite persistent enemy fire, the men pushed forward into their new positions, relieved that they were no longer in the defensive positions they had previously held. Even though the old positions had been laboriously constructed and were known intimately by every step and turn, the situation demanded progress. The enemy's advance had to be stopped, and every effort was made to fortify the new positions and continue the fight.

The battle rages on as the Hauptmann Olnnen Battalion continues to advance. Regiment 1056 also reports their first successful reconnaissance patrols and raids. The situation is becoming increasingly tense. From the north, the 116th Panzer Division advances towards Vossenack. The closure of the front lines is evident in the south. The enemy attempts to break through at multiple points with all their might but is repelled everywhere. Parts of the battalions led by Hauptmann Wolf and Hauptmann Schütz have penetrated deeply into the heart of Kommerscheidt, offering fierce resistance. The battle fluctuates with unpredictable intensity. Explosions echo continuously, and enemy artillery fires sporadically from hidden positions or behind cover.

An American battalion was reported to be moving towards Kommerscheidt in the late afternoon hours. Enemy tanks also make repeated attempts to break through, but they cannot shake the determination of our men. The first prisoners are captured. They are transporters who have attempted to move from Schmidt into the dense woods near Schaidt. Prisoners are also returned from Kommerscheidt. The numbers slowly rise: first seven, then nine, then fifteen. Among them are those who were missing in action since 1942. In the midst of the battle, known for its fierce skirmishes, two prisoners are killed, one wounded, and one elderly civilian is accidentally injured. In the dark, reconnaissance patrols continue to engage the enemy, but they can't find a moment of peace. Our artillery also joins in with persistent and precise counter-battery fire to disrupt the enemy's movements.

On November 6, the weather has become clearer. Allied fighter-bombers take advantage of the sunny day to launch relentless attacks. The men of the Schindler Battalion fight fiercely and gain ground against Olnnen and Wißchewatz. At around 2:30 PM, the enemy attacks from the north towards Kommerscheidt. Earlier, as reported, heavy fire was directed towards Schmidt and the densely wooded areas behind our positions. However, our artillery continues its work unabated. Thick smoke billows over the landscape as the fighting intensifies. Sometimes, the smoke obscures visibility to less than 100 or 200 meters. Under the cover of the dense smoke, movements from Kommerscheidt towards Lendersdorf or Hürtgen can hardly be detected.

At the right time, we launch our attack, with about 200 men moving in to disrupt the enemy's rear lines. The enemy at Vossenack, despite all efforts, fails to bring about any significant change in their situation. However, it's not all smooth sailing. At 3:00 PM, the message comes through the wires that the battle for Kommerscheidt has been successfully concluded. Over the past few days alone, 260 prisoners have been captured, with 100 confirmed fatalities. Eleven tanks have been destroyed, with two more likely, and two have surrendered. Some smaller pockets of resistance still hold out, but the pressure against these resistance nests continues. Our infantry, along with tanks and grenadiers, who have been engaged in continuous combat for almost a day without a moment of respite, persist against the enemy. Finally, after the long struggle, the resistance pockets are defeated, and the front lines are completely secured.

On November 8, during the actual combat operations for the clearing of the forest by Terraced Groups, we encounter an attack. The battalion leader of the 3rd Battalion of Regiment 1056 takes action once again, this time on the Kesternich hill, with renewed vigor. Once again, the enemy assaults the position, which had received no resupply for several days and had barely any time for rest. Despite the difficult circumstances, the attack is repelled in a coordinated manner, with the support of the 1st Company of the 1st Battalion, 189th Regiment, and the pioneers of the regiment. The enemy is repelled with hand grenades and machine pistols. Eighty enemy soldiers are killed, and twenty-seven prisoners and wounded are taken, marking a significant success for our forces.

Against a larger group of scattered artillerymen, the area around Schmidt, where just a few days ago the Luftwaffe had already brought out a portion of the prisoners, another operation is launched, this time with the support of two assault guns. The infantry, under the strong leadership of the officers, advances through the dense forest towards Lendersdorf. Even though the last scattered enemy resistance pockets are eliminated, the outcome of this often bitterly fought struggle justifies the sacrifices made, both on our side and on the side of the enemy. In this engagement, the enemy lost twice as many prisoners and dead as we have had soldiers in action since the beginning of the battles when the Kessel von Kommerscheidt was formed. Five hundred thirty-five prisoners, 280 confirmed enemy dead, twenty-six enemy tanks destroyed, two more captured, four self-propelled guns, four trucks, one medical tank, one antitank gun, and a vast amount of small arms, ammunition, and supplies testify to the numerical success of this battle. But even more important is its operational success. The enemy's intended breakthrough through the Eifel into the hinterland beyond was prevented; the incursion into the Kommerscheidt and Schmidt area was contained; and the encircled enemy, trapped in multiple fierce battles (the struggle in Kommerscheidt alone lasted five days), was annihilated.

Thus, the division has achieved new and enduring glory. All this was only possible through the close cooperation of all subordinate units and their reliance on cooperation with the division. Within the division, the spirit of the fighters from La Salle, combined with the audacity and attack momentum of the young Luftwaffe personnel and the battalions newly arrived in the Westernwall, has been unified. In the crucible of battle in Kommerscheidt, amidst loss and danger, blood and sacrifice, our 89th Infantry Division will continue to defy all enemy attacks in the future and will not rest until victory is ours.[1]

16

Analyses and Lessons Learned

German Generalmajor Rudolf-Christoph Freiherr von Gersdorff's account of the Battle of the Hürtgen Forest

On October 22, 1944, the Fifth Panzer Army, commanded by General Manteuffel, was placed in a position on the right flank of Army Group B, commanded by General Model. This was at approximately the time when the second battle for Aachen had ended: At this time only the command staff of the Fifth Panzer Army was present.

In broad outline it was believed that the American advance could be halted. However, it was felt that it would not be successful to eliminate the penetrations that had been made on both sides of Aachen, nor would it be possible to push the enemy forces west to the boundary of Germany. The city of Aachen was finally lost to the American forces October 20, 1944.

The intelligence reports of the German army made clear the fact that in the Aachen-Liege sector the purpose of the American drive was the Ruhr industrial area with the cities of Cologne and Dusseldorf as the primary objectives. On the north we felt that the British, in a coordinated action, would also drive for the Ruhr, sweeping down from the north. The results of consideration on the above point revealed to us that the right flank of the American attack (north) would be just north of Monschau. We felt that the main effort would be directed at the Hürtgen-Monschau-Düren road for the purpose of (1) capturing Düren and (2) seizing the Roer Dams. The following were the reasons that influenced us in the decision of committing the Fifth Panzer Army:

1. The length of the front of the Seventh Army (from Gelsenkirchen to Trier) was too broad to effectively handle the disposition of the tasks at Army level.

2. During the battles east of Aachen more and more mobile troops were brought into the area (Panzergrenadier units). Also other forces of a highly mobile type were brought forward. This made it necessary to place such forces under an Army that was qualified to direct them. That was the Fifth Panzer Army.
3. The Ardennes Offensive, which had been planned at this time, also influenced placing of the Fifth Panzer Army in the line of defense. It was believed that this would hide the preparations that were being made for the December attack.

The boundary between the Fifth Panzer Army and the Seventh Army was the same as the one between the LXXXI Corps and the LXXIV Corps and ran on a line from Vicht-Schevenhütte to just north of Düren-Brühl. The Fifth Panzer Army, at the same time this line became effective, took control of the LXXXI Corps. (This was on October 22, 1944.)

This line was not satisfactory to the Seventh Army because it ran on an angle to the northeast. It was assumed that, when the American attack drove to the east, the forces north of the line would withdraw in that direction and those south would withdraw to the east. That would leave an open corner in the direction to Düren-Cologne through which the American forces could penetrate. An attempt by the Seventh Army to have the boundary between the two armies changed to a more satisfactory position was not given favorable consideration by the Army Group. In the beginning of November, therefore, the right wing of the Seventh Army was in the Hürtgen Forest engaged in what the Germans termed the third phase of the battle for Aachen.

The infantry divisions of the corps (275th and 89th) possessed the faults of being organized hurriedly while holding a front in the Siegfried Line. Many improvisations were necessary and there existed insufficient quantity of materiel for future action. The strength of the infantry divisions was complete but the distribution of material among the sub-units was unsatisfactory. The personnel of the units were not soldiers. They were support troops, previously assigned to supply duties, and had no combat experience. The officers and noncommissioned officers were not satisfactory and left much to be desired. The weapons were unsatisfactory and not uniform. The artillery regiments were composed of guns of German, Russian, Italian, and French origin. For some of these foreign guns there was an insufficient supply of ammunition, i.e., the 122mm Russian howitzer. There were also very few anti-tank weapons, but a sufficient supply of bazookas and Panzerfausts. Especially distressing was the personal clothing of the soldiers. This was especially felt when the weather became cold and wet and we incurred a large number of non-battle casualties.

From the beginning of November and the operations which developed until the Ardennes Offensive, it is necessary to consider the reasons given before to fully appreciate the difficulties of the fighting. The men and officers were fully cognizant of the importance of this zone of operation and did their very best in its defense. Therefore, there existed bitter fighting for every foot of ground and resulted in the counterattacks which at times were successful as well as unsuccessful. It is a fact that, as the strength and bitterness of the fighting increased, coupled with the conditions of the ground and the weather and the effects on all arms, there was a similarity that was noticeable between this fighting and that of the last years of the first World War.

For the Seventh Army the Hürtgen area was always an "open wound," and was a very disturbing factor in the planning for the Ardennes Offensive. Because of the continued fighting, Seventh Army was always forced to attempt to bring forward reserve troops for the battle in the Hürtgen. Those Volksgrenadier divisions that were in the area could not be utilized because they had been earmarked for the Ardennes. (Panzer and SS units were already under control of the armies that were going to fight in the Ardennes.) These divisions had to finish their organization and instructions behind the front, or in the inactive sectors, the only zones we were permitted to commit them. As an example of this, the 47th Volksgrenadier Division might be cited. (The 47th Volksgrenadier Division was almost completely destroyed in about three days just north of Schevenhütte in about mid-November, when it was committed in a critical sector with incomplete preparation.) Furthermore, it might be said that the Siegfried Line divisions, which possessed secondary troops and poor weapons, were likewise unqualified for commitment in the difficult fighting of the Hürtgen. One of the big problems was the consistent lack of ammunition of artillery caliber. Because of that we were restricted to firing only about one fourth to one fifth the amount of ammunition that the Americans fired. In spite of that we successfully maintained offensive and defensive action west of the Roer, so that the initial phase of the Ardennes Offensive was insured. (General Gersdorff pointed out that had the Roer River been crossed by the American forces, the Ardennes Offensive would not have been possible to execute as originally planned.)

The fact of the American attack was no surprise—only its timing. Observed movement of American troops in the rear of Roetgen, obviously (by pattern of air bursts) preplanned artillery fires, agent reports, and other signs led us to believe that an attack was imminent. The anticipated direction of the attack was towards Germeter and Lammersdorf. The deep penetration in the direction of Hürtgen and Vossenack assured us that the attack was headed for the roads to Düren, the Roer, and the dams. Since the Army reserves were too weak, we initiated a request to Army Group for troops with which to counterattack and reduce the penetration. By unusual chance both the Army Commander and his Chief of Staff were in conference with the Army Group Commander, Field

Marshall Modl at Castle Schlenderhan. Army Group initially gave one battle group and later in the day released the entire 116th Panzer Division, whose commander, General von Waldenburg, was present at the conference. The decisions, orders, and execution were accelerated by this chance gathering of the commanders.

The Army decided to move the bulk of the 116th Panzer Division over the shortest route from Düren to Hürtgen. The counterattack itself was to be organized in the woods south of Hürtgen. The Army ordered that the shoulders of the penetration—northwest of and south of Germeter—be held strongly. With the rapid advance of the Americans to the east and southeast of Vossenack, parts of the 116th Panzer Division were positioned around the perimeter ready to launch a concentric counterattack. Since the deep valley between Vossenack and the Brandenberg-Bergstein ridge offered us considerable protection, our greatest fears were for the axis Vossenack-Kommerscheidt-Schmidt. We expected a rapid advance in that direction to the dams. Near the Mestrenger Mühle were only weak elements of the 89th Infantry Division. The reconnaissance battalion of the 116th Panzer Division was ordered to this point.

Because the woods north and east of Vossenack prevented armored employment, the tank regiment of the 116th Panzer Division was sent to the vicinity of Schmidt, attached to the 89th Division. Both these forces, however, were so restricted by the air situation and by the condition of the road that they arrived too late to perform their initial tasks. The Reconnaissance Battalion, however, was successful, in coordination with the 89th Infantry Division, in retaking the Mestrenger Mühle and thereby severing the connection between leading elements and those in Vossenack. At this time the Army ordered LXXIV Corps to launch two attacks. The first attack, employing the 89th Infantry Division, reinforced with the tank regiment of the 116th Panzer Division, and assault gun brigade (fifteen guns) was to retake Schmidt and Kommerscheidt.

The second attack, employing the remainder of the 116th Panzer Division, was to be a concentric squeeze on Vossenack. All possible support—artillery, assault guns, and heavy weapons—were given to these attacks. The divisional artillery of the 272nd Volksgrenadier Division, less one battalion, was displaced to the north and added its fires. This artillery disposition was ordered by the Corps artillery commander.

The first part of the mission given to LXXIV Corps can be considered successful. By November 7, the Corps had destroyed the American forces which had gotten to the vicinity of Schmidt. After heavy fighting in both Schmidt and Kommerscheidt, the American tanks had been destroyed and the infantry could only pass individually back through the woods to Vossenack. The three most important reasons for our success in this engagement were: the steepness of our supply route from Vossenack to Kommerscheidt, the availability to us of roads capable of supporting an armored attack, and the effective massing of our artillery fire.

The second part of the mission was not so successful. The 116th Panzer Division was able to reach the church in Vossenack but they could neither capitalize on nor retain this advantage. Without armored support, operating on open ground which left us at the mercy of aircraft and artillery, lacking reserves, and facing an excellent, spirited defense, our attack could go no further. In spite of heavy artillery support and repeated assaults, we made no success. When we saw that our attack to cut off the penetration had no chance of completion, we ordered that the troops establish a defense along the edge of the woods. In this process the 116th Panzer Division was replaced by parts of the 89th Infantry Division and the 275th Volksgrenadier Division.

The Panzer Division then assembled near Hürtgen in preparation for a new attack, designed to go along the Hürtgen-Germeter road to the edge of the woods south of Germeter. Such an attack would cut off the Vossenack bulge. The tank regiment was to remain east of the Kall while the two Panzergrenadier regiments and the assault gun brigade were moved to Hürtgen. The artillery displaced to support the new attack. All elements of the 275th Volksgrenadier Division which were in the zone of attack became attached to the 116th Panzer Division.

The American renewal of the attack on November 7 had been stopped by the effective use of extensive minefields, by the artillery and by the employment of a mortar battalion. When the 116th Panzer Division launched its attack southwest of Hürtgen on November 10, it met a new American Division, the 4th, which was also attacking. The arrival of this unit was a surprise to us. The Panzer Division was successful in stopping the attack of the new American forces but could not effect a breakthrough. The attack of the 116th Panzer Division in the woods succeeded in pinching off the salient of the American troops but we were unable to prevent withdrawal to the south. The American troops could pass through the thick woods undetected. The special character of forest-fighting was illustrated in another episode east of the Germeter-Hürtgen road. Here an American attack was launched along a division boundary into the woods south of Hürtgen. There the enemy established a defensive position which, after repeated attempts, we could not reduce. The 89th Infantry Division considered the ejection of this force to be a point of honor, but they were never able to dispose of them. This typically confused example of forest-fighting may be likened to a contest of "cat and mouse".

The Army now realized that the possibility of regaining the lost ground was now dim. Orders were therefore issued changing the mission from offensive to defensive. In this connection we consistently tried to keep control of the dominating terrain and to establish the front lines in the woods. On November 16 the expected large scale American offensive began, striking the Army's northern flank with the American right wing. At this time the strong American attacks by the 4th Division were launched, first in the woods against Weisser Weh and Rother Weh. The defending elements of the 275th Infantry Division could not prevent the advance of the 4th Division towards Grosshau. At this time, against our strongest wishes, we were again forced to commit the 116th Panzer Division to prevent American troops from spilling out of the woods onto the open ground. The Division should have been withdrawn from the line and rehabilitated for the Ardennes Offensive. The ever-pressing problem confronting us at Army was the reinforcement of the heavily engaged right flank of the LXXIV Corps. Since reserves were not available we adopted an expedient solution. The 272nd and 277th Volksgrenadier divisions were periodically required to leapfrog their right flank battalion during the night to occupy the positions of their neighbor to the north. In this way we were able, bit by bit, to shift the weight north. The right boundary of the 272nd Volksgrenadier Division, for example, initially was north of Monschau and ultimately was edged up to Zweifallshammer.

The Army consistently tried this method to milk reserves from the LXVI and LXXX Corps. At first we were able to free only single battalions, separate field artillery battalions, etc. Now began a series of moves in which newly arrived Volksgrenadier divisions on the Eifel front relieved the Panzer divisions located there. The 18th and 26th Volksgrenadier divisions had, in early November, relieved the 2nd SS Panzer Division and 2nd Panzer Division, respectively. The two Panzer divisions were not available for our use, since they had to be readied for the Ardennes Offensive.

The 18th and 26th divisions in mid-November each extended their interior flanks, thereby pinching out the 344th Division, which was in the center of LXVI Corps. The 344th Division thus became available for employment in the north. A few days later the 352nd Volksgrenadier Division replaced the 353rd Division in the LXXX Corps zone. The 353rd Division then moved north and was committed on November 20 to further bolster the right flank of LXXIV Corps. Not an integral part of this shift to the north but indicative of the readjustment of units at this time was the insertion of the 212th Volksgrenadier Division above Trier. This division relieved the 36th Volksgrenadier Division, which in turn was dispatched to the Saar front. These two divisions—the 353rd and 344th—were committed in mid-November in the Hürtgen Forest.

The 344th Division was originally known as the 91st Air Landing Division, which had been reportedly destroyed. A new designation was therefore applied. It was clear to the Army that units like the 344th and 353rd infantry divisions had little combat value in the unusually bitter fighting of the Hürtgen Forest. Since no other troops were available, we had to content ourselves with what we had. With the arrival of these two divisions we were enabled, however, to withdraw the 116th Panzer Division in preparation for its role in the coming Ardennes Offensive.

The Panzer Division artillery remained several extra days in position partially because there were no replacements and partially because we did not want to inform you of their withdrawal. Later, however, the Division once again had to detach a combat group to the south flank of the Fifteenth Army. The arrival of the two divisions also enabled us to withdraw the staff, key commanders, non-coms, and the supply echelons of the 275th Infantry Division. The remnants of the infantry troops were absorbed by the 353rd, 344th, and 89th divisions, as was the artillery.

All these complicated changes and reinforcements were accomplished during the relentless, bitter fighting of the Hürtgen Forest. In a steady, slow, meter-by-meter advance, the numerically superior enemy forces were able to shove the front line back through the woods and into the cleared space of Hürtgen and Kleinhau.

The defense now gripped onto the battered towns of Hürtgen, Kleinhau, Grosshau to protect the critical hills east of those towns. When the 89th Infantry Division was broken through north of Vossenack and the town of Hürtgen threatened from several sides, the defense was unhinged. The attack of an American armored group in the direction of Brandenberg in early December was of critical importance. This thrust threatened a deep penetration with a consequent extension of our thinly spread forces. Every effort was, therefore, made to repel this lunge by counterattacks.

Having no other reserves available, the Seventh Army, with concurrence of Army Group, decided to commit the 272nd Volksgrenadier Division assisted by assault gun units. It was an unwelcome decision for both the Army and Army Group. The Division was scheduled to participate in the Ardennes Offensive and it was recognized that heavy casualties in this engagement would seriously hamper its effectiveness. The projection, however, of the American attack on through Bergstein to the Roer River would jeopardize the execution of the Ardennes Offensive. For this reason Army Group released the 47th Volksgrenadier Division for the specified purpose of defending east of the Roer River. This Division was in the process of absorbing replacements after its heavy engagement farther north. By these measures a new American breakthrough was prevented but repeated counterattacks against Brandenberg, Bergstein, and Hill 400 [the name given by Allied forces during World War II to a 1,300ft.-high hill located 0.62 miles east of the village center of Bergstein] enjoyed no success.

Meanwhile, in the north the right flank of the Army had been slowly retiring before the repeated assaults that also drove back the southern flank of the Fifteenth Army. But at Gey—considered the focal point of the defense, since it controlled the debouchment of American forces from the woods—we made special efforts to hold the ground. Army Group considered the threat of a breakthrough, Gey to Düren, so important that they assigned to the Seventh Army a task force of the 3rd Parachute Division—again with specific limitations. The task force was to form a second line of defense running generally north-south through Birgel.

On December 10, Seventh Army was relieved in the Düren-Bergstein area by the Fifteenth Army and on its southern front by the Fifth Panzer Army. Seventh Army then took over its Vianden-Trier sector. Although we left a dangerously weak front manned by exhausted troops, we felt that we had prevented a strategic penetration in the Hürtgen area.

The fighting in Hürtgen had cost us dearly in casualties yet we were certain that we had inflicted commensurate losses on the enemy in men and materiel. In what was probably the heaviest fighting in the war, soldiers of both sides performed, under unbelievable hardships, acts of great gallantry and perseverance.[1]

Lieutenant Colonel Kenneth McMillin's account of the reasons behind the Battle of the Hürtgen Forest

Historian Martin Blumensen proposed that the unexpected success of the Allied breakout and the subsequent chase of the German army through France led Eisenhower and his top generals to underestimate the German threat. This sense of optimism persisted through the Allied advance in France, waning only when they encountered the Westwall.

Blumensen noted that Eisenhower and Bradley were already planning future operations into Germany before they had fully defeated the German forces in the Falaise pocket. Bradley was focused on crossing the Rhine, while Eisenhower aimed for Berlin. Blumensen criticized the Allied planners for their terrain-focused approach in setting objectives, which led to tactical and operational lapses and a misunderstanding of what was necessary to defeat the enemy.

Blumensen also suggested that the "miracle of the West" might not have occurred if the German staff had been destroyed or captured, as many German units had been in the Falaise-Argentan Gap. He argued, "Conditioned by Overlord planning, which focused on securing the lodgment area as the goal, the three Allied leaders [Eisenhower, Montgomery, and Bradley] neglected a fundamental principle of warfare. They thought that capturing terrain, rather than destroying the enemy, was the proper way to win the war."

The lack of a detailed Allied plan to incapacitate the enemy's ability to continue fighting after the Normandy breakout also played a role in the subsequent battles of the Hürtgen. During the Battle of Hürtgen Forest, the Americans struggled with tactics that had previously been effective during their advance through France—specifically, combined arms operations.

The forest's road network was unsuitable for armor, and American tanks faced difficulties due to narrow trails and the need for infantry support. German artillery had targeted key crossroads, clearings, and other strategic terrain features throughout the forest. Poor weather conditions hindered air support, and the Germans had adapted by moving their units primarily at night to avoid air attacks. The challenging forest terrain and well-fortified German positions diminished the impact of Allied air support compared to earlier in the campaign. Additionally, the Americans lost their artillery advantage during the attacks because observers could only see a short distance in front of them, and the Germans effectively utilized bunkers and pillboxes.

Why did Lieutenant General Hodges keep sending unit after unit into the Hürtgen Forest, and why did none of his subordinate commanders attempt to persuade him otherwise? In a 1983 interview, Collins said: "The Germans didn't launch counterattacks on my flank because we had troops in the Hürtgen that prevented them from doing so. If we had withdrawn from the Hürtgen, the Germans could have attacked my flank. It's easy to second-guess decisions with hindsight and say that we shouldn't have done that. But then, what would you have done instead? Who would have cleared the area? How long would it have taken?"

Collins is right; it's easy to second guess decisions made nearly forty years ago. In 1944, both Hodges and Collins were under immense pressure to advance across the Roer River and into Germany's industrial heartland. However, repeatedly committing divisions to the Hürtgen Forest raises questions that remain unresolved. One factor might have been US intelligence shortcomings and the forest's challenging terrain, which hindered effective reconnaissance to assess the German forces defending it.

Why didn't the Americans deploy a blocking force in the northern part of the forest to guard against German attacks on the northern flank? Generalmajor von Gersdorff remarked that there was no benefit in the Americans pushing through the Hürtgen Forest, suggesting that circumventing it on both sides would have met with little resistance. While this may have been true in early September 1944, the situation was complicated by the arrival of German reinforcements.

The primary reason the Americans did not advance through the Stolberg Corridor or the Monschau Corridor in the south early in September 1944 was due to severe logistical shortages affecting the Allied armies in Europe. The lack of supplies halted the Twelfth Army Group's efforts to push further into Germany. If adequate supplies had been available, Hodges might have been able to bypass the Hürtgen Forest entirely. Once the First Army became bogged down due to shortages of gasoline, artillery ammunition, and other essential supplies, it was too late; the German defenses had already solidified.

There are also the lingering questions over the American failure to prioritize the Roer River dams as key operational objectives until November 1944. The initial goal was to clear the forest and establish supply routes for crossing the Roer River.

As previously mentioned, Eisenhower and Bradley were overly optimistic and failed to focus on intermediate objectives necessary to achieve their strategic goals. Blumensen criticized the Americans for focusing on terrain rather than on the crucial task of destroying the German army. Historian Russell Weigley attributed the failure to identify the dams as key objectives early in the campaign to a broader "pattern of uninquisitive headquarters planning" among the Allies in late autumn. Once the battle of attrition began in the forest, it posed the classic dilemma of knowing when to stop and how to gauge success. In this respect, the US army faced several challenges.

One major issue was the lack of forward leadership. Few division commanders were recorded as having personally surveyed the Hürtgen Forest. Unlike line officers, division and corps staff officers were not typically exposed to the dangers of the front lines, allowing them to devise new plans for gaining ground while the soldiers tasked with executing these plans often lasted only a few days before being wounded or killed.

Another reason American leadership did not view the casualties in the forest as excessive was the steady flow of replacements. These replacements often consisted of inexperienced personnel, such as reclassified cooks, clerks, drivers, and air defense and aircrew members, drawn from rear-echelon units. The situation was further exacerbated by the loss of seasoned riflemen and noncommissioned officers. Integrating new recruits into squads and platoons is challenging in any combat environment, but in the Hürtgen Forest, it was nearly impossible. Many replacements became casualties so quickly that they did not even know the platoon, company, or battalion to which they belonged, for example, upon reaching aid stations. Throughout the battle, many subordinate commanders "painted a rosy picture" of progress to higher headquarters, a task made easier by the availability of replacements.

Finally, American leadership remained hopeful that just one more fresh division would be enough to drive the Germans out of the forest. During the battle, the Americans deployed five infantry divisions, a combat command of armor, an additional armored infantry battalion, and a ranger battalion. As First Army G-3 Brigadier General Thorsen described it, "We had the bear by the tail, and we just couldn't turn it loose."

Neither Bradley, Hodges, nor their staff had a clear vision for the ultimate goal of the advance to the Ruhr. Had they attacked Aachen immediately and then moved through the Stolberg Corridor, they could have saved significant time and manpower that would be needed later in the year. Additionally, they did not designate the Roer River dams as operational objectives until late November. As long as victory seemed imminent, it was easier to dismiss the dams as a concern rather than create a detailed plan for their capture. Weigley notes that caution was the downfall of Bradley, Collins, and Hodges. If the dams had been identified as operational objectives earlier, "the full-scale clearing of the forest and the bitter combat for every obscure crossroads" could have been avoided.

Regarding the decision to attack directly into the forest and the Westwall, Hodges likely intended to break through the Westwall, secure it, and allow his armor to push through to the Rhine before needing to pause and refit. Hodges and his commanders believed the Westwall was heavily defended and planned their attack accordingly.

However, he still needed to secure his flank and rear in the Hürtgen Forest. Could he have attacked just enough into the forest to secure his flank and enable his more mobile armor units to advance through the Stolberg Corridor?

The German defenders had limited mobility and likely could not have mounted a significant counterattack. Alternatively, could Hodges have redirected the V Corps' main effort to the south and attacked through the Monschau Corridor? He would still have needed to secure his northern flank in the southern part of the Hürtgen Forest. These are hypothetical scenarios, but either approach could have reduced the attrition battles in the forest itself.

The Germans managed to reach their border first and, with some luck and fresh reinforcements, stopped the American advance short of the Roer River before the Ardennes Offensive. The fighting in the Hürtgen Forest was costly for both sides, but the Germans suffered more from the loss of their trained officers and noncommissioned officers, as they were no longer able to replace them.

From September until December 16, the American First Army incurred 7,024 killed in action, 35,115 wounded, and 4,860 missing or captured. Although German casualty records were destroyed at the end of the war, making it difficult to determine their losses, the Americans had severely weakened at least six German divisions, eliminated hundreds of individual replacements, and forced the Germans to deploy forces that were originally intended for the Ardennes Counteroffensive.

The battle of the Hürtgen Forest inflicted significant casualties on the Germans, contributing to the broader strategic goal of weakening the German army, but at a considerable cost. However, in terms of destroying Germany's ability to continue the war, no strategic objectives were achieved. Even the crucial operational goal of capturing the Roer River dams was overlooked until the Americans were deeply mired in the forest.

The Hürtgen Forest battle was reminiscent of the Meuse-Argonne Offensive in World War One or Grant's Battle of the Wilderness in the Civil War—each resulting in horrendous casualties and little tangible gain. The Hürtgen was arguably a greater American military tragedy than either the Wilderness or the Argonne.[2]

Epilogue

The 28th Infantry Division suffered around 6,180 casualties during its deployment in the Hürtgen Forest. The 112th Infantry Regiment lost 2,100 of these men. It is noteworthy that 554 112th casualties were non-combat. Mental breakdowns, illnesses, hypothermia, so-called "trench foot," feet bruised by wet boots with non-healing wounds.

As the 28th Infantry withdrew, Combat Reporter Ivan H. Peterman was witness and wrote the following report:

> As Cy Peterson observed, the survivors left the Hürtgen Forest in silence, too traumatized and grief-stricken to speak of heroism after losing so many comrades. Physically and emotionally shattered, they wanted nothing more to do with the forest, which they had come to hate for its harsh conditions, constant danger, and relentless toll on their unit.
>
> The sounds of battle—gunfire and the cries of men—dissolved into the hush of the Hürtgen Forest, but the wounds it inflicted on both the terrain and those who fought there endured long after the fighting ceased. As the war pressed deeper into Germany, the Hürtgen Forest remained a somber and often overlooked chapter in American military history, etched deeply in the memories of those who survived its ordeal. In the years that followed, many veterans of the 28th Division returned home, their faces marked by the shadows of what they had witnessed. The stories of bravery and terror shared only among the few who had stood shoulder to shoulder in that brutal landscape remained largely untold to the world. Families welcomed them back with open arms, but the unshakeable burden of memory weighed heavily on their hearts. The forest, once alive with the sounds of battle, gradually reclaimed its serenity. Nature's resilience masked the memories of anguish; trees grew tall and wild, their roots entwined with the remnants of old war machines and forgotten dreams. Over time, the locals turned the battle-scarred terrain into a site of reflection, honoring

the sacrifices made there with monuments that stood as quiet witnesses to a past that was both revered and reviled.

As history began to acknowledge the Hürtgen Forest and the battles fought within, the lessons learned there became a crucial part of military training, emphasizing the need for unity and adaptability in the face of insurmountable odds. Scholars and historians sought to uncover the details long buried beneath layers of neglect, illuminating the complexities of the engagement and the indomitable spirit of the soldiers who fought through mud, rain, and fear.

For those who had endured the hardships, the bonds formed in the depths of the Hürtgen Forest forged friendships that would last a lifetime. Gatherings of veterans became a cherished tradition, where laughter mingled with tears as they shared their stories of resilience and the ghosts that continued to haunt them. Together, they navigated the fragile line between remembrance and moving forward, understanding that while the past could not be changed, it could be honored.

In the end, the Hürtgen Forest stood not only as a testament to the fierce combat fought within its borders but also as a symbol of humanity's capacity for endurance, empathy, and reconciliation. Through the shadows of its history, a glimmer of hope emerged—a reminder that even in the darkest of places, light could break through, illuminating the paths of those who dared to face the unknown.

The men who fought and died in the woods of the Hürtgen Forest in November 1944 deserve at least a reflective look. This grueling conflict, marked by dense fog, treacherous terrain, and fierce resistance, tested the resolve and endurance of those who served. Each soldier, facing unimaginable challenges, carried with them hopes, fears, and dreams, often cut short by the harsh realities of war.

As we remember their sacrifices, it is crucial to consider not only the strategic implications of the battle but also the human stories that unfolded within these dark, cold woods. Their bravery and camaraderie in the face of overwhelming odds reflect the profound complexities of courage and the cost of freedom. A reflective look at their experiences reminds us of the heavy toll of conflict and the enduring legacy of those who fought. By honoring their memory, we acknowledge the lessons learned and the forgotten sacrifices made, ensuring that their stories are never forgotten.[1]

Appendix A

Letter of Instruction from V Corps to Commanding Generals of 4th, 9th, 28th Infantry and 5th Armored Divisions, and V Corps Artillery

28th Division will attack on Corps Order (Target date November 1), to secure the high ground vicinity of SCHMIDT. It will maintain contact with units of the VII Corps on the North and South. When VOSSENACK-SCHMIDT (F0629) line is secured the Division will attack Southwest and secure the general line LAMMERSDORF-TOLLESBROICH-STRAUCH-STECKENBOR. Plans for the above operations will be submitted to this headquarters by 300800A October.

The following instructions are issued for operation of Corps Artillery.
Organization for combat:

190th FA Group
- 190th FA Bn (155 G)
- 997th FA Bn (6" H)

187th FA Group
- 167th FA Bn (155 H)
- 953rd FA Bn (155 H)

HQ V Corps Arty (less Det)
17th FA Cbsn Bn (less Battery B)

406th FA Group
- 186th FA Bn (155 H)
- 955th FA Bn (155 H)
- 941st FA Bn (4.5 G)
- 200th FA Bn (155 G)
- 272nd FA Bn (240 H)

Battery B, 17th FA Cbsn Bn
Detachment HQ V Corps Arty

Corps Artillery, less 406th FA Group, direct support 28th Inf. Div. and reinforce fires of 4th Cavalry Group Commanding General V Corps Artillery will coordinate fires of VII Corps Artillery units remaining in support of V Corps. 406th FA Group general support of Corps zone South of MONSCHAU.

893rd Tank Destroyer Battalion detached 4th Infantry Division and attached 9th Infantry Division on completion of relief of 4th Infantry Division by 9th Infantry Division.

382nd Medical Collection Company reverts to 53rd Medical Battalion effective 231200A October.

117th Engineer C Group less 668th Engineer Topographic Company attached to 28th Infantry Division effective 231200A October.

Provisional Military Government Police Force will operate in new zone as Directed.

All front-line units will continue active and aggressive patrolling and harassing fires to continue impression that attack will be made in present sector.

Radio silence lifted immediately for V Corps. Normal radio operations for all units. 4th Infantry Division will maintain radio silence in its relief until released by Commanding General VII Corps.

Headquarters V Corps moves to vicinity EUPEN (K8027), date and time of opening to be announced. (Actually, the Corps Forward Echelon moved on 28th October to EUPEN by Command of Major General GEROW.)

O. C. Wood, Col. GSC, C/S

Source: First Army Report of Operations, August 1, 1944 to February 22, 1945, (Washington, D,C,: U.S. Government Printing Office, 1945).

Appendix B

M29 Weasel

The M29 Weasel was designed and produced by the Studebaker Company in South Bend, Indiana from 1942 through 1945. It was initially conceived by British inventor Geoffrey Pyke to support proposed Allied attacks on Axis forces and industrial installations in Norway. A combination of low vehicle weight and comparatively wide track pads gave the Weasel low ground pressure, providing superior cross country movement in snow, sand, and muddy conditions. This allowed the Weasel to travel in terrain and weather conditions that most other vehicles couldn't. Some sources claim that Weasels were able to safely cross live minefields due to its low ground pressure. This characteristic made the Weasel a favored vehicle during its service in Italy, Northwest Europe, and throughout the Pacific islands.

The M29 Weasel is small for a fully tracked vehicle, measuring only 10 feet 6 inches long, 4 feet 3 inches wide, and 5 feet tall, weighing only 1.8 tons. The combination size and light weight makes the Weasel highly transportable, while retaining sturdy and reliable performance. Powered by a Model 6-170 Champion, a 6-cylinder 169.6 cu in (2,779 cc) cubic inch 4-stroke engine running on 72 octane gasoline delivering 70 bhp at 3,600 rpm, the M29 Wesel could travel at 36 mph on improved road surfaces. Its 35-gallon fuel tank could range 165 miles (266 km). The M29 Weasel is operated by a single driver and can carry three additional passengers.

Comparing the M29 to similar contemporary vehicles finds the Weasel as a middling vehicle in size, weight, capacity, and production next to the British Universal (AKA Bren) Gun Carrier and the German Kettenkraftrad. Like its contemporary vehicles, the Weasel was adopted for numerous roles beyond basic transport. The Weasel commonly served as a command and control vehicle, medical evacuation vehicle, communication wire dispenser (with a large wire spool attached to the rear), and messenger / courier. How it was used was limited only to the imagination of the GIs in the field.

The standard M29 Weasel began production in 1943 with 523 produced, followed by another 2,951 produced in 1944. Later in 1944, an improved version of the Weasel (the M29C) was developed with taller side boards, and additional floatation sections added to the front and rear to improve its amphibious performance. 4,201 M29Cs were produced in 1944 and another 6,446 produced in 1945.

Characteristics
Design: Fully tracked
Length: 10' 6" (3.20m)
Width: 5' (1.8m)
Height: 4' 3" (1.5m)
Weight: 1.8 tons
Road Speed: 36 mph (58 km/h)
Capacity: 1 driver, 3 passengers
Number Built: 15,892 (Sources vary on the exact number produced for the M29 and the improved M29C)

Source: Technical Manual, Series Number 6020, US WWII Studebaker M29 and M29C Weasel, (Erlangen, Germany: Tankograd Publishing, 2010).

Appendix C

M4 Sherman Tank

The Sherman was the most commonly used American tank in World War II. More than 50,000 Shermans were produced between 1942 and 1945. They were used in all combat theaters—not only by the United States, but also by Great Britain, the Free French, China, and even the Soviet Union. Initially developed to replace the M3 "Grant/Lee" medium tank, the first Shermans were manufactured in 1942, and some early production examples saw combat in North Africa in 1943. The model proved itself somewhat effective against German Mk II and Mk IV Panzers, but it was thoroughly outclassed by the Tiger, Panther, and King Tiger tanks. Notorious for their flammability, Shermans were nicknamed "Ronsons" after a lighter with the slogan "lights every time."

The Sherman tank's primary role was infantry support, spearheading attacks as well as bolstering defensive positions. Though frequently outgunned by their German counterparts, Shermans proved easier to maintain—often fixed on the battlefield. This particular tank, a rare M4A3E9 model (only a few hundred were built), carries appliqué armor for additional protection.

Statistics:
Type: Medium Tank

Production:
Date Produced: 1943
Manufacturer: Ford Motor Company
Number Produced: 12,500+

Specifications (M4A3):
Crew: 5 (Commander, Loader, Gunner, Driver, and Assistant Driver)
Speed (sustained, level ground): 26 miles per hour
Engine: Ford GAA-V8 4-cycle, 8-cylinder (500 hp)

Weight: 68,000+ pounds
Armament: One 75mm main gun; two .30 caliber machine guns; one .50 caliber machine gun

Source: M4 Sherman Tank—The Online Tank Museum (https://tanks-encyclopedia.com /ww2/ us/m4_sherman) Accessed: January 20, 2018.

Appendix D

M10 Tank Destroyer

The M10 tank destroyer, formally known as "3-inch Gun Motor Carriage M10" or "M10 GMC," was an American World War II tank destroyer. After US entry into World War II and the formation of the Tank Destroyer Force, a suitable vehicle was needed to equip the new battalions. By November 1941, the army requested a vehicle with a gun in a fully rotating turret, after other interim models were criticized for being poorly designed. The prototype of the M10 was conceived in early 1942 and delivered in April that year. After appropriate changes to the hull and turret were made, the modified version was selected for production in June 1942 as the "3-inch Gun Motor Carriage M10". It mounted the 3-inch (76.2mm) gun M7 in a rotating turret on a modified M4 Sherman tank chassis.

Statistics:
Designed: 1942
Manufacturer: Fisher Body division of General Motors, Ford Motor Company
Number built: 6,406

Specifications:
Mass: 29.1 metric tons (65,000 lbs.)
Length: 22 ft., 5 in. (including gun)
Width: 10 ft.
Height: 9 ft., 6 in.
Crew: 5 (Commander, gunner, driver, loader, assistant driver)
Armament: 76.2 mm (3 in.) M5 gun

Source: TM 9-752A—tank-afv.com (https://tank-afv.com/ww2/US/M10_Wolverine.php# google_vignette) Accessed: January 20, 2018.

Appendix E

28th Infantry Division Casualties

November 2–14, 1944: 6,184 Battle and Non-battle Casualties

109th Infantry Regiment: (Original strength: 3,142)
112 Killed in Action
801 Wounded in Action
10 Prisoners of War
352 Non-battle Related Casualties (sickness, combat fatigue, etc.)
Total casualties: 1,275

110th Infantry Regiment: (Original strength: 3,202)
65 Killed in Action
1,624 Wounded in Action
253 Prisoners of War
288 Missing in Action
86 Non-battle Related casualties (sickness, combat fatigue, etc.)
Total casualties: 2,316

112th Infantry Regiment: (Original strength: 3,100)
167 Killed in Action
719 Wounded in Action
232 Prisoners of War
431 Missing in Action (later confirmed killed in action)
544 Non-battle Related (sickness, combat fatigue, etc.)
Total casualties: 2,093

630th Tank Destroyer Battalion
707th Tank Battalion

893rd Tank Destroyer Battalion
20th Engineer Battalion
146th Engineer Combat Battalion
340th Engineer Combat Battalion
1340th Engineer Combat Battalion
Total casualties for these units: 500

Main combat vehicle losses:
16 of 24 M10 tank destroyers (893rd Tank Destroyer Battalion)
31 of 50 M4 Sherman tanks (707th Tank Battalion)

Source: 28th Infantry Division Historical Summary (Pennsylvania National Guard Military Museum: Fort Indiantown Gap), p. 188.

Endnotes

Preface

1. R. W. Thompson, *The Battle of the Rhineland* (Westholme Publishing: Yardley, 2012), p. 14.

Introduction

1. R. Atkinson, *The Guns at Last Light: The War in Western Europe, 1944–1945* (Picador, New York, 2014), p. 44. Note: The Third Battle of Ypres also known as the Battle of Passchendaele was a campaign of the First World War, fought by the Allies against the German Empire.
2. "9th Infantry Division, Report of Operations, September 1–30, 1944, October 1, 1944"; "Report of Operations, October 1–31, 1944, November 1, 1944" (Pennsylvania National Guard Military Museum: Fort Indiantown Gap).
3. "After Action Report for November 1944, G-3 Summary, 1944," *Headquarters, U. S. V Corps*, (Pennsylvania National Guard Military Museum: Fort Indiantown Gap), p. 2.
4. Ibid.
5. O. A. Kensler, Private, Company B, 112th Infantry Regiment, Unpublished Diary, (Pennsylvania National Guard Military Museum: Fort Indiantown Gap).
6. C. Whiting, *Siegfried: The Nazis' Last Stand* (Stein and Day: New York: 1982), pp. 58–59.
7. Ibid.
8. Ibid.
9. "After Action Report for November 1944," *Headquarters, U. S. V Corps*, (Pennsylvania National Guard Military Museum: Fort Indiantown Gap).

10. Ibid.
11. Ibid.
12. Ibid.
13. "Unit Report Number 5, December 6, 1944 for period November 1–30, 1944 inclusive" *28th Infantry Division* (Pennsylvania National Guard Military Museum: Fort Indiantown Gap), p. 28.
14. *28th Division Infantry Historical Summary*, p. 149.
15. Ibid.
16. Ibid., p. 99.
17. C. B. Curry, *Follow Me and Die: The Destruction of an American Division in World War II* (Stein and Day Publishers: Briarcliff Manor, 1984), p. 97.
18. Ibid, p. 98.
19. Unit Report 5. 110th Infantry Regiment, 1944 (Pennsylvania National Guard Military Museum: Fort Indiantown Gap), p. 2.
20. Ibid.
21. Curry, p. 17.
22. Ibid.
23. Ibid.
24. *28th Infantry Division Historical Summary* (Pennsylvania National Guard Military Museum: Fort Indiantown Gap), p. 157.
25. Ibid.
26. Ibid.
27. Ibid.
28. Ibid.
29. Ibid.
30. H. W. Morrison, *Report of Medical Evacuation, November 11, 1944* sent to 28th Division Surgeon, 28th Division Archives (Fort Indiantown Gap: Pennsylvania National Guard Military Museum).
31. Ibid.
32. Unit Report 5, p. 5.
33. Ibid.
34. *28th Infantry Division Historical Summary*, p. 151.
35. Unit Report 5, p. 6.
36. *28th Infantry Division Historical Summary*, p. 151.
37. Morrison, 155.
38. *28th Infantry Division Historical Summary*, p. 155.
39. Ibid.
40. Morrison, 155.
41. Fuller interview by Cecil B. Curry, Washington, Pennsylvania, 1979 (Pennsylvania National Guard Military Museum: Fort Indiantown Gap).

42. 112th Infantry Regiment, Unit Report, 1944 (Pennsylvania National Guard Military Museum: Fort Indiantown Gap).
43. Unit Report 5, p. 15.
44. 28th Division G1 Documents, November 01–30, 1944 (Pennsylvania National Guard Military Museum: Fort Indiantown Gap).
45. "The Battle of the Hürtgen Forest." DOCFILM. Deutsche Welle. https://www.dw. com/en/the-battle-of-hürtgen-forest/av-53307984. Accessed: January 3, 2019.
46. 28th Division G3 Report to VIII Corps G3.
47. Ibid.
48. 28th Division G1 Documents, November 01–30, 1944.
49. I. Peterman, 'Great Unsung Battle of the 28th Division: Pennsylvanians on the Western Front,' *Philadelphia Inquirer, January 1944*. Robert H. Henschen Collection, Series #272.99, Manuscript Group 272 (Military Museum Collection, Pennsylvania State Archives: Harrisburg).

Chapter 1

1. O. Bradley, *A Soldier's Story* (The Modern Library: New York 1999), pp. 434–35.
2. C. B. McDonald, *The Siegfried Line Campaign* (Office of the Chief of Military History, Department of the Army, Washington D.C., 1963), p. 326.
3. Bradley, p. 442.
4. McDonald, 324.
5. Ibid.
6. FUSA G-2 Per Report 171, as cited in VII Corps G-2 Per Report 164, November 28,
7. FUSA G-2 Tac. Jnl. file, Nov. 29, 1944 (US Army Center of Military History: Washington, D.C., 1944).
8. Memo, XIX Corps Engineer for XIX Corps G-3, 8 Oct, XIX Corps G-3 Jnl file, Oct. 12, 1944(US Army Center of Military History: Washington, D.C., 1944).
9. Ibid.
10. V Corps Operations in the ETO (US Army Center of Military History: Washington, D.C., 1944), pp. 272–78.
11. FUSA G-2 Per Report,
12. V Corps Operations,, p. 278.
13. Message, SHAEF (MAIN) to Twelfth Army Group, 20 Oct, FUSA G-2 Tac Jnl file, Oct 20–21, 1944,US Army Center of Military History: Washington, D.C., 1944).

14. Twelfth Army Group Weekly Intel Summaries 11 and 12 for weeks ending 21 and Oct. 28, dtd. Oct. 22 and 29, respectively, Twelfth Army Group G-2 AAR, Oct 1944 (US Army Center of Military History: Washington, D.C., 1944)
15. McDonald, 328.

Chapter 2

1. C. B. MacDonald, *The Siegfried Line Campaign* (US Army Center of Military History: Washington, D.C., 1990), pp. 70–72.
2. Ibid.
3. Ibid.
4. S. J. Newland and C. K. S. Chun. "The Hürtgen Campaign." *The European Campaign: Its Origins and Conduct*. Strategic Studies Institute, US Army War College: Carlisle, 2011. http://www.jstor.org/stable/resrep12096.12.
5. MacDonald, 81.
6. I. Werstein, *The Battle of Aachen* (Thomas Crowell Company: New York, 1962), p. 22.
7. Ibid.
8. Ibid.
9. Ibid.
10. MacDonald, 302.
11. US Department of Defense, Department of the Army, 1st Infantry Division, Intelligence Activities (October 1 to October 31, 1944), Headquarters, 1st Infantry Division, APO # 1 US Army, November 1, 1944, p. 1.
12. Ibid.
13. D. M. Daniel, *The Capture of Aachen*, a monograph prepared for the (Command and General Staff College Regular Course, Fort Leavenworth, 10–October 21, 1944), p. 6.
14. Ibid.
15. Ibid.
16. Ibid. NOTE: A typical RCT consisted of an infantry regiment, a field artillery battalion, a combat engineer company, a medical company, and a signals platoon. However the organization could be tailored to fit its mission and might include additional units, such as a company from a separate tank battalion, a company from a tank destroyer battalion, and a battery from an anti-aircraft artillery battalion.
17. Ibid.
18. Werstein, p. 63.
19. Ibid.
20. Ibid.

Chapter 3

1. P. Bruckner, "Tab J to Appendix 1 to Advance Sheet, Lesson 1." *The Battle of Hürtgenwald* (US Army Command and General Staff College: Leavenworth, June 1982), p. 63.
2. Ibid.
3. R. A. Johnson, "Soldier's Story, 1941–1946," *Unpublished Memoir* (Pennsylvania National Guard Military Museum: Fort Indiantown Gap).
4. Bruckner, p. 66.
5. Ibid.
6. Ibid.
7. H. Guderian, *Struggles of the 116th Panzer Division in the period from March 24–April 16, 1945* (US Army Command and General Staff College: Leavenworth).
8. Ibid.
9. Ibid.
10. *28th Infantry Division Historical Summary*, (Pennsylvania National Guard Military Museum: Fort Indiantown Gap).
11. Guderian.
12. Ibid.
13 Ibid.
14. Ibid.
15. Ibid.

Chapter 4

1. Unit Report 5, 109th Infantry Regiment for 1–November 30, 1944. Submitted to G-3, 28th Infantry Division December 4, 1944. (Pennsylvania National Guard Military Museum: Fort Indiantown Gap), p. 2.
2. Ibid.
3. Ibid.
4. Ibid.
5. Ibid.
6. Ibid.
7. Unit Report 5, p. 3.
8. Ibid.
9. Ibid.
10. Ibid.
11. Ibid.
12. Ibid.
13. Ibid.

14. G. M. Dix, *Company M, 109th Infantry Silver Star Award, March 6, 1945* 28th Infantry Division Archives (Pennsylvania National Guard Military Museum: Fort Indiantown Gap).
15. Unit Report 5, p. 4.
16. Ibid.
17. Ibid.
18. Ibid.
19. C. B. McDonald, *The Siegfried Line Campaign*. European Theater of Operations. US Army in World War II, 1963. (US Army Center of Military History: Washington, D.C., 1963), p. 365.
21. Ibid.
22. Unit Report 5, p. 5.
23. '109th Infantry Regiment Awards and Decorations, Topping.' *28th Infantry Division Public Affairs Office, July 12, 1945* (Pennsylvania National Guard Military Museum: Fort Indiantown Gap).
24. Ibid.
25. E. R. Corbett, II, Private, 109th Infantry, 28th Infantry Division, letter to his wife, November 8, 1944, (Elliott R. Corbett II commemoration website, the Netherlands, www.elliott-r-corbett-ii.com/publications).
26. Ibid.
27. T. W. Hickman, Unpublished Diary (Pennsylvania National Guard Military Museum: Fort Indiantown Gap), p. 40. Note: Hickman was a Battalion Scout with the 1st Battalion of the 109th Infantry.
28. Unit Report 5, p. 6.
29. Ibid.
30. Ibid.
31. Ibid.
32. Ibid.
33. Ibid.

Chapter 5

1. "Unit Report 5, 110th Infantry Regiment for 1–November 30, 1944." Submitted to G-3, 28th Infantry Division, December4, 1944 (Pennsylvania National Guard Military Museum: Fort Indiantown Gap), p. 2.
2. Ibid.
3. Nikola, Private, 110th Infantry Regiment, 28th Infantry Division, Silver Star Award' (Pennsylvania National Guard Military Museum: Fort Indiantown Gap).
4. Unit Report 5, p. 3.
5. Ibid.

6. Ibid.
7. Ibid.
8. Ibid.
9. Ibid.
10. R. Arford, Company G, 110th Infantry, Unpublished Journal. (Pennsylvania National Guard Military Museum: Fort Indiantown Gap).
11. Unit Report 5, p. 4.
12. Ibid.
13. Ibid.

Chapter 6

1. A. E. Drapeau, *Dark November*, Unpublished Manuscript (Pennsylvania National Guard Military Museum: Fort Indiantown Gap, 1993).
2. P. A. Troup, *The Operations of the 112th Infantry in the Hürtgen Forest, Germany, November 2–November 14, 1944*. Advanced Infantry Officers Course. (The Infantry School: Fort Benning, 1947–1948), p. 8.
3. "112th Infantry Regiment Awards and Decorations, Kauffman." *28th Infantry Division Public Affairs Office, July 12, 1945* (Pennsylvania National Guard Military Museum: Fort Indiantown Gap).
4. C. B. Curry, *Follow Me and Die: The Destruction of an American Division in World War II* (Stein and Day Publishers: Briarcliff Manor, 1984), p. 97.
5. "110th Infantry Regiment Awards and Decorations, Welc." 28th Infantry Division Public Affairs Office, July 12, 1945 (Pennsylvania National Guard Military Museum: Fort Indiantown Gap).
6. Troup, p. 9
7. "R. J. Esterly, Company I, 112th Infantry, Silver Star Award." Press release for First Army By 28th Division Public Relations Office, November 20, 1944. 28th Infantry Division Public Relations Section. APO 28, U. S. Army Europe, September 28, 1945. 28th Infantry Division Archives. (Pennsylvania National Guard Military Museum: Fort Indiantown Gap).
8. Troup, p. 10
9. Drapeau.
10. Ibid.
11. Troup, p. 11.
12. P. O. Meyer, *The Shadow of Death: The Hürtgen Forest, Luxemburg, Battle of the Bulge, Stalag XIIA and Stalag IIA, Arbeit Kommandos*, as told to her by Robert W. Meyer Jr., Company A, 109th Infantry Regiment (Self-published, 1999), p. 59.
13. Troup, p. 11.

14. Ibid.
15. "Unit Report 5, November 1–30," 28th Infantry Division, November 20, 1944 (Pennsylvania National Guard Military Museum: Fort Indiantown Gap), p. 1.
16. Ibid.
17. Ibid.
18. Ibid.
19. Troup, p. 11.
20. Ibid.
21. C. Skains, Company M, 112th Infantry, Unpublished Journal. (Pennsylvania National Guard Military Museum: Fort Indiantown Gap).
22. O. A. Kensler, Private, Company B, 112th Infantry Regiment, Unpublished Diary (Pennsylvania National Guard Military Museum: Fort Indiantown Gap).
23. R. A. Johnson, *Soldier's Story, 1941–1946*, Unpublished Memoir (Pennsylvania National Guard Military Museum: Fort Indiantown Gap).
24. Unit Report 5, p. 5.

Chapter 7

1. G. Gillot, *The 707th Tank Battalion in Support of the 28th Infantry Division* (European Center of Military History: Jalhay, Belgium, 2017).
2. Ibid.
3. Ibid.
4. Ibid.
5. Ibid.
6. Ibid.
7. J. F. Marshall, 'The 707th Tank Battalion,' Unpublished Memoir (Pennsylvania National Guard Military Museum: Fort Indiantown Gap).
8. Ibid.
9. Ibid.
10. Ibid.
11. Ibid.
12. Ibid.
13. Gillot.
14. Ibid.
15. Ibid.
16. Ibid.
17. Marshall.
18. Ibid.
19. Ibid.

20. Ibid.
21. Ibid.
22. Ibid.

Chapter 8

1. J. W. Cooper, *Commander, Unit Report 5, 630th Tank Destroyer Battalion, November 1–30, 1944* (Dwight D. Eisenhower Presidential Library: Abilene), p. 3.
2. Ibid.
3. Ibid.
4. Ibid.
5. Ibid.
6. Ibid.
7. Ibid.
8. Ibid.
9. Ibid.
10. Ibid.
11. Ibid.

Chapter 9

1. W. E. Nash, S-3, *893rd Tank Destroyer Battalion, After Action Report from November 1–30, 1944* (Adjutant General: Washington, D.C., December 6, 1944).
2. Ibid.

Chapter 10

1. T. F. Creegan, and C. B. Setterberg, *Interview by V Corps Captain W. J. Fox about Operations of 1340th Engineer Combat Battalion* (Pennsylvania National Guard Military Museum: Fort Indiantown Gap), p. 1.
2. Ibid.
3. Ibid.
4. Ibid.
5. Ibid.
6. Ibid.
7. Ibid.
8. Ibid.

Chapter 11

1. J. E. Sonnefield, Commander, *Statement of 20th Engineer Combat Battalion Operation, November 6–10, 1944* (Pennsylvania National Guard Military Museum: Fort Indiantown Gap), p. 1.
2. Ibid.
3. Ibid.
4. Ibid.
5. Ibid

Chapter 12

1. H. Ball, Commander A Company, *146th Engineer Combat Battalion Interview with V Corps Captain William J Fox, November 27, 1944*. Battalion (Pennsylvania National Guard Military Museum: Fort Indiantown Gap), p. 1.
2. Ibid.
3. Ibid.
4. Ibid.
5. Ibid.
6. Ibid.
7. Ibid.
8. Ibid.
9. Ibid.
10. Ibid.

Chapter 13

1. R. T. Bradicich, Company E, 2nd Battalion, 110th Infantry, Unpublished Memoirs (Pennsylvania National Guard Military Museum: Fort Indiantown Gap).
2. A. W. Burghart, Company K, 110th Infantry, Unpublished Memoirs (Pennsylvania National Guard Military Museum: Fort Indiantown Gap).
3. J. J. Farrell, Company I, 3rd Battalion, 112th Infantry, Unpublished Memoirs (Pennsylvania National Guard Military Museum: Fort Indiantown Gap).
4. G. W. Grizzle, Company E, 2nd Battalion, 112th Infantry, Unpublished Memoirs (Pennsylvania National Guard Military Museum: Fort Indiantown Gap). NOTE: Private First Class George Grizzle was a machine gunner in the 112th Regiment of the 28th Division. He had been sent to the unit in late July as a replacement. When he and the remaining nine survivors of the November 2–7 assault were captured, he was the second-most-senior man. He spent six months at Neubrandenburg and Dannenwalde POW camps.

5. R. F. Leach, Company D, 109th Infantry, Unpublished Memoirs (Pennsylvania National Guard Military Museum: Fort Indiantown Gap).
6. G. Mass, Company K, (Heavy Weapons), *110th Infantry War Diary* (Pennsylvania National Guard Military Museum: Fort Indiantown Gap).
7. J. F. Marshall, Company B, 707th Tank Destroyer Battalion, Unpublished Memoirs (Pennsylvania National Guard Military Museum: Fort Indiantown Gap).
8. H. Rallard, Company B, 110th Infantry, Unpublished Memoirs (Pennsylvania National Guard Military Museum: Fort Indiantown Gap).
9. W. F. Train, 112th Infantry, *My Memories of the Battle of the Bulge* (Pennsylvania National Guard Military Museum: Fort Indiantown Gap).
10. H. Gees, Fusilier Battalion, 275th Infantry Division, Unpublished Memoirs (Pennsylvania National Guard Military Museum: Fort Indiantown Gap).
11. A. Güvert, 116th Panzer Division, Unpublished Memoirs (Bundesarchiv: Koblenz, Germany). Note: For this attack, August Güvert was awarded the Iron Cross. He and his comrades named in the report were also entered in the Honorary Sheet of the 116th Panzer Division.
12. E. Kreßmann, "Tank Destroyer Division 519," Unpublished Memoirs (Bundesarchiv: Koblenz, Germany).
13. H. Kunst, "1st Artillery Regiment 189, with the 89th Infantry Division," Unpublished Memoirs (Bundesarchiv: Koblenz, Germany).
14. G. Schmidt, "272nd Volksgrenadier Division," Unpublished Memoirs (Bundesarchiv: Koblenz, Germany).

Chapter 14

1. A. L. Berndt, *112th Infantry Medical Evacuation Report to 28th Infantry Division Surgeon, November 10, 1944* (Record Group 407, Box 24032, National Archives and Records Administration, at College Park, 1944),p.1.
2. Ibid.
3. Ibid.
4. Ibid.
5. Ibid.
6. Ibid.

Chapter 15

1. "A Report on the Fights Near Schmidt and Kommerscheidt," 89th Division Newsletter, vol. 2, November 9, 1944, (Pennsylvania National Guard Military Museum: Fort Indiantown Gap), p. 1. NOTE: The "89th Division Mirror, Volume 2", published on November 9, 1944, was intended to give the members

of the division an impression of the heavy and bitter fighting in the area of Kommerscheidt and Vossenack, where a stronger enemy (American) force was encircled and destroyed on November 11, 1944.

Chapter 16

1. R. F. von Gersdorff, *Account of the Battle of the Hürtgen Forest Analysis* (Bundesarchiv: Koblenz, Germany, December 12, 1945), p. 1. NOTE: Translated from the German text by General Gersdorff in the presence of Captains. N. B. Sigband and F. Mahin, USFET Historical Officers. Minor paraphrasing and additions were made by the historical officers, all of which were approved by General Gersdorff at a final reading, December 121945). Following the war, Gersdorff participated in the work of the US Army Historical Division, in which, under the guidance of Franz Halder, German generals wrote World War II operational studies for the US army, first as POWs and then as employees.
2. K. McMillin, "The Battle of the Hürtgen Forest: Why?" *U. S. Army War College Class of 2001 Strategy Research Project,* (U. S. Army War College: Carlisle, 2001), p. 1. NOTE: Approved for public release. Distribution is unlimited.

Epilogue

1. I. Peterman, "Great Unsung Battle of the 28th Division: Pennsylvanians on the Western Front," *Philadelphia Inquirer, January 1944*, Robert H. Henschen Collection, Series #272.99, Manuscript Group.

Bibliography

9th Infantry Division, Report of Operations, September 1–30, 1944, October 11944; Report of Operations, October 1–31, 1944, November 1, 1944 (Fort Indiantown Gap: Pennsylvania National Guard Military Museum)

Twelfth Army Group Weekly Intel Summaries 11 and 12 for weeks ending Oct. 21 and 28, dtd Oct. 22 and 29, respectively, Twelfth Army Group G-2 AAR, Oct 1944 (Washington, D.C.: US Army Center of Military History, 1944)

89th Division Newsletter, vol. 2, November 9, 1944, *A Report on the Fights Near Schmidt and Kommerscheidt* (Fort Indiantown Gap: Pennsylvania National Guard Military Museum)

109th Infantry Regiment Awards and Decorations, Topping. 28th Infantry Division Public Affairs Office, July 12, 1945 (Fort Indiantown Gap: Pennsylvania National Guard Military Museum)

109th Infantry Regiment, Unit Report, 1944 (Fort Indiantown Gap: Pennsylvania National Guard Military Museum)

110th Infantry Regiment Awards and Decorations, Welc. 28th Infantry Division Public Affairs Office, July 12, 1945 (Fort Indiantown Gap: Pennsylvania National Guard Military Museum)

112th Infantry Regiment Awards and Decorations, Kauffman. 28th Infantry Division Public Affairs Office, July 12, 1945 (Fort Indiantown Gap: Pennsylvania National Guard Military Museum)

112th Infantry Regiment Awards and Decorations, Hackard. 28th Infantry Division Public Affairs Office, July 12, 1945 (Fort Indiantown Gap: Pennsylvania National Guard Military Museum)

112th Infantry Regiment, *Unit Report*, 1944 (Fort Indiantown Gap: Pennsylvania National Guard Military Museum)

28 Signal Company Unit History, November 01, 1944 to January 01, 1945 (Fort Indiantown Gap: Pennsylvania National Guard Military Museum)

28th Division Surgeon's Report of Casualties, November 1, 1944 to April 30, 1945 (Washington, D.C.: US Army Center of Military History, 1945)

28th Division G1 Documents, 01–November 30, 1944 (Fort Indiantown Gap: Pennsylvania National Guard Military Museum)

28th Division G3 Report to VIII Corps G3, 1944 (Fort Indiantown Gap: Pennsylvania National Guard Military Museum)

28th Infantry Division Historical Summary, (Pennsylvania National Guard Military Museum: Fort Indiantown Gap)

"After Action Report for November 1944," *Headquarters, U. S. V Corps*, (Pennsylvania National Guard Military Museum: Fort Indiantown Gap)

Arford, R., Company G, 110th Infantry, *Unpublished Journal* (Fort Indiantown Gap: Pennsylvania National Guard Military Museum)

Atkinson, R., *The Guns at Last Light: The War in Western Europe, 1944–1945* (New York: Picador, 2014)

Ball, H., Commander A Company, 146th Engineer Combat Battalion Interview with V Corps Captain William J Fox, November 27, 1944. Battalion (Fort Indiantown Gap: Pennsylvania National Guard Military Museum)

Berndt, A. L., 112th Infantry Medical Evacuation Report to 28th Infantry Division Surgeon, November 10, 1944. Record Group 407, Box 24032, (College Park: National Archives and Records Administration, 1944)

Bradicich, R. T., Company E, 2nd Battalion, 110th Infantry, *Unpublished Memoirs* (Fort Indiantown Gap: Pennsylvania National Guard Military Museum)

Bradley O., *A Soldier's Story* (New York: The Modern Library, 1999)

Bruckner, P., Lieutenant Colonel. "Tab J to Appendix 1 to Advanced Sheet, Lesson 1." *The Battle of Hürtgenwald* (Fort Leavenworth: US Army Command and General Staff College, 1982)

Buckler, Tech Sergeant, Company C, 1st Battalion, 112th Infantry Regiment, 28th Infantry Division. *Personal History Of the Men Who Marched in the Paris Parade*, 28th Infantry Division Public Relations Section, 1945 (Fort Indiantown Gap: Pennsylvania National Guard Military Museum)

Burghart, A. W., Company K, 110th Infantry, *Unpublished Memoirs* (Fort Indiantown Gap: Pennsylvania National Guard Military Museum:)

Cooper, J. W., Commander, *Unit Report 5, 630th Tank Destroyer Battalion, November 1–30 1944.* (Abilene: Dwight D. Eisenhower Presidential Library)

Corbett, E. R., II, Private, "109th Infantry, 28th Infantry Division," letter to his wife, November 8, 1944, (Elliott R. Corbett II commemoration website, the Netherlands, www.elliott-r-corbett-ii.com/publications)

Creegan, T. F. and Setterberg, C. B., Interview by V Corps Captain W. J. Fox about *Operations of 1340th Engineer Combat Battalion* (Fort Indiantown Gap: Pennsylvania National Guard Military Museum)

Curry, C. B., *Follow Me and Die: The Destruction of an American Division in World War II* (Briarcliff Manor: Stein and Day Publishers, 1984)

Daniel, D. M., *The Capture of Aachen*, a monograph prepared for the (Fort Leavenworth: Command and General Staff College Regular Course, October 10–21, 1944)

Dix, G. M., Company M, 109th Infantry *Silver Star Award*, March 6, 1945, 28th Infantry Division Archives (Fort Indiantown Gap: Pennsylvania National Guard Military Museum)

Drapeau, A. E., *Dark November*, *Unpublished Manuscript* (Fort Indiantown Gap: Pennsylvania National Guard Military Museum, 1993)

Esterly, Robert J. Company I, 112th Infantry, *Silver Star Award*. Press release for First Army by 28th Division Public Relations Office, November 20, 1944. 28th Infantry Division Public Relations Section. APO 28, U. S. Army Europe, September 28, 1945. 28th Infantry Division Archives. (Fort Indiantown Gap: Pennsylvania National Guard Military Museum)

Farrell, J. J., Company I, 3rd Battalion, 112th Infantry, Unpublished Memoirs (Fort Indiantown Gap: Pennsylvania National Guard Military Museum)

First Army Report of Operations, August 1, 1944 to February 22, 1945, (Washington, DC: U.S. Government Printing Office, 1945)

FUSA G-2 Per Report 171, as cited in VII Corps G-2 Per Report 164, November 28, FUSA G-2 Tac Jnl file, 29 Nov 1944 (Washington, D.C.: US Army Center of Military History, 1944)

Gees, H., Fusilier Battalion, 275th Infantry Division, Unpublished Memoirs (Fort Indiantown Gap: Pennsylvania National Guard Military Museum)

Gillot, G. *The 707th Tank Battalion in Support of the 28th Infantry Division* (Jalhay, Belgium: European Center of Military History, 2017)

Grizzle, G. W., Company E, 2nd Battalion, 112th Infantry, Unpublished Memoirs (Fort Indiantown Gap: Pennsylvania National Guard Military Museum)

Guderian, H., *Struggles of the 116th Panzer Division in the period from March 24–April 16, 1945* (Leavenworth: US Army Command and General Staff College)

Güvert, A., 116th Panzer Division, Unpublished Memoirs (Koblenz, Germany: Bundesarchiv)

Headquarters, U. S. V Corps, *After Action Report for November 1944* (Fort Indiantown Gap: Pennsylvania National Guard Military Museum)

Headquarters, U. S. V Corps, *After Action Report for November 1944*, G-3 Summary, 1944 (Fort Indiantown Gap: Pennsylvania National Guard Military Museum)

Hickman, T. W., *Unpublished Diary* (Fort Indiantown Gap: Pennsylvania National Guard Military Museum)

Hubner, C., *Unpublished Diary* (Fort Indiantown Gap: Pennsylvania National Guard Military Museum)

Johnson, R., *A Soldier's Story, 1941–1946,* Unpublished Memoir (Fort Indiantown Gap: Pennsylvania National Guard Military Museum)

Kensler, O. A., Private, Company B, 112th Infantry Regiment, Unpublished Diary (Fort Indiantown Gap: Pennsylvania National Guard Military Museum)

Kreßmann, E., Tank Destroyer Division 519, Unpublished Memoirs (Koblenz, Germany: Bundesarchiv)

Kunst, H., 1st Artillery Regiment 189, with the 89th Infantry Division, Unpublished Memoirs (Koblenz, Germany: Bundesarchiv)

Leach, R. F., Company D, 109th Infantry, Unpublished Memoirs (Fort Indiantown Gap: Pennsylvania National Guard Military Museum)

M4 Sherman Tank —The Online Tank Museum (https://tanks-encyclopedia.com/ww2/us/m4_sherman)

Marshall, J. F., Company B, 707th Tank Destroyer Battalion, Unpublished Memoirs (Fort Indiantown Gap: Pennsylvania National Guard Military Museum)

Mass, G., Company K, (Heavy Weapons), 110th Infantry, War Diary (Fort Indiantown Gap: Pennsylvania National Guard Military Museum)

McDaniel, D., Company A, 1340th Engineer Battalion, Unpublished Journal (Fort Indiantown Gap: Pennsylvania National Guard Military Museum)

McDonald, C. B., *The Siegfried Line Campaign* (Washington D.C.: Office of the Chief of Military History, Department of the Army, 1963)

Mcmillin, K., U. S. Army War College Class of 2001 Strategy Research Project: *The Battle of the Hürtgen Forest: Why?* (Carlisle: U. S. Army War College, 2001)

Morrison, H. W., *Report of Medical Evacuation, November 11, 1944 sent to 28th Division Surgeon.* 28th Division Archives (Fort Indiantown Gap: Pennsylvania National Guard Military Museum)

Memo, XIX Corps Engineer for XIX Corps G-3, Oct. 8, XIX Corps G-3 Jnl file, Oct. 12, 1944 (Washington, D.C.: US Army Center of Military History, 1944)

Message, SHAEF (MAIN) to Twelfth Army Group, 20 Oct, FUSA G-2 Tac Jnl file, Oct. 20–21, 1944 (Washington, D.C.US Army Center of Military History, 1944)

Meyer, P. O., *The Shadow of Death: The Hürtgen Forest, Luxemburg, Battle of the Bulge, Stalag XIIA, Stalag IIA, Arbeit Kommandos*, as told to her by Robert W. Meyer Jr., Company A, 109th Infantry Regiment (Self-published, 1999)

Nash, W. E., S-3, 893rd Tank Destroyer Battalion, After Action Report from November 1–30, 1944 (Washington, D.C.: Adjutant General, December 6, 1944)

Newland, Samuel J., and Clayton K. S. Chun. *The Hürtgen Campaign*. The European Campaign: Its Origins and Conduct. Strategic Studies Institute, (Carlisle: US Army War College, 2011). http://www.jstor.org/stable/resrep12096.12.

Nikola, G., Private, 110th Infantry Regiment, 28th Infantry Division, *Silver Star Award* (Fort Indiantown Gap: Pennsylvania National Guard Military Museum)

Peterman, Ivan, *Great Unsung Battle of the 28th Division: Pennsylvanians on the Western Front*, Philadelphia Inquirer, January 1944, Robert H. Henschen Collection, Series #272.99, Manuscript Group 272. (Harrisburg: Pennsylvania Military Museum Collection, Pennsylvania State Archives, 1944)

Rallard, H., Company B, 110th Infantry, Unpublished Memoirs (Fort Indiantown Gap: Pennsylvania National Guard Military Museum)

Schmidt, G., 272nd Volksgrenadier Division, Unpublished Memoirs (Koblenz, Germany: Bundesarchiv)

Setliffe, T., Lieutenant Colonel, 1340 Combat Engineer Battalion, *After Action Report*, 1944 (Fort Indiantown Gap: Pennsylvania National Guard Military Museum)

Skains, C., Company M, 112th Infantry, Unpublished Journal (Fort Indiantown Gap: Pennsylvania National Guard Military Museum)

Sonnefield, J. E., Commander, *Statement of 20th Engineer Combat Battalion Operation, November 6–10, 1944*(Fort Indiantown Gap: Pennsylvania National Guard Military Museum)

tank-afv.com (https://tank-afv.com/ww2/US/M10_Wolverine.php#google_vignette)

Technical Manual, Series Number 6020, US WWII Studebaker M29 and M29C Weasel, (Erlangen, Germany: Tankograd Publishing, 2010)

The Battle of the Hürtgen Forest, *DOCFILM*. Deutsche Welle. https://www.dw.com/en/the-battle-of-hürtgen-forest/av-53307984.

Tankograd Technical Manual, Series Number 6020, US WWII Studebaker M29 and M29C Weasel.

Thompson, R. W., *The Battle of the Rhineland* (Yardley: Westholme Publishing, 2012)

Train, W. F., 112th Infantry, *My Memories of the Battle of the Bulge* (Fort Indiantown Gap: Pennsylvania National Guard Military Museum)

Troup, P. A., *The Operations of the 112th Infantry in the Hürtgen Forest, Germany, November 2–November 14, 1944*. Advanced Infantry Officers Course. (Fort Benning: The Infantry School, 1947–48)

Unit Report 5, *109th Infantry Regiment for November 1–30, 1944*. Submitted to G-3, 28th Infantry Division December 4, 1944. (Fort Indiantown Gap: Pennsylvania National Guard Military Museum)

Unit Report 5. *110th Infantry Regiment, 1944* (Fort Indiantown Gap: Pennsylvania National Guard Military Museum)

Unit Report Number 5, 28th Infantry Division, December 6, 1944 for period November 1–30, 1944 inclusive (Fort Indiantown Gap: Pennsylvania National Guard Military Museum)

US Department of Defense, Department of the Army, 1st Infantry Division, Intelligence Activities (October 1 to October 31, 1944), Headquarters, 1st Infantry Division, APO # 1 US Army, November 1, 1944

V Corps Operations in the ETO (Washington, D.C.: US Army Center of Military History, 1944)

von Gersdorff, R. F., *Account of the Battle of the Hürtgen Forest Analysis* (Koblenz, Germany: Bundesarchiv, December 12, 1945)
Wells, R. C., Interview by Cecil B. Curry, Washington, Pennsylvania, 1979 (Fort Indiantown Gap: Pennsylvania National Guard Military Museum)
Werstein, I., *The Battle of Aachen* (New York: Thomas Crowell Company, 1962)
Whiting, C., *Siegfried: The Nazis' Last Stand* (New York: Stein and Day, 1982)